THE RESTORATION OF THE MONASTERY OF
SAINT MARTIN OF TOURNAI

HERMAN OF TOURNAI

THE RESTORATION OF
THE MONASTERY
OF SAINT MARTIN
OF TOURNAI

TRANSLATED WITH AN INTRODUCTION
AND NOTES BY LYNN H. NELSON

THE CATHOLIC UNIVERSITY
OF AMERICA PRESS
WASHINGTON, D.C.

The paper used in this publication meets the minimum requirements of American National Standards for Information Science—Permanence of Paper for Printed Library materials, ANSI Z39.48-1984.
∞

LIBRARY OF CONGRESS CATALOGING-IN-PUBLICATION DATA

Herman, of Tournai, 12th cent.
    [Liber de restauratione Monasterii Sancti Martini Tornacensis. English]
    The restoration of the Monastery of Saint Martin of Tournai /
Herman of Tournai ; translated with introduction and notes by Lynn H. Nelson.
      p. cm.
    Includes bibliographical references and index.
    1. Abbaye de Saint-Martin de Tournai (Tournai, Belgium). 2. Tournai (Belgium)—Church history. 1. Nelson, Lynn H. (Lynn Harry), 1931– .
11. Title.
    BX2612.T6H4713 1996
    271'.14049342—dc20
    95-40170
    ISBN 0-8132-0850-5 (cloth : alk. paper)
    ISBN 0-8132-0851-3 (pbk. : alk. paper)

CONTENTS

PREFACE

One might imagine the monks in a twelfth-century Cluniac monastery to have been stern and silent men, and so they may have been in some abbeys. In Saint Martin's of Tournai, however, they took great delight in talk, and they told and retold their anecdotes until each was polished and well-worn. Growing up in such company, Herman of Tournai could not help but become an accomplished storyteller, and he had an ample fund of tales from which to draw when he came to write the story—or rather the stories—of the re-establishment of the monastery of Saint Martin's.[1]

He writes with a deceptive simplicity and an eye for the telling detail, and the reader is soon drawn into his world, admiring a scriptorium at work, digging for buried treasure, longing for dinner at the Council of Reims, wandering through a lost village, watching a tragic tournament, opening the tomb of a murdered count, attending a lecture on astronomy, searching for purloined parchments, eavesdropping on a couple planning to renounce the world, dining on oats and straw during a famine, listening to King Henry and Archbishop Anselm argue about a Scottish princess, joining a midnight migration of monks, tracing a schoolmaster's erratic path to sainthood, and much more.

His anecdotes and digressions are woven into a suggestive account of the complex personal motives, political undercurrents, and social conflicts that surrounded the establishment of a monastic community in a derelict church just outside the town of Tournai. The work is entertaining and stimulating at first reading, but it also rewards careful re-reading. There are few sources that offer such a wealth of personal glimpses into the world of the twelfth century, and one might well be content with that. But Herman has more to say than first appears, and the patient reader will soon be absorbed in the puzzles posed by his steady stream of digressions, puns, incongruities, and omissions. Most things are not exactly what they first appear to be; anything that Herman writes may have a hidden meaning or, again, it may not.

I have attempted to provide sufficient materials for the reader to penetrate beneath the surface of Herman's account. The chapter headings (composed by me) are intended to offer a running guide to the apparent meanderings of the narrative, and the chronology may help the reader to keep events in some order. The introduction provides a context for readers who may lack an extensive knowledge of the place or period, and the notes offer specific information to illuminate some of the more cryptic passages. I have not attempted to explain all such passages, however, nor have I tried to clarify all of the levels of narrative and comment lying beneath Herman's main account. Any attempt to do so would be bound to fail since many of his allusions and puns appear to have been based upon shared but unrecorded experiences of the monks of St. Martin's and upon a world which we can recapture only imperfectly. In any event, it is perhaps best that some puzzles be left for the reader to solve.

I have provided an epilogue drawn primarily from the anonymous continuation to Herman's work in order to bring the account, which Herman terminated in a sudden fashion, to a conclusion. In addition to this, a series of appendices provide more extended historical background for some of the central issues in Herman's account, and offer selected relevant bibliography. There are certain points crucial to Herman's narrative that cannot be appreciated without considerable reflection and numerous re-readings, and these points should not be beyond the reach of the reader without the time to invest in this manner. On the other hand, some readers may find this a challenge and wish to solve the puzzles on their own. Consequently, I have placed the discussions of these matters among the appendices, and the reader may turn to them whenever he or she is inclined to do so.

A NOTE ON TEXT AND TRANSLATION

The translation is based on the edition prepared by Georg Waitz and published in the *Monumenta Germaniae Historica* in 1883.[2] The base manuscript for this edition was codex 69 of the Municipal Library of Tournai, written sometime in the late twelfth or early thirteenth centuries. British Library MS Harleian 4441, ff. 447–486 offered yet another source. Written in a sixteenth-century hand, it bears the notation that it came from the library of the abbey of Tournai; it was probably acquired in the years during which Tournai was Henry VIII's "French" capital. It contains several passages not found in the earlier text and which are probably additions and clarifications to the base from which it was copied. I have included within the text those passages that provide useful information or clarify the original material without citation, but have set those additions in italics.

Herman's narrative style varies somewhat but is generally discursive and familiar in tone. He seems to have been averse to drama and emotion, often defusing passionate scenes and events with a joke or the observation that his readers would not really want to read or hear that sort of thing. I have accepted such sentiments and his own references to his account as indicating that he sought an easy-going and playful style in which literary cliches and rhetoric would not distract his audience from the implications of his words. I have attempted to recreate that tone in English. This has required the simplification of many sentences, the transposition of word order, and the reduction of ambiguities and indefinite antecedents. This practice is not without a price, however, since many of Herman's ambiguities and obscurities were doubtless intentional. I have noted where this seems to be the case and have suggested the tenor of the Latin text.

Finally, a word about names. Both Germanic and Romance personal and place names were current in twelfth-century Tournai, and the matter was complicated still further by the uncertain orthography with which they were recorded. The modern names of places, some French and others Flemish, are used when identification is possible, and I have used the English forms of personal names wherever it was clearly appropriate to do so. The retention of archaic names has the virtue of lending color to a translation, but it is a practice that erects a needless wall of difference between the reader and the characters about whom he or she is reading. Thus Abbot Haimericus will be referred to as Emory, Radulfus as Ralph, and so on. Some names with no common English equivalent have been left unchanged, and well-known names such as Thierry of Ypres have been retained even when an English form, Theodoric, has been applied to other characters with the same name in the account. The result may appear inconsistent but so too was contemporary usage.

Family names were not yet used in the region, and so I have had to supply them. Odo and Bishop Radbod were members of a family that had established its seat at Avesnes and, by the late twelfth century, had adopted that name as its own. The naming of Herman's kindred is more arbitrary. Herman referred to his father occasionally as Radulfus de Osmunt and so, on the analogy of Avesnes, I have accepted Osmunt as the family name but changed it to an English equivalent of Osmond. Although this family name would, at best, have applied only to that branch of the family in Noyon, I have applied it to the entire kindred

It is my hope that readers will find *The Restoration of the Monastery of Saint Martin of Tournai* a rewarding work and will derive as much pleasure in reading it as I did in preparing this translation.

Lynn H. Nelson
The University of Kansas

INTRODUCTION

HERMAN OF TOURNAI[1]

Herman was born in Tournai in about 1090, the second of the four sons of Ralph of Noyon and Mainsendis, members of the Flemish lower nobility. Ralph owned the brewing monopoly in the city and was a man of substance. He was also a member of a rich and influential kindred that controlled the government of the city and district, and he had become the advocate of Radbod, bishop of Tournai and Noyon. Mainsendis was the daughter of a prior of the famous monastery of Saint Amand and had been reared in the abbey. Both of Herman's parents took their religion seriously. In 1095 and under dramatic circumstances, they abandoned the secular world and entered the recently reestablished abbey of Saint Martin, just outside the walls of the city and a short walk from their home.

Herman was reared by his uncle, Theodoric, coiner of the money of Tournai and reputedly the richest man in the city, but entered the monastery as soon as he had passed out of infancy, and was educated there under Odo, its abbot and the former master of the cathedral school of St. Mary's of Tournai. In the course of time, Herman followed his father as prior in charge of the monastery's ex-

ternal affairs and became its third abbot in 1127. Some accounts
state that he was stricken by paralysis and could no longer rule
the congregation, while others record that he was lax in maintaining discipline and resigned the office when censured for this
flaw. Whatever the reason, he stepped down after governing St.
Martin's for ten years and became an ecclesiastical man of affairs.

In 1142, he was dispatched to Rome by the canons of Tournai
to petition Pope Innocent II to end the peculiar arrangement by
which the diocese of Tournai and that of Noyon, over a hundred
miles to the south, were ruled by a single bishop. Rome was no-
toriously deliberate in dealing with such matters, and, on 26
April, Herman learned that he would have to wait some seven
weeks for the papal decision. The fiftieth anniversary of the
reestablishment of Saint Martin's fell on 2 May of that year, and
Herman decided to fill his enforced idleness by writing a history
of the restoration of the abbey.

HISTORICAL BACKGROUND[2]

Tournai arose as a town on the Roman military road that led
from the fortress city of Cologne on the lower Rhine to the naval
base at Boulogne. It was surrounded by rich fields, and the
marshes to the west provided flax and sheep's wool that the
women of the town wove into cloth and made into military uni-
forms. Legend had it that Piatus, a missionary from Benevento in
Italy, had spread Christianity through the district before being
beheaded in Diocletian's great pogrom against the Christians in
287. Whatever the truth of the matter, Christianity had made relatively little progress when the pagan Franks began moving
southward along the Scheldt river in about the year 350. By 400,
Tournai and its district were under Frankish rule, and what
Christianity existed there was of the Arian variety preferred by
many German tribesmen.

Clovis, the first king of a unified Frankish people, converted to Catholicism in 496, and a second Christian era began in Tournai. It was at this time that Tournai was made a bishopric by Eleutherius, the second apostle to the district. Upon Eleutherius's death in 532, the episcopal see was offered to Medard, the bishop of Noyon, who accepted Tournai without giving up Noyon. The two dioceses, separated by well over a hundred miles, were united almost accidentally, but this inconvenient union would persist for more than six centuries. Tournai was at this time the lesser of the two cities and was located in a virtual wilderness. The lands of northern Flanders, lying to the north of Tournai, were periodically inundated, and were marshlands and open water during much of the sixth century. The sea retreated during the seventh century and once again left Flanders open to settlement and development.

Supported by the Merovingian monarchs, the bishops of Tournai-Noyon began to develop the marshes and to bring the True Faith to their inhabitants. This was an heroic age of Christian conversion in which the Flemish saints Omer, Bertin, Vaast, and Amand led the work of ecclesiastical settlement. English and Irish monks sponsored by the bishops of Tournai converted most of the still-pagan Franks in the area north of Tournai and extended the boundaries of the diocese to the mouth of the Scheldt and the beaches of the North Sea. This was an era of monastic establishment, and Tournai was not exempt. Bishop Eligius, the martyred St. Eloy, was popularly believed to have established a monastery dedicated to St. Martin of Tours just outside the walls of the city.

The decay of Carolingian authority in the course of the ninth century marked the end of a golden age for Tournai and its district. The nobility of the area became embroiled in the intermittent civil wars of the time, and Norse sea raiders launched attacks upon the region throughout the century. The destruction caused by the Norse was appalling, reaching its peak in the period 879–884, when many of the churches and abbeys of the region were abandoned or destroyed. The monasteries of the Scheldt valley were sacked, and Tournai itself was ravaged and burned.[3]

The bishops assumed leadership in Tournai, partly because there was no other authority capable of doing so. As in other cities of the region, they used church lands as fiefs to secure the services of "advocates," warriors who managed the defense of the district and provided the military service that powerful lords sometimes demanded of the bishops in exchange for allowing them to retain the secular authority they had assumed.

Although the tenth century was hardly a peaceful era, the city recovered steadily under the rule of a series of able bishops. Local manufacturing and processing developed to serve the immediate market area, and some merchants of Tournai began participating in a growing trade along the Scheldt. By the early eleventh century, a substantial merchant community had arisen, and tensions had begun to arise between the townsmen and their ecclesiastical overlords. In common with the burghers of the rest of Western Europe, the citizens of Tournai were anxious to be freed of the restrictions of a society dominated by a rural, land-owning Church and aristocracy that had little understanding of, or appreciation for, the realities of commercial life.[4]

These tensions were contained, at least to a certain extent, by the growing power of the counts of Flanders. In the course of the eleventh century, the counts established their authority in the frontier towns of Flanders in the person of the castellan. The castellan held the local castle in the name of the count and was provided with extensive lands as fiefs. He maintained his own professional fighting force and developed a town militia to act as a comital defense force. He was responsible for maintaining order and administering justice and usually performed the latter function by presiding over a court of citizen representatives, called *scabini* or *iudici*. The counts were not themselves prone to grant the privileges that the middle class craved, however, so the presence of the castellan only served to introduce another element into the currents of conflict that characterized urban life at that period.

Certain factors made the tensions in Tournai even more complex. In the first place, the powers of the bishop had become dispersed. The bishops relied upon their advocates to back them up with force should it become necessary. The office of advocate had long since become hereditary, however, and the advocates often operated as independent authorities, usually but not always in alliance with the bishop. The eleventh-century ecclesiastical reform that attempted to extend monasticism to the secular clergy introduced yet another complicating factor. This reform had been accepted at Tournai, and most of the cathedral staff had been organized into a monastic corporation supposedly living under the relatively mild restraints of the Rule of St. Augustine. The properties and revenues of the diocese had been divided between the bishop and his personal assistants on the one hand and the cathedral canons on the other.

The canons had continued to marry and hold private property, however, and clergy and even laymen could become canons if they could gain the approval of the chapter and increase its endowments sufficiently. The canons thus became much like a private club but one with extensive public powers. These powers were accentuated by the fact that it was necessary for the bishops of Tournai to spend at least half of their time in Noyon. The chapter of canons of St. Mary's of Tournai constituted the permanent religious authority in the diocese, and frictions between the cathedral and the town were primarily those between the canons and the citizens.

The townsmen, for their part, were no more unified than the cathedral. The social distinctions among the secular inhabitants of Tournai were both great and complicated. The citizenry was divided into nobles and commoners, but that division was not as clear as the social distinction warranted. Nobility and commoners intermingled in daily life, in economic pursuits, and often in political activities.

Nobility in Flanders was a matter of birth, not of wealth or occupation. Although Flanders was unusual in that noble status required both parents to have been noble, the Flemish aristocracy was relatively large. Near the close of the eleventh century, this small county could put fifteen hundred knights in the field. The aristocracy was itself divided, however. The highest level was composed of the peers of the county, of whom there were probably not more than twelve or fifteen at any one time. These men held extensive properties in their own right, some of which they granted as fiefs to secure the services of a military following, and they also held fiefs and offices from the count. The second level of the aristocracy comprised those men who held fiefs in addition to their modest personal properties and exercised some authority in the name of their overlords. The mass of the aristocracy consisted of the *milites*, or knights, who held property of their own and were always prepared to advance their status by accepting a fief and becoming a vassal.

Relatively few of the knightly class reached that goal, however, but sought a living in whatever way presented itself. Many became the salaried warriors of members of the upper nobility, and many others emigrated, often in the capacity of mercenaries. Most, however, remained at home. Since it was not considered demeaning for a Flemish noble to do so, many engaged in trade and manufacturing or received an education that prepared them for entry into the Church. The result was that many of the townsmen of Tournai belonged to the noble class but shared the trades, occupations, and concerns of their commoner neighbors. Nevertheless, this does not mean that the distinction between noble and commoner was not important or that it was not keenly felt.

This was yet another contribution to the undercurrent of so-

cial stress in late eleventh-century Tournai. As the counts of Flanders had extended their power in the course of the tenth and
eleventh centuries, they had sometimes granted lands and authority to their servants, some of whom had been commoners or even
serfs. Some of these appointees had succeeded in passing on their
positions to their descendants, and the servile origins of these
families had become obscured with the passage of time. Noble
families had intermarried with those of the counts' "new men,"
with the result that many of the Flemish aristocracy did not in
fact meet the criterion of noble descent in both the maternal and
the paternal lines. This fact was a more or less open secret, and
wealthy and able commoners had every reason to chafe at the
privileges enjoyed by nobles whose claims to noble status were
often suspect.

With such social tensions, it is not surprising that Flemish society generally, and that of Tournai specifically, should have been
violent or that the law was enforced sporadically at best. Civil institutions were unable to protect the individual, and so the individual relied upon his or her family for support. Kindreds com-
peted for authority and power; since the bishops, advocates,
canons, citizens' court, and castellan were all drawn from the
same broad noble class, families of that class contended for control of these offices. The civil and ecclesiastical discords that
marked the end of the eleventh century in Tournai were family
feuds as well as class conflicts. Politics was a family affair, and an
understanding of the principal kindred of Tournai does much to
explain the troubled situation into which Herman was born.

In the year 953, Fulcher, reputed to be the son of the chief
cook of Louis IV, aspired to be a bishop. The king's favor and the
support of influential members of the royal court gained him the
appointment and placed him deeply in their debt. He discharged
his obligations by abolishing three of the churches in his new see
of Noyon and distributing their properties to those to whom he

owed his appointment. He then wished to go to Tournai, thinking that its extensive diocese would be a source of great wealth, but he realized that he would not likely be received with acclaim. He attempted to interest some of the knights of Noyon in accompanying him by offering them the opportunity of seizing lands in what he described as a veritable paradise. The nobles were not swayed by Fulcher's rhetoric until he promised that he would grant them properties if they would accompany him. And so four nobles and their followers escorted him to Tournai.

Once in Tournai, Fulcher repeated the process that had won him Noyon by abolishing two churches and confiscating their lands. He added to these the properties of the abbey of St Martin, which had been abandoned in the Viking attacks of the late ninth century and had lain unoccupied since then. After distributing these holdings to his followers, he returned to Noyon and left the knights in Tournai to hold the city for him. All of Fulcher's contriving had gained him little real advantage, however, since his episcopacy ended with his death after only eighteen months from the time of his consecration. At least one of the knights of Noyon, however, remained in Tournai. Having been endowed with fertile fields and vineyards south of the city, he prospered and his offspring grew into a numerous and powerful kindred I have called the Osmonds.

The Osmonds were not the only influential family in the district; other family groups gained power during this period as well. In the tumultuous times that saw the fall of Carolingian authority and the onslaught of the Vikings and Magyars, local strong men arose to defend and dominate their localities. One such man was Guerric le-Sor, a resident of Leuze, a small town about six miles east of Tournai. He gathered some fighting men about him, kept a rough peace, and required nearby villages to pay him tribute. By the time of his great-great-grandson, Guerric ad Barbam, the family had established an hereditary claim to the district of Leuze and had become its lords. The counts of Hainaut, in whose territory Leuze was located, were interested in strengthening their southern frontiers, and Guerric ad Barbam was chosen as a likely person to accomplish this. He was consequently given an extensive and fertile tract of land between the Helpe Mineure and Helpe Majeure rivers in fealty and homage to the count who held the castle of Mons and controlled Hainaut.

Guerric encountered a slight problem in that most of the land was held by the monastery of St. Hildtrud by right of an ancient royal grant. Evidence of the grant had been buried with the saint, and so the monks opened her tomb and extracted her testament to support their claim. The same night that they did so, a fierce fire broke out in the monastery, both the testament and the monastery itself were consumed, and Guerric ad Barbam settled down to defend his fiefs. He constructed a small tower at the village of Avesnes, where the main road from Mons to Reims crossed the Helpe Majeure, and this became the seat of the family. The Avesnes clan became wealthy and powerful, and its marriages allied it with a number of the noble families of northern France. Although the major holdings of the Avesnes lay some fifty miles to the south, the family continued to hold Leuze and its district, and its members exerted considerable influence in Tournai.[5]

There were a few other relatively important clans. The St. Piats appear to have been residents of Tournai itself, and the kindred of Mortain held sway in a fortress a few miles south of the town. The principal competitors for influence and wealth were the Avesnes and Osmonds, however. Over the years, the two divided the available offices and established an acceptable balance of power. The post of episcopal advocate, the most powerful secular official in Tournai, was usually held by a member of the Avesnes family, while Osmonds usually occupied the post of dean of a chapter of canons accustomed to act with considerable independence. Since the bishop was often in residence in Noyon, the city and diocese was in effect ruled through an alliance of the Avesnes and Osmond families. During the latter half of the eleventh century, a number of factors arose to disrupt relations between these two kindred and among their members.

In 1068, Radbod, a ecclesiastic with powerful family connections in both Flanders and France and a member of the Avesnes family, became bishop of Tournai-Noyon, a dignity that he was later accused of having purchased. His power was rather limited by the fact that members of the Osmond family held the most important of the ecclesiastical offices other than that of the bishop himself. Herman Osmond was prior of the chapter, and his brother, Siger, held the important post of cantor. The bishop could balance the power of the Osmonds, however, with that of his advocate and kinsman, Fastrad, commander of the bishop's corps of professional fighting men and head of the civil court of Tournai. This was a precarious balance and one that was soon upset.

Civil war broke out in Flanders in 1071, when Robert "the Frisian" gained the support of the German Emperor and a number of Flemish nobles and challenged the rule of the count of Flanders, his nephew Arnulf III. The war ended with Robert's complete victory at the battle of Kassel; Arnulf's supporters were scattered, and Robert's followers gained wealth and position. Advocate Fastrad appears to have taken Arnulf's side; at any rate he disappears from the sources after the year 1071, and his place is taken by Baldwin Osmond, a supporter of Count Robert. Both secular and ecclesiastical power were now monopolized by the Osmond family and Bishop Radbod of the Avesnes was isolated.

The Osmonds took advantage of this unusual opportunity, and, over the next few years, several members of the family benefited by grants extracted from the bishop. Baldwin's brother, Tetbert, was advanced to the post of episcopal prior, with oversight of the episcopal lands, tenants, and revenues; another brother, Theodoric, was given the post of minter; and Ralph, yet another brother, was granted hereditary right to the bishop's brewery. The Osmonds were accounted the richest family in Tournai and were soon connected by marriage to several other wealthy members of the knightly class. By 1075, the Osmonds were in almost complete control of both cathedral and town.

The same disturbances that had given the Osmonds this near-monopoly of authority soon ended it. The German emperor had ceded the rich district of Aalst, situated between the Scheldt and Dender rivers, to Count Robert who compensated many of his followers with fiefs in the area. This territorial acquisition was a disadvantage to one group of Flemish nobles, however. For many years, noble families had held the frontier along the Scheldt against German incursions from Aalst, and they now found themselves without a function. Bishop Radbod's sister had married one of these nobles, Alard of Petegem and Eine, and Bishop Radbod no doubt played a hand in aiding Alard's son, Everard Ralph, and his followers, in establishing themselves at Tournai. Everard soon seized the castle of Mortain, located across the frontier in the county of Hainaut and dominating the confluence of the Scheldt and Scarpe rivers. On the basis of this conquest, Everard was able to establish himself as castellan of Tournai.

The post of castellan was rather new in Flanders and represented an extension of the power of the counts over local districts. In Tournai, Everard represented the authority of the count of Flanders and as such was superior to the episcopal advocate. Advocate Baldwin had little apparent desire to contest the matter. In 1082, he relinquished the post of advocate and entered the Norman monastery of Bec, and Bishop Radbod quickly filled the vacant advocacy with Fastrad's son and namesake. This erosion in the position of the Osmond family was only temporary. Advocate Fastrad found that his authority was limited by Prior Tetbert's control of the episcopal lands and tenants of the region, and determined to eliminate that constraint. In 1084, he treacherously had Tetbert murdered, and, as a result, the Osmonds began a feud against Fastrad and his followers. Fastrad fled to the safety of Avesnes, but his kindred were not inclined to support him in this dispute. The bishop immediately appointed Tetbert's brother, Ralph, as advocate, and, after killing of two of Fastrad's knights, the Osmonds allowed the matter to rest.

Bishop Radbod then turned his attention to the cathedral chapter, the other base of Osmond authority. For some years, Tournai had experienced stirrings of the religious renewal now generally known as the Gregorian Reforms. Perhaps the most significant of several manifestations of this religious zeal in Tournai had been in 1072 when Otfrid of Tournai and some of his disciples had retired to a spot near the village of Watten. They established a community of regular canons living under a rigorous interpretation of the Rule of St Augustine, the first such canonry in the province of Reims. The chapter of canons of the cathedral of St. Mary of Tournai was a poor reflection of this new religious fervor. Although they professed the Augustinian Rule, it was interpreted rather loosely. The canons did not lead a communal life but had separate residences, owned and managed personal property, married, and took an active role in civil and family affairs. Since they also accepted wealthy and influential laymen into their company, the chapter house must have had the air of the exclusive and influential gentlemen's clubs of Victorian London. Not all within the chapter were happy with this state of affairs, however, and there was a significant minority of the canons who would have preferred greater clerical discipline and spirituality.

In 1079, Pope Gregory VII issued a decree that all cathedral churches should maintain a school for the instruction of letters in which one could read the traditional curriculum of grammar, rhetoric, logic (the *trivium*) and arithmetic, geometry, astronomy, and music (the *quadrivium*). Bishop Radbod was slow to comply with this requirement, but in 1086, he finally secured the services of Odo of Orléans, a recognized scholar and a kinsman. More to the point, Odo had been a teacher in the cathedral school of Toul. Bishop Bruno of Toul, who had become Pope Leo IX (1049–1054), had initiated the diocesan reform movement that had led to the divided sentiments of the canons of Tournai. Toul had remained a famous center of reform, and Odo consequently represented a point of view with which most of the canons were not in agreement.

In the year 1090, a famine was beginning to spread over the low countries. An early sign of this shortfall in the food supply was seen in the appearance of a malady that the people of Tournai called "The Fires of Hell." Those living on charity were being given bread made of old and spoiled rye, and they were being poisoned by ergot toxin, an agonizing and often deadly affliction. So many flocked into the cathedral of Saint Mary's of Tournai that the canons decided to expel those who were beyond help. This callous lack of Christian charity set in motion the events that were to lead to the restoration of the abandoned abbey of Saint Martin's.

FLANDERS

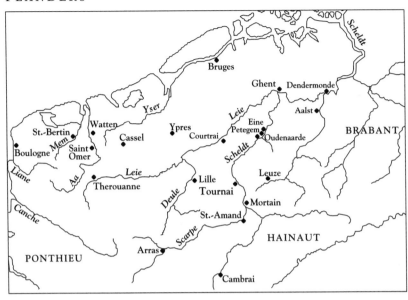

CITY OF TOURNAI

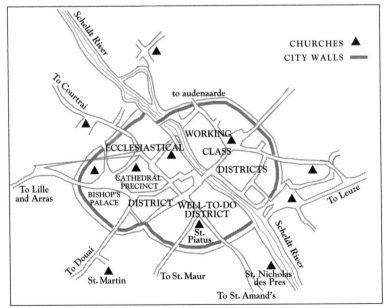

DESCENT OF COUNT ROBERT I THE FRISIAN

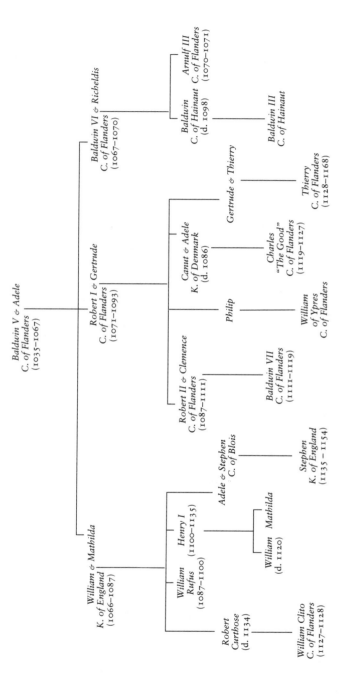

Baldwin V & Adele
C. of Flanders
(1035–1067)

William & Mathilda
K. of England
(1066–1087)

Robert I & Gertrude
C. of Flanders
(1071–1093)

Baldwin VI & Richeldis
C. of Flanders
(1067–1070)

Baldwin
C. of Hainaut
(d. 1098)

Arnulf III
C. of Flanders
(1070–1071)

Baldwin III
C. of Hainaut

Canut & Adele
K. of Denmark
(d. 1086)

Gertrude & Thierry

Charles
"The Good"
C. of Flanders
(1119–1127)

Thierry
C. of Flanders
(1128–1168)

Robert II & Clemence
C. of Flanders
(1087–1111)

Philip

William
of Ypres
C. of Flanders

Baldwin VII
C. of Flanders
(1111–1119)

William Rufus
(1087–1100)

Henry I
(1100–1135)

Adele & Stephen
C. of Blois

Mathilda

William
(d. 1120)

Stephen
K. of England
(1135–1154)

Robert
Curthose
(d. 1134)

William Clito
C. of Flanders
(1127–1128)

THE OSMOND CLAN

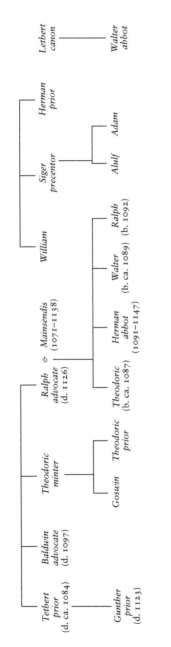

THE AVESNES CLAN

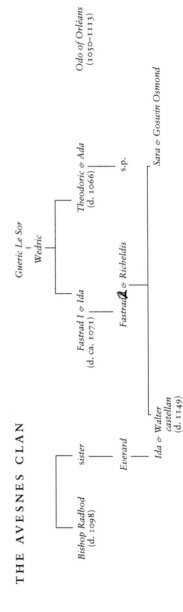

THE RESTORATION OF THE MONASTERY OF SAINT MARTIN OF TOURNAI

CHAPTER HEADINGS IN THE TEXT

PROLOGUE: BROTHER HERMAN TO ALL THE MONKS OF ST. MARTIN'S OF TOURNAI

Above the waters of Babylon and forever recalling Zion, Brother Herman, the least of your servants; to all the most beloved reverend fathers, brothers, and sons, the monks of the abbey of St. Martin's of Tournai.

I offer thanks to God and to you all for the love that you have shown me from my infancy and for the sincere and unstinted obedience that all of you, both present and departed, constantly gave me throughout the time that I consented to be your abbot. I beg the Lord for charity, so that He might reward you on my behalf.

You have asked me a number of times to enlighten both those who are present as well as those who are to come by committing to writing the manner in which our abbey was built and reestablished. I am now quite willing to satisfy your request. I know that a full knowledge of those who have gone before benefits their successors, and that time and again an ignorance of one's predecessors has caused considerable harm.[1]

You should be aware that I have wanted to do this since I was only a boy. I even wrote down a certain amount on tablets, but when I stopped to consider that the founders of our community were still active, I was afraid that I would be considered just a flatterer if I were found writing down their deeds while they were still alive.[2] So I erased what I had started. But now, since I succeeded as the third abbot when the first two were already dead, and since I see that few, if any, of the early monks survive; and also since I am not unaware that the fiftieth year of the restoration of our house is now passing, I can agree to your request with less concern. In fact, if I put it off any longer, many things that need to be written down about those bygone times will gradually be forgotten.[3]

As you know, I returned from Rome shortly after Christmas with letters from the reverend Pope Innocent.[4] I delivered them to Sampson, our lord archbishop of Reims, at Tournai. The canons anticipated there that they would win the right of selecting their bishop themselves and of being completely freed from obedience to the bishop of Noyon. They therefore chose Absalom, lord abbot of St. Amand, as bishop, and I was immediately asked to return to Rome on his behalf.[5]

I see now that I will be detained here in Rome from the octaves of Easter until the octaves of Pentecost awaiting the response of the lord Pope.[6] Lest I should starve mentally from such a long period of boredom or perish from inactivity here in the Lateran Palace, I am undertaking to write a narrative of the restoration of our abbey, and I wish to send the work to you. If it should happen that this Roman heat should grow worse and cause my death, which I very much fear, I earnestly beg you to commend through your prayers the soul of your humble servant to God.[7] I urge the brethren to persevere constantly in two things above all, in religion and in mutual love. Through these two, with the aid of God, you will be able to progress both internally and externally.[8] When we have held firmly to these two principles, we have scorned the outside world and have been contemptuous of the storms that raged in it; and, by scorning the outside world, we have trodden it beneath our feet. But when we have thoughtlessly let these things grow cold among us, we have found that no material prosperity has brought us comfort.

But this preface is already long enough; now let it be joined to a most truthful tale.

THIS PROLOGUE IS COMPLETED;
HERE BEGINS THE BOOK OF LORD ABBOT
HERMAN ON THE RESTORATION OF THE
MONASTERY OF SAINT MARTIN OF TOURNAI[9]

1. Odo of Orléans; His Teaching and Scholarship[1]

In the days when the scepter of the kingdom of the French was borne by Philip, son of Henry, son of Robert, son of that Hugh Capet who had expelled the kings of the lineage of the famous Charles from the realm and achieved dominion,[2] there was a cleric by the name of Odo, a native of Orléans and the son of Gerard and Cecilia. He had been diligently absorbed in the study of the liberal arts from childhood and by the time he was a young man, he had achieved such learning that he was considered second to none of the Frenchmen of his time in scholarship. For this reason, he was better suited for the title of "master" than that of "student." First he instructed scholars in the city of Toul and was then called by the canons of St. Mary's of the city of Tournai to become the master of their school.[3] He directed this school for almost five years, and his reputation spread to such an extent that crowds of different clerics came, not only from France, Flanders, and Normandy, but also from distant and remote Italy, Saxony, and Burgundy.[4] Every day they crowded in to listen to him. If you had seen the flocks of debaters pacing around the city squares, you would have thought that all the citizens had abandoned their other work and had given themselves over completely to philosophy. If you had gone near the school then, you would have seen Master Odo, sometimes walking around with his students and teaching according to the custom of the Peripatetics; at other times sitting and answering various questions after the fashion of the Stoics; and then discoursing in front of the church doors from the evening hours deep into the night, and showing his students the course of the stars with his outstretched finger and tracing the differences between the zodiac and the Milky Way.[5] When his students were giving him a number of presents, one of them gave him a gold ring on which this little verse was appropriately engraved: "A golden ring befits Odo of Orleans."[6]

Although he was learned in all seven liberal arts, Odo particularly excelled in dialectics, and the largest crowd of clerics gathered about him for this subject. He wrote two books on the subject. He entitled the first, which is very useful for recognizing and avoiding logical fallacies, *Sophistem.* He called another book *Complexionem,* and he composed a third on *res* and *ente,* in which he solved whether one and the same could be both Substance and Essence.[7] When the opportunity presented itself for introducing his name in these three little books and in his other works, he did not use the name Odo, but Odard, as everyone then called him.[8]

2. Odo's Philosophy and Teaching Methods Are Attacked by Masters of Other Schools; a Canon Consults a Diviner as to whether Odo's Teachings Are the Best

You must understand that this master did not lecture to his students about words, like some modern teachers, but, like Boëthius and the other doctors of antiquity, he lectured about things.[1] For this reason, Master Rainbert, who lectured on dialectics at the time and in the modern fashion to his students in the town of Lille, was jealous, as were a great many other masters who were not the equals of Odard. They criticized his lectures, saying that their own were better. Some of the clerics were confused by this and uncertain as to whom they should believe. They saw that Master Odard did not stray from the doctrines of the ancients. Nevertheless, because of human curiosity, some of them were always eager, like the Athenians, to hear and learn something new, and praised the other masters.[2] They said particularly that the lectures of the other masters were more valuable for the exercise of disputation and eloquence, as well as for fullness and readiness of speech.

One of the cathedral canons was Galbert, who later became our monk and then an abbot in the diocese of Châlons-sur-Marne. He was disturbed by the excessive variety of opinions and vagaries of the clerics. He secretly brought in a deformed deaf-mute who was quite famous in the city for his divination. Galbert began to ask him by signs of his fingers and nods of his head in which of the masters it would be better to believe.[3] Marvelous to say, the deaf-mute immediately understood his question. Drawing his right hand over his left palm as if cleaving the earth with a plow, and extending his finger toward Master Odo's school, he indicated that Odo's doctrine was most correct. Extending his finger toward the city of Lille, by contrast, he applied his hand to his mouth and, by blowing, indicated that the lectures of Master Rainbert were nothing but windy chatter.[4]

I have not told you this because I believe that diviners should be consulted or that, contrary to holy precept, they are to be believed. I do wish to reprove the excessive presumption of certain arrogant people who want nothing more than to be thought to be educated and would sooner have their newfangled novelties read to them from the books of Aristotle or Porphyry than hear an exposition of Boëthius and other ancient authors.[5] Finally, in a book that he wrote dealing with the Incarnation of the Word, the reverend Anselm, archbishop of Canterbury, did not call dialecticians of this sort clerics, but heretics through dialectics, ". . . who only through arrogance," he says, "consider universals to be substances." He also says that people with this sort of learning deserve to be despised.[6]

3. Odo's Strictness as Master of the School

Although Master Odo was justly praised everywhere for his learning, his religious propriety was so great that he was no less celebrated and universally famous for this. When there was a procession of an army of almost two hundred clerics heading toward the church, it was his custom to follow behind as the very last one in line. You could hardly have found better discipline in any of the strictest monastic communities. No one dared to speak to his companion; no one dared to laugh; no one dared to mutter. No one presumed to turn his eyes to the left or to the right even a little. Indeed, if someone broke wind in the choir, you could not have asked for greater strictness in a Cluniac monk. It is unnecessary to speak about visiting women or about the irregularities in hair, dress, and the like that we see being practiced everywhere today. Odo would either have rid the school of plagues of this kind or he would have resigned the mastership.[1]

Moreover, discipline was so strict that no layman was permitted for any reason to enter the cloister during the lecture hour. Before Odo's arrival, the knights and citizens were accustomed by tradition to make full use of the canons' cloister to hear and determine legal cases. Odo now barred them all, even Everard, the exceedingly powerful castellan of the city, from the interior. It was at that time that Everard captured the castle of Mortain by armed assault, a fortress that had previously been considered impregnable, and had added it to the domain of Tournai.[2] Not even for such a reason did Odo allow the castellan to occupy the cloister until a given hour, although he knew that Everard was more than a little offended. There was nothing that Odo feared less than the unjust anger of the rich and powerful, and he used to say that it was a great dishonor for a man of learning to stray even slightly from the path of rectitude for the favor or gratitude of a prince.[3]

He was highly regarded for such character not only by the canons, but by Lord Radbod, the venerable bishop of the city at the time, and by all the citizens; and he was honored because of his merit. A few people, however, said that he did not practice such severity because of religious zeal but rather because such was the custom of the philosophers of antiquity.[4] Nevertheless, the reader can easily imagine what someone who had conducted himself with such rigor in secular life would be like when he had renounced the world. But let what I have already said about the things he did in school be sufficient; let us now come to the story of his conversion.

4. Odo Decides to Renounce Secular Life

He had been master of the school of Tournai for almost five years when he purchased Augustine's book on free will from one of the clerics. Since he was given to worldly learning and took greater delight in reading Plato than Augustine, he had bought the book only as an addition to his library and tossed it into his bookcase along with some others.[1] Almost two months later, he was lecturing to his students from Boëthius on *The Consolation of Philosophy* and had come to the fourth book, in which he was about to examine free will.[2] He remembered the book he had purchased and wondered if something worth remembering might be found in it since, from its title, it dealt with the same topic. He called his assistant and ordered the book to be brought to him. After opening the book and reading two or three pages, he gradually began to take delight in the beauty of its eloquence.

He immediately convened the clerics, since he did not wish them to be jealous, but to be partners in the treasure he had discovered.[3] "Truly," he said, "I did not know until now how great and how delightful Augustine's eloquence was." He said this and immediately began to read the book chapter by chapter. Not only then but on the next day too, he read the chapters eagerly and began to expound diligently on the more obscure passages. He had arrived in his reading at the third book, where the aforesaid doctor compares sinful souls who have lost celestial glory because of their wicked ways to a slave who once enjoyed status but is then beaten for his crimes and set to cleaning sewers. Those sinful souls likewise embellish this disgusting and sewer-like world, as long as they live in it.[4]

As Master Odard read these words to his listening students, he was struck with a great pain in his innermost heart. Heaving great sighs from his breast, he said, "Alas! How harshly we are condemned by this sentence![5] It really seems to me to suit us as fittingly as if it were written for us alone. We do adorn this foul world in some little way with our learning, but in truth we shall not be worthy of celestial glory after death because we do no service to God nor do we employ our learning in His work. We devote our learning wholly to worldly vanities, seeking after corrupt and worldly praise." Having said this, he arose, completely soaked with tears, and went into the church.[6] The entire school was immediately thrown into turmoil, and the congregation of canons was shaken with astonishment.

Odo gradually began to absent himself from classes after this; to frequent the church more by himself; to give the money collected from everyone to certain beggars,[7] but particularly to needy clerics; and to attempt the rigors of fasting. He would often hold his bread in his fist and cut away at it with a little knife he had purchased outside, keeping nothing more to eat than what remained in his fist. He had been portly and elegant, and he had a milky complexion, but how swiftly he was worn away by the anguish of fasting and transformed in a few days into a gaunt and wasted man, dry and skinny, with protruding bones! Those who were accustomed to seeing him thought that he had been changed into a different person, and many people could now scarcely recognize him.

The news of Master Odo's total renunciation of the world quickly spread through the region. In the wake of this news, four of the clerics, who followed Odo and cherished him, promised him that they would be his inseparable followers wherever he might go. He told them that he would do nothing without their common consent. And we consider ourselves in the debt of those men, who were called by these names: Abbot Odo, whose anniversary is 19 June; Gerbert, who died 10 April; Ralph, who died 26 February; William, who died 22 April. Their fifth comrade, Lamfred, failed, ran away, and died.[8]

Soon the abbots of the entire province, both those of monks and of canons, came one after the other to Tournai, and each one invited Master Odo and his comrades to join his community.[9] Actually, the clerics would have preferred for Odo to choose a canonical order rather than a monastic one, because they considered the canons' regimen, both in ecclesiastical offices as well as in daily food and clothing, to be more tolerable than that of monks.[10] For this reason, they set out to visit the canonry of Mont-Saint-Eloy first, and then went to Watten, where the canons endured a stricter way of life. They carefully considered in which place it would be best for them to stay, but Divine Will now ordained something different for them.

5. The Abandoned Church of St. Martin's

In those days, there was an undistinguished church that had been built in honor of St. Martin on a slight hill outside the south gate of the city.[1] According to tradition, it had been a monastery in ancient times but, along with many other churches of Gaul, it had been devastated by pagans at the time of the Vandal persecution and had crumbled away into nothingness.[2] Nevertheless, there were still some lands in the province that everyone called

"St. Martin's lands." These lands had come into the possession of laymen, however, who held them as benefices from the hand of the bishop.

In fact, the little church had been reduced to such a forlorn state that no divine offices were performed in it at all.[3] The priests who held the parish churches in the city were not willing to sing a mass in it since there were no visitors there who might give them something. Only paupers who had nothing at all— those who had died at some distance from the parish churches and did not have anyone to carry their bodies to them—were taken to the little church of St. Martin, simply because it was closer. The priest of the neighboring church of St. Piatus used to come over and bury them.[4] If by chance he received some donation from one of the faithful, he would take it away with him.[5]

6. The Plague of the Fires of Hell (1090); the Canons Force Dying Men and Women from the Cathedral and They Are Taken to Die and Be Buried at St. Martin's; Bishop Radbod Institutes the Great Procession

Through divine judgment at that time, the province was greatly troubled by the burning plague. The feet of many people were seen to be burned by an invisible fire that was called the "fires of Hell."[1] Every day, crowds of people being consumed in this fashion came to the cathedral of St. Mary, built in the city of Tournai, because it had been established and widely reported that many people had already been cured there through Her mercy. They came not only from this province but also from remote and far-distant regions. But when the cathedral had been completely filled with their numbers, there arose an intense stink just like that of burning human flesh, or, to speak more politely, an "odor" that allowed hardly anyone to enter.[2] The canons were forced to order those whose feet had been burned away, and whose shins were now being burned so that no hope remained of their recovery, to be ejected from the church.[3]

Since they were not accepted in the other parish churches because of their intolerable odor, those who had been evicted from the cathedral were hauled to the church of St. Martin because it was empty and away from the vicinity of the canons. Here the dead, consumed at last by their burning, were buried.

Moved by the savagery of the plague, the venerable bishop Radbod, who was mentioned above, had the populace of the entire province gather at St. Mary's. After he had preached a general sermon and everyone was quite terrified, he cut the hair of over a thousand young men and also cut short the robes that flowed down to the ground and served fashion (actually, whim) more than need. Then he commanded everyone, even infants still suckling, to fast en masse all Saturday until nightfall. Moreover, he established that on the following Feast of the Exaltation of the Holy Cross [14 September], the entire population should form a procession and that, walking with bare feet and carrying the reliquaries of their saints, they should circle the outside of the city.

Everyone thus worked collectively to convert the anger of God into mercy, and many prayers and acts of charity were performed toward this end.[4] This procession around the city on the Exaltation of the Holy Cross is observed in the present day. Almost a hundred thousand people of various sexes and ages have been seen to gather from adjacent regions. Now, however, they do not walk in their bare feet, but knights and young men play games of diverse vanities in the procession and race their horses. Today one finds more gaiety than religion and devotion. The necessity and cause of the first procession should be taught to the numerous people who are now ignorant of these things because of the passage of time.[5]

7. The Laity Call for the Restoration of St. Martin's

Those who were sick were consumed by the flames of an invisible fire in this world but, so we believe, were purged of their sins by this same punishment.[1] When the lords and citizens of the town saw them carried off to the church of St. Martin's,[2] they were moved by compassion. They poured forth tears and ordered the whole city treasury to be carried to St. Martin's. In their hearts, the faithful joined in the prayers of those buried here that God might more swiftly have mercy on his church and restore it.[3] Their pious faith did not disappoint them.

8. An Old Man Predicts the Restoration of St. Martin's and Confounds the Prior of the Canons of the Cathedral of St. Mary

There was a old man by the name of Vidal, *father of that Bernard of whom we made mention in the first arrangement,*[1] who was poor in goods but rich in character. When he saw youngsters coming here on feast days, since it was a spacious and solitary spot, to engage in various games, races, and playful clamor, he would scold them, saying, "Dearest children, you don't want to disturb the souls of those at rest here. Come, I will tell you something that is true. Because their prayers have appeased God, within a short time something great will come to pass in this place." Since the old man often declared this before all who were listening, the prior of the canons, a brisk man by the name of Herman, laughing at him as if he were senile, playfully asked Vidal what this great thing might be, the future of which he was predicting so frequently. Vidal answered him straightaway by saying in front of everybody, "It is certain that you will see it with your own eyes, but I shall not see it."[2] The way things turned out proved that this had been the truth. Prior Herman, together with his brother, Sigebert, precentor of the canons, later became a monk in our monastery and lived for many years, and he often told us what the old man had predicted for him.

9. The Advocate's Wife Distributes Some of St. Martin's Lands and Her Husband Prophesizes That She Will Come to Regret Her Act; the Advocate Prays for the Restoration of St. Martin's and Promises to Give It all His Lands, but Is Murdered before the Monastery Is Restored

Another thing happened shortly afterward. Fastrad was the advocate of the city who held the lands of this church as a benefice from the hand of the bishop. He saw his wife, Ida, sister of Theodoric of Avesnes, distributing these lands to his peasants to live on and farm, and he told her that she would be doing an evil thing if she handed out St. Martin's lands to other people.[1]

He further said that she would regret that she had done it before she died, because divine kindness would quickly come to the aid of the little church.[2] The outcome of the matter proved this to have been true. After the death of her husband, Ida became a nun with us.[3] She beat her breast with hard blows when she saw the same peasants to whom she had given those lands come to contend with us for their redemption. Lamenting the fact that the responsibility for this matter was hers, she revealed that her husband had often predicted this to her.

Many times, when he was riding with his fighting men and passing by this little church, Fastrad would lift his eyes and hands toward its doors and would say with tears, "Oh, Saint Martin! Why don't you have some regard for this church of yours, desolate for so long? I ask for your pity now; grant that it be restored!" When his men had heard such prayers so often, they urged him to install some monks there from monasteries in the neighboring provinces. He answered that no one willing to enter into such poverty was to be found. "If I were to find one man among them who was willing to reside here and to restore this little church, I swear to God and His saints, that I would not leave a single foot of my lands to my children, but I would turn over everything that I possess wholly to this church."[4] Fastrad was killed by his enemies on the feast of St. Medard, however, before the arrival of Lord Odo, so that he was not able to see what he long desired. Nor did he bequeath his sons or even his good will to our house when it came into existence.[5]

10. A Child and His Mother Dream That Two Knights, Walter, Son of Hubert, and Ralph Osmond, Are Rebuilding the Church of St. Martin's; the Mother Predicts That St. Martin's Will Be Restored and That Walter and Ralph Will Do Its Church Much Good

Two knights lived in the city of Tournai. One, by the name of Walter, son of Hubert, was regarded as one of the more powerful nobles of the province. The other, called Ralph of Osmunt, was considered inferior to no one in the city.[1] A certain young boy in his dreams saw these two knights in this church of St. Martin's toiling to restore its ancient ruins. When he awoke, he told this to his mother, and she immediately told him a similar tale, saying "Believe this, my son. That church will soon be restored through the mercy of God, and those two knights will be of great benefit to that abbey." This is just what later happened, for both became monks in the congregation of St. Martin's. The work that they accomplished in it and for it is evidenced by that very thing for which they labored.[2]

11. A Delegation of Citizens Requests That St. Martin's Be Given to Odo and His Followers; Odo and the Bishop Negotiate, and Odo Asks for Exemption from Ecclesiastical Taxes; the Canons Refuse to Agree, but the Bishop Forces Them to Do So; St. Martin's Is Restored under the Rule of St. Augustine and with Odo as Its Abbot on 2 May 1092

As reports of this sort from several different sources in the region of Tournai were foretelling the restoration of the church, the citizens learned that Master Odo and his five clerics proposed to renounce secular life but had not yet decided where they would go. The citizens went to the reverend Bishop Radbod and unanimously requested that Odo and his companions be urged to remain in Tournai, in the church of St. Martin's. The citizens promised that they would not lack the support of the entire city. The bishop rejoiced and, having called them to a private meeting, he revealed the citizens' petition to them and added a great deal of persuasive talk of his own. The four clerics responded that they would accept whatever Master Odo decided; all important negotiations rested on his judgment.

The bishop redoubled his prayers that if Odo should be so brave as to undertake such great good, he might prevail upon him. Odo, however, seeing that the place consisted of nothing but a little church, at one and the same time old and almost in ruins, was apprehensive about accepting such a heavy burden. He left the bishop's palace without having given a definite answer. The bishop kept trying again and again to arouse his soul into undertaking this work. When he saw that he was not making sufficient progress, he summoned a devout priest named Gilbert, who was honored at the time as a sort of prophet in the region and lies buried in front of the altar of the church of St. Peter of Elnon.[1]

Having enlisted Gilbert's aid, the bishop again tried with all his might to enflame the soul of Master Odo. He advanced the proposition of the apostle that he who had labored more would receive a greater reward and "because it is proper that through many tribulations we should enter into the kingdom of God."[2] He urged Odo by pointing out that it would be more advantageous and honorable with God and among men if he were to bring about the establishment of a new congregation than if he were to build upon another's foundations by entering a monastery already constructed.[3] Overwhelmed by the darts of so many and such weighty arguments, Odo finally answered that he would remain if the abbey were turned over to him freed of all obligations by an episcopal charter.

The bishop was greatly pleased and called a meeting of the canons to convince them to grant this request in a generous manner. They somehow guessed at what the future held and absolutely refused to agree. They said that the residents of the diocese would desert the mother church and would frequent St. Martin's because of the piety of its inhabitants. They themselves would be diminished and those of St. Martin's would be raised above them.

The bishop saw that such objections would stall his request for several days, and he feared that it would strike Master Odo to set out elsewhere during these delays. He called the canons together again and, when he saw that all his entreaties were being poured forth in vain, he grew somewhat angry. "Eya," he said, "now then, in the name of the Lord and by virtue of obedience, I command you to tell me if it is not permissible for me to deliver this church—which is under my control and does not in any way belong to your congregation—to those who would serve God in it and are eager to build it to the honor of God?" They were then constrained by the bonds of obedience, knowing that the church was in the hand of the bishop and that he could legitimately do whatever he wished with it. Since they could not oppose any of this by canon law, they finally accepted his counsel. They said that they would be co-donors, because it pleased the bishop, but with the condition that he should not allow any of their parishioners who might die in secular life to be buried at St. Martin's without their permission.[4]

The bishop was greatly gratified and, on the following Sunday, which was the second of May, the Eve of the Apostles Philip and James, he led Master Odo and his four clerics, with an immense crowd of all the canons and people, in a procession to the church that had been founded in honor of Christ the Confessor and of Bishop Martin and had been destroyed by the barbarian attacks of early times and the undisciplined flight of the monks serving there under an abbot. He transferred it to them quit of episcopal obligations and confirmed this with an episcopal charter in the presence of all.[5]

And thus he left them there to serve God canonically in clerical habit under the rule of St. Augustine. This occurred in the one thousand and ninety-second year of the Incarnation of the Lord; Pope Urban presiding in the apostolic seat; Rainald, archbishop of Reims; Radbod, lord bishop of Tournai and Noyon; Philip ruling the kingdom of the Franks; Henry, emperor of the Romans; the English governed by the renowned King William, son of Count Robert of the Normans, who subjugated England to himself by force when Harold and his army had been overthrown; the country of Flanders held by the younger Robert, son of the Frisian.[6]

12. Count Robert of Flanders, Lord of Tournai (1071–1092)[1]

Robert was the son of Count Baldwin [V, 1035–1067], who built the church of St. Peter's in the fortress of Lille, placed canons in it, and commanded that he be buried there. When he died, his son Baldwin, brother of the aforesaid Robert, succeeded him [Baldwin VI, 1067–1070]. He constructed the church of St. Peter's of Hasnon, in which he placed monks, and directed that he be buried there.[2]

By precept of Count Baldwin, his father, this Baldwin took as his wife Richeldis, the widow of Count Herman of Hainaut.[3] He sired two sons by her, Baldwin and Arnold. The quarrels that had persisted for a long time between Flanders and Hainaut having been thus composed, he ruled both counties. When Leo [IX (1049–1054)], who was the Roman pope at the time and who had previously been the bishop of Toul and was called Bruno,[4] heard this, he said that the marriage was not legitimate because their lineages were within the limits of consanguinity. He prophesied that Baldwin's posterity would not possess either county for long. The way it turned out proved the truth of this; for the Baldwin who lies at Lille, fearing lest dissension should arise after his death between his sons, Baldwin and Robert, gave all of his land during his lifetime to Baldwin, and he had his nobles pledge homage and fidelity to him. At Audenarde, publicly in the presence of the father and son and many princes, Robert swore upon the relics of saints that he would not harm either Baldwin himself or his heirs in the county of Flanders in any fashion. When he had completed his oath, he left Flanders and withdrew into Frisia.

13. A Respectable Woman Predicts the Future of Flanders (1071)

After several years, Robert heard that his brother Baldwin was dead and buried in the monastery of Hasnon and that his son Arnold had now been made count of Flanders [Arnold III, 1070–1071]. He secretly gathered certain of the Flemish nobles and, having promised them many gifts, he invaded Flanders. Neglecting the oath he had made, he openly prepared for war against his nephew. When Arnold learned of this, he allied with King Philip of France, from whose hand he accepted the land. He did battle with his uncle Robert at the fortress of Kassel. When the battle had been joined and Arnold had been killed, Robert obtained Flanders. Richeldis, Arnold's mother, was driven from Flanders and returned to the county of Hainaut with her other son, Baldwin. Thus it became clear that the prophesy of Pope Leo had been true.

Robert immediately sent legates to Emperor Henry [IV, 1056–1105], asking the emperor to be his ally if it should be necessary. One of these legates was Baldwin, advocate of Tournai,[1] and later a monk of Lord Anselm, archbishop of Canterbury. He told how, when they were nearing Cologne, they met a respectable but unknown matron, who asked them who they were, where they were going, and what they intended to do. They were unwilling to reveal such things to her, but she said, "I know that you are legates from Robert, count of Flanders, who broke the oath that he made to his father regarding his brother, killed his brother's son, and invaded his land. And you are now going to Emperor Henry to obtain his grace and friendship. You may know, therefore, that your path is prosperous and you will obtain the grace of Caesar. Robert and his son shall hold Flanders in peace, but his grandson, who shall be begotten by his son, will die without children. A handsome youth coming from Dacia will succeed to the county, but he too shall die without issue. After him, two other men from Flanders will contend, and one of them will kill the other. The victor will obtain Flanders, and his heirs will hold it until the time of the Anti-Christ." I heard Baldwin, the advocate of Tournai who was one of those legates, tell this tale when I was still a small boy; and now that I am verging on old age, I see with my own eyes that what he said was true.

14. The History of the Sons of William the Conqueror; William II Is Killed While Hunting and Henry I Gains the Throne; Robert Curthose, Count of Normandy, Disputes the Succession; Henry I Defeats Robert in Battle and Keeps Him a Prisoner for the Rest of His Life; England and Normandy Reunited under Henry

Robert held Flanders in great peace. He was so powerful that Philip, king of the French, married his step-daughter, from whom he fathered King Louis [VI, 1108–1137].[1] Robert's sister [Matilda] was wed to William, count of Normandy. When King Harold of England was killed and England taken by force, William held two dominions, being count of the Normans and king of the English. On one side of his seal, he sat on a horse as a count, and, on the other side, with a scepter upon a throne as a king. He fathered three sons from Mathilda, daughter of the count of Flanders, namely, William [William I Rufus, 1087–1100], who first succeeded him as king of England; and Robert [Robert II Curthose, 1087–1106], to whom he gave the county of the Normans. His third son was Henry, who at first had nothing, so that he appeared to be nothing more than one knight among many others when his father, the renowned King William, had died.[2]

Henry had marvelous luck, however. After a reign of almost ten years, his brother, King William, went into the woods to hunt with some young men. He saw a stag running past them and ordered one of his knights, Walter Tyrell, who was standing opposite him with a bow and arrow, not to let the stag get past. The knight had his bow drawn and shot an arrow at the deer, but he struck the king in the heart, and he died instantly. And so his brother, Henry, who had nothing before, succeeded him in the realm [Henry II, 1100–1135].

Henry's brother, Robert, rebelled against him and claimed the realm of England because he was the elder son and ought to have succeeded his brother by right of majority.[3] Henry gathered an army when he learned of this, and he crossed the sea and invaded Normandy. Henry defeated Robert in battle and took him prisoner.[4] He took Robert back to England and kept him confined in a castle until the end of his days. Nevertheless, Henry commanded that Robert was to be supplied and provided with whatever was necessary in creature comforts as if they were for himself. Thus a single person again held the kingdom of England and the county of Normandy, and Henry ordered the paternal seal to be made for him. Since I have mentioned Henry and there will be no other passage referring to him, I may appear to have digressed considerably from the narrative I have undertaken, but I shall have some things to say that will be worth remembering.

15. Henry Wishes to Marry a Scottish Princess; Anselm Objects Because She Is a Nun; an Ecclesiastical Council Is Held; the Tale of Princess Edith and the Nun's Veil; the Council Decides That Henry May Marry Her, but Anselm Predicts That They Will Have Few Children

When he had been confirmed in his realm, Henry wanted to marry the daughter of King David of Scotland.[1] He spoke with Lord Anselm, the reverend archbishop of the city of Canterbury at the time,[2] and asked him to bless her and unite them in marriage in a solemn wedding ceremony. The archbishop replied that he refused to bless her and that he advised the king not to marry her. He said that he had been told by a reliable source that she had worn upon her head the veil of a nun, by which she had shown herself to be the wife of a heavenly, rather than an earthly, king. The king argued that he had promised that he would marry her and had even sworn an oath to her father, King David. In order to keep his oath, he declared, he would not repudiate her unless it should be so decided by canon law.

He ordered the distant archbishop of York to assemble a council of the bishops, abbots, and ecclesiastics of all of England to determine such an important affair by ecclesiastical judgment. In the general council, the abbess in whose convent the girl had been reared was asked whether the placing of the nun's veil upon the girl's head had in fact been consecrated by an episcopal blessing according to custom. The abbess answered candidly and in the presence of everyone, "In truth, King David, her father, did not commend her to me so that she would become a nun, but only so that she could be reared safely in our convent with other little girls her own age and be taught her letters."

"When she had become a young woman, I was informed one day that King William, the brother of my lord King Henry, who was alive at that time, had come in order to take a look at her.

He and his knights had already dismounted before the gates of our convent, and the gates had been opened to him at his request. I was terrified when I heard this. He was a young king and untamed, and he wanted to do immediately whatever came into his head. Since he had come so suddenly and unexpectedly in order to look at the girl, I was afraid that he might perhaps do some illicit violence to her when he saw her beauty. I led her into a inner room and I explained to her just how matters stood. With her permission, I placed a veil on her head so that the king would be recalled from his forbidden passion when he saw it. Nor did my hope fail me."

"The king had entered our cloister as if for the purpose of inspecting our roses and other flowering herbs.[3] As soon as he saw her with our other girls wearing a veil on her head, he withdrew from the cloister and left the convent, and so openly revealed that he had come for no other reason than her. When King David, the girl's father, came to our convent within the week and saw the veil upon his daughter's head, he was angry.[4] He tore the veil into pieces, threw them on the ground, and trampled them under his feet. He then took his daughter away with him." The abbess was next asked how many years old the girl was at the time. She answered that she might have been twelve.

The king then instructed the archbishop to order a judgment to be made in this matter. The bishops and the abbots, taking counsel and reading various chapters of the canon, decided in common that the girl should not be prohibited from marrying because of an event of this sort. As long as she was under legal age, she was under the tutelage of her father and could do nothing legally without his consent.

When this judgment had been rendered, the king asked the archbishop if he wish to challenge anything in it. Lord Anselm replied that he would not challenge it because the council had in fact judged correctly according to the decrees of the canon. Then the king said, "Since you approve of the judgment that has been made, I would like you to marry me to the girl." But Lord Anselm said, "I do not disapprove of the judgment, but if your Majesty would trust me, I would advise you not to marry her. However it may have happened, she has nevertheless worn a nun's veil; you could find a more suitable match among the daughters of kings and counts." The king persevered in what he had undertaken, and that most holy man added, "You are ignoring my counsel, my lord king, and you are going to do what you please, but I believe that, as long as you live, you will not see England rejoice for long because of a child that might born of her." I heard him say this when I was a youth; now I see that it has, for the most part, come to pass.[5]

16. The Anarchy of King Stephen (1136–1154); Three Prophecies

The king fathered two sons and a daughter from her. When his sons were young men and were returning from Normandy, their ship broke up, and they perished in the sea with many others.[1] He sent his daughter, along with great riches, to Henry, emperor of the Romans, who took her as his wife and celebrated his nuptials with great glory at Liege. But a swift death came before he had fathered a single child by her and he left her a widow.[2] Having been widowed, she married the count of Anjou.

When King Henry died suddenly at Rouen [1134], the English nobles established Stephen, count of Boulogne and brother of Count Theobald of Champagne, as king.[3] Robert [of Gloucester], King Henry's son by a concubine, was greatly indignant at this and rose in open revolt against Stephen. He took Stephen prisoner in a battle and confined the defeated king in a castle that his father [King Henry] had given him. He [Robert] then ordered his sister to come quickly with her son [the future Henry II] to England and receive the paternal realm. Thinking that her restoration would be entirely prosperous, she [Matilda] quickly returned, but she found things quite different from what she had anticipated. Stephen's wife had assembled the nobles and opposed her staunchly. After a few days, Matilda and Stephen were reconciled by Robert, and agreements were made between the two. Freed from his chains, Stephen once again assumed the rule of England. And so Henry's cheated daughter was left to sigh over her vain hopes.[4]

Although we are uncertain of the future, we see this one thing clearly: that, in accordance with the prophecy of Lord Anselm, England did not rejoice for long because of the offspring of the queen whom Henry had married after she had worn the nun's veil. On the contrary, England sank from its earlier wealth into great poverty because of the devastation and expense of persistent dissension. The words of wise men and of prelates of the Church are therefore not to be condemned, but rather venerated and feared. The truth of this has been demonstrated by an account of the prophecy of Pope Leo concerning Robert, the count of Flanders who married his kinswoman, followed by that of Lord Anselm concerning the king of England. Now let us return to what the unknown woman prophesied to the legates regarding Robert, count of Flanders, and we shall explain in brief how true it was.

17. Count Henry of Brabant is Killed at Play (1095)

As we have already said, Count Robert gave his step-daughter in marriage to King Philip of France; his sister to Count William of Normandy; one of his two daughters to King Canute of Denmark, from whom Charles was born; and the other to Count Henry of Brabant.[1]

When Count Henry heard that Everard, the castellan of Tournai, had very able knights, he came to Tournai to test their mettle. One day, when he had gone out and was youthfully exulting in his strength,[2] he called for a man on the other side, named Goswin of Forest, to come at him alone. Goswin answered that he would not charge him because Henry was his lord, and he was afraid that he might accidentally hurt him. Again and again the count provoked him by calling him timid and cowardly, goading him with such insults so that he would charge. The knight was finally driven to action by these repeated affronts. He raised his lance, spurred his horse violently, and charged against the count. He wished only to knock the count from his horse in war-like play, but instead fixed his lance in his heart. The count died instantly. His name and reputation were so great at the time that the entire region was filled with grief.

He had driven robbers and thieves from the land so completely that in no other land could there be found greater peace than in his. He died through such foolishness—or stupidity—and left no heir. His wife was left a widow, married Duke Simon of Alsace near Saxony, and bore him many children.[3]

18. Clemence of Burgundy and the Perils of Contraception

Having provided so nobly for his daughters, Count Robert left all of Flanders to his son, Robert, upon his death.[1] It was in the younger Robert's time that Lord Odo and his clerics renounced the world and entered the church of St. Martin's of Tournai. Odo found the count and his wife, Clemence, to be generous supporters of St. Martin's. Clemence was a native of Burgundy, of course, the daughter of William, duke of Burgundy, and the sister of Guy, the archbishop of Vienne who was later made pope of the Romans and called Calixtus.[2] Calixtus held a general council at Reims in the time of Archbishop Ralph, called "Green" [1119]. Ralph's successor was Manasses, the predecessor of Rainald, bishop of Anjou.

When she had borne three of Count Robert's children in less than three years, Clemence was afraid that if she bore any more, they would fight among themselves for Flanders. She employed a female art so that she could no longer become pregnant. This was punished by divine vengeance in that all of her children died a long time before she. Later, in her widowhood, seeing other women's sons as counts and suffering many evils from them, she bewailed too late that she and her offspring should be disinherited.[3]

19. Count Robert of Flanders on the First Crusade (1096–1100)

In a council at Clermont two and a half years after lord Odo's conversion, Pope Urban admonished all the bishops to enjoin the people subject to them to go to Jerusalem for the remission of their sins and to free the Holy Sepulcher and the city from the power of the pagans. Then indeed, you might have seen a countless multitude from the West abandon their native lands and head for Jerusalem as if by divine command. Count Robert, together with Count Godfrey of Bouillon, Count Robert of Normandy, Count Raymond of St. Gilles, Count Hugh of Vermandois, Count Baldwin of Hainaut, Anselm of Ribemont, Clarenbald of Vendeuil, and many other nobles left Flanders on this occasion and set out with the people of God.[1] Antioch was besieged and captured together with many other cities, and, with the aid of God, Count Robert finally entered Jerusalem victoriously. When the pagans had been either expelled or killed, Christians settled in the city, and a king had been appointed, he returned to Flanders. Having obtained great renown, he ruled the province for almost twelve more years.

20. The Death of Count Robert and Accession of Baldwin VII (1111)

Count Robert was then called by his sister's son, King Louis of France, to the assault of a castle called Dam-martin.[1] He fought bravely in the battle, as was his custom, and drove back the enemies of the king. Exhausted by this extreme effort, he was carried to his bed and, after three days there, he was dead. He was carried by the king and nobles of the realm to Arras and was interred in the church of St. Vaast with great mourning.[2] Immediately after the count's burial, the king summoned Baldwin, the count's quite youthful son [who had not yet been made a knight] along with the boy's mother and handed over all of his father's lands to him. He ordered the nobles of Flanders to render Baldwin public homage, and then returned to France.

What then shall I say of Baldwin, who at heart was still of a tender age?

21. Young Count Baldwin VII, (1111–1119) Orders the Nobles to Keep the Peace

When the king returned to France, Count Baldwin summoned his nobles, informed them that he intended to keep the peace, and asked them to assist in this cause. He warned them that whoever was the first to violate the peace would have justice done upon him for that reason. None of them, however, undertook to swear to keep the peace. The nobles promised to observe it, and so the court adjourned, with many saying that the peace would not be easily kept by such a child because no one feared him.[1]

22. Count Baldwin's Justice: A Knight Is Boiled Alive

After almost two months, a poor little woman was robbed by a thief of two cows, complained loudly to the count, and showed him where the culprit would be staying for the night. The young count immediately took the robber to Bruges as a prisoner. When everyone begged him not to order the knight to be hanged or to have his eyes gouged out, he answered that he would do neither. He immediately directed that a huge copper vessel, which is popularly called a kettle or cauldron, should be hung high up in the square, in full public view, and that it should be filled with water.

A great fire was set beneath it, and when the water had come to a hard boil, he had the knight thrown into the cauldron still fully clothed and still belted with his sword.[1] He killed him in boiling water. Everyone was immediately struck with such fear that, from that time on, no one in all Flanders dared to steal anything.

23. Count Baldwin's Justice: An Old Woman Is Heard

One day, the count entered the church of St. Peter's in Ghent in order to hear vespers when a poor little woman suddenly began to complain that her cow had been stolen from her. When the count politely asked her to wait for him at the porch until he had heard vespers, she said that she would not get another chance of talking to him because of the crowd of knights and princes that would be standing around him. He immediately took off his cloak and gave it to her, telling her to keep it for him until after vespers. When vespers were finished and the nobles gathered around him wanted the count to talk about other business, he swore that he would not talk to anyone until the poor little woman's cow had been returned to her. And so he satisfied her plea and was blessed a thousand times by her.

24. Count Baldwin's Justice: Nine Knights Hang Each Other, and the Last Hangs Himself (with a Little Help)

Each year on the Feast of St. John, a great market was customarily held in the village of Thourout.[1] They tell this story about the count. Ten knights trusted by their kinsmen stole something from the pack of a merchant going to the market. The count immediately went out, took them prisoner, and shut them up in a house.

Their families were quite frightened and quickly went to the count to beg his mercy. They promised to pay however much he wished in money or horses just so long as he did not hang them. Pretending to be satisfied by the prices to be paid for them, the count told their families that they should wait a little while, until he had entered the house and spoken with the accused, when he would return to them. He spoke and immediately going in with a few men, he ordered the prisoners to be hanged inside the house. Since his men pleaded with him to excuse them and not force them to incur the eternal wrath of the kindred of the accused, he let them leave.[2]

He advised the prisoners that anyone who wished to escape should hang his comrade. Nine of them were hanged in this fashion,[3] and the count commanded the remaining man to throw a rope over a beam, stand on a stool, and place a rope noose around his neck. When he had done this, the count shoved the stool with his foot and left the man hanging two cubits from the earth. And so he went out with his men and back to the prisoners' families. "Eya," he said, "go on in and bring them out, and, when you have brought them out, warn them not to steal anything else in my lands." He spoke, and immediately mounted his horse and left that place.[4]

The kinsmen entered the house and found all their relatives hanged and already dead. Terrified, they fled.

The count drove all robbers out of his lands by such actions. Not only did no one dare to steal anything, but if someone found a precious tapestry or a golden bowl lying in the road, he would not dare to pick it up. Flanders might have called itself happy if it had deserved to have such a ruler for long. When such a peace had been established that he saw that no one had brought a complaint to him for an entire year, Count Baldwin counted it a disgrace to remain quietly at home. Being youthful, scarcely thirty years old, he began to train himself in the use of arms, and whenever he heard that soldiers had gathered somewhere for the sake of a fight, he yearned to be there also.

25. Count Baldwin Invades Normandy and Liberates a Few Deer

At this time, King Henry of England invaded Normandy, waged war on his brother, Count Robert, and sent him defeated to England. Robert's son, William [Clito], a ten-year old boy, was disinherited and fled to Count Baldwin of Flanders.[1] The count reared him and made him a knight when he turned fourteen. He then advised William to rebel against his uncle, the king of England, who held his father prisoner. The count repeatedly undertook to attack Normandy along with William. [Through an envoy,] King Henry commanded the count to desist from such attacks, or he should see him coming to Bruges with his army. The count immediately replied that Henry should not put himself to so much trouble, since it would be better for the king to see him attacking Rouen.

He said that, and the royal envoy was immediately followed by five hundred knights. The count arrived at the city of Rouen, where Henry was staying, fixed his lance firmly in the city gate, and called out to the citizens that they should tell the king that the count of Flanders had come. The king had two thousand men with him, but like a most prudent man, he would not sally out against an irrational youth. He told all of his knights that no one should presume to go out through the gate. He advised them to stroll around, ". . . because," he said, "when he grows tired, he will withdraw and he will take nothing from my land with him." The count was very gloomy because he could not draw out anyone when he went around the city walls shouting. He did not know what he might do, since he could not take such a great city with so few knights. He saw in the distance a herd of deer that the king had shut up in a nearby wood, and the young man exclaimed, "If I can do nothing else, at least I will drag those deer from their pens and set them free." He said this and immediately went running with his knights with their swords drawn. He cut down a very strong fence made of tree-trunks that held the deer captive, and scattered the deer across the fields. And so he returned to Flanders having accomplished nothing.

26. Count Baldwin Dies and Appoints Charles His Successor (1119)

Meanwhile, Charles, his paternal aunt's son, whom she conceived by King Canute of Denmark, came to him at the death of his father, and Count Baldwin generously kept him.[1] He arranged his marriage to the sister of Count Ralph of Verdun. He commended Charles, so that he should keep Flanders while he himself was absent, and he then began to raid Normandy in greater security. Although this exercise in arms and warfare gave him great pleasure, just as it should afford a young man, it nevertheless caused monks, clerics, and other wise men the greatest sadness, for everyone declared that he could not live for long among such dangers. Nor were they mistaken in this opinion, but rather the contrary; the fearsome thing that they feared befell them and that about which they were concerned happened.

While the count was attacking Normandy with great tenacity, a knight wounded him over the nose with a sword. The count would not leave the fight because of the wound, but, in addition to his injury, he was struck by the excessive heat of the sun. When the wound began swelling, he was taken back to Arras against his will. Here the doctors agreed that he would be easily cured if he were willing to abstain from noxious food. Since he would not give up goose flesh and similar things, the patient was weakened by his wound and was confined to his bed for the entire year. He nevertheless often had himself carried from place to place in a litter in order to avoid boredom. Finally, when he saw that he could not avoid it, he established Charles as his successor and turned Flanders over to him. He was made a monk at St. Bertin and was dead within eight days. He left a legacy of immense grief and sadness to all the churches, and he demonstrated most thoroughly that no one should confide in his own powers.

His kinsman, Charles, succeeded him as count [Charles I the Good, 1119–1127]. He was not a bit less understanding of justice than Baldwin, and, because he was a little older, he was wholly superior to him in prudence and caution. He protected the churches so well that he was soon called the Father of Churches. I shall relate one thing concerning this that comes to mind, so that, since it concerns his devoutness, he might be recognized for this.

27. Count Charles Reproves the Abbot of St. Bertin

When he saw Abbot John of St. Bertin enter his court at Bergues St. Winnoc on the day of Epiphany,[1] he immediately asked him, "Lord abbot, who sang high mass today in the church of St. Bertin?" The abbot replied that they did not lack someone who would sing it respectably, since there were more than a hundred monks in his monastery. The count replied, "You yourself ought to have sung it with great solemnity, eaten with the brothers in the refectory, and provided good sustenance to those who stood vigil all night until matins from those things that the counts who preceded me gave you, and not have attended my court." The abbot responded that he would rather have sung the mass than have come to that place, but that he had been compelled to come because of a knight who had taken as his own certain lands that the monastery had possessed peacefully for more than sixty years. The count rejoined, "And why did you not entrust this to me on behalf of your community? It is your job to pray for me, and it is mine to protect and defend churches." He spoke, and the knight was soon admitted. The count asked him why he had disturbed St. Bertin for land that they had possessed for so long. The knight answered that the monastery had held it unjustly because it should have been his by law.² The count said, "Since your father was silent about this, you also will be quiet, because I swear by the soul of Count Baldwin that if I hear any further complaint about this, I shall not do anything to you but what Count Baldwin did to the man in Bruges whom he boiled in a cauldron." Abbot John told me how he was granted peace by the count.

28. The Murder of Count Charles the Good (2 March 1127)

Because Flanders was not worthy of such a ruler, Bertulf, prior of the church of Bruges, and his kinsmen, impious men who denied that they were servants of the count, united and secretly conspired against him because of the judgments that he was making.¹ When this was announced to the count at Ypres, many people warned him not to go to Bruges. He answered that he was prepared to die for justice, if God so wished, rather than be kept from doing what was right. He immediately went to Bruges with his knights, burned down a fortification that the conspirators had erected, and went to his own house. He arose at dawn the next morning and went from his palace grounds to the church of St. Donatian. He ordered his chaplain to sing mass for him there, for it was the fourth feria of the second week of Lent.² When the speech of Esther in the Epistle was being read, and the count was prostrate in prayer, with an open psalter so that he might read Psalms, a poor little woman came up and begged alms from him. She accepted from his hand one of the thirteen pennies that the count placed upon the psalter according to his custom. When she had taken it, she exclaimed to him, "Lord count, look out!" The count lifted his head to see what it was. Behold Burcard, the nephew of the prior, who had come up to him silently, in armor and with his sword drawn! He thrust his sword into the count's forehead and added many other wounds, murdering him there in front of the altar. He killed a man who was with the count, and the others who were there were frightened and ran away. The sad news straightaway filled the country that the glorious Count Charles had been killed in church.[3]

29. The Lame Beggar Who Ran (2 March 1127)

Lord Gilbert, abbot of St. Peter's of Ghent, a most truthful and religious man, told me and asserted under a vow of truth, that there was a lame pauper, well-known to him, in Bruges at the time to whom the count had often given alms.[1] When beggar heard the sad news, he went to the church sobbing and wailing with a great clamor. Laboriously crawling on his hands and knees, he climbed up the stone stairs to the chair of state at which the count had been killed.[2] He found the count's corpse unattended, lying there stained with blood. Astonished at how quickly and completely everyone had abandoned the body, he rested beside it and gave voice to loud moans and words from the great pain of his heart. He began to smear his feet and legs with the blood that was flowing copiously. He did not do this, so he said, because he had any hope that he would be cured, but only because of the sweetness and love of the man who had done so many good things for him. Suddenly, he felt himself to be perfectly cured by divine mercy, and went down the stairs and through the doors like a goat. He ran the circuit of the entire town, showing all of the populace that he was cured.

This cast a great cloud of confusion over the murderers. It might have been greater still, except that the pauper was terrified of their power. He went out to make a public speech but ran away instead. The conspirators had embezzled great wealth from the rents of the count over which he had set them. Moreover, shortly before his death, the count had set the day of their hearing at the fortress of Kassel [in Flanders], where they might prove themselves not to be his serfs by the judgment of the count's nobles. Bertulf, prior of the same church and uncle of Burcard, had openly brought three thousand soldiers with him. Since the count feared that so many people might start a riot, he had postponed the case to another day.

30. Chaos in Flanders

The body of the count could not be buried at St Donatian's since, just as soon as lord Bishop Simon, whose sister the count had married, had heard of such great wickedness, he had placed an interdict upon all sacred offices in that church. But the provincial bishops would by no means suffer the body to be moved to another church. Prior Bertulf, wishing to excuse himself from the count's death as much as he could, quickly had a sepulcher built for him, made of precious marble columns, and located in the very place on the balcony where he had been killed. The body was placed there and remained for almost sixty days. There was such a sudden and great disturbance in all of Flanders that what one reads in the Apocalypse, "After a thousand years the devil will be set free" [Rev. 20:7], appeared to happen in that province to the letter, or at least two-thirds of the letter.[1] One saw everywhere only plundering, robbing, and even killing. It was then so evident that even the most simple person could easily see how much had depended on the power of that ruler alone, who had compelled such a turbulent folk to be as quiet as cloistered monks.

31. Baldwin of Ghent Establishes a Peace and Attacks Bruges (1127)

Seeing such a great disturbance, the lords of Flanders, primarily Baldwin of Ghent, brother of Ivo Nigel, who is now count of Soissons, met upon an agreed day and arranged a peace among themselves. Since such a crime as the murder of their count, if it remained unpunished, would be a lasting disgrace to them, they gathered an army and headed for Bruges. The murderers, with many supporters aiding them, went out with a great force of knights and foot soldiers to do battle against them.

Baldwin, protected by a breastplate and helmet, shouted out in a loud voice, "We do not come against you, citizens, nor do we wish to destroy the fortress of Bruges. We do wish to avenge the unjust death of our lord, lest we also might be accused of his betrayal and be called traitors. If you therefore come to do battle against us, you are allowing yourselves to become participants in this great crime, and you will be much hated for that. I advise you and warn you that it would be better for you to be with us and aid us in confounding the betrayers of our lord."[1]

When he had said these things, the crowd cried out deafeningly, joined Baldwin, and fought against those with whom they had come. Soon the murderers and their supporters turned in flight. Since they had no other avenue of escape, they fled back into the city. They went into the count's tower, where they were shut up by Baldwin and were besieged for almost two months.

32. King Louis of France Seeks a New Count of Flanders (1127)

Meanwhile, King Louis of France, the son of Charles's maternal aunt, of whom we spoke above, was shocked by such grim news regarding his cousin and went to Arras. Since Charles had died without an heir, the king asked the Flemish nobles whom they wished to have as count. The king could not be said to have been particularly close to any of them, and since he had many sons, it was suggested that he should give Flanders to one of them. But the king, turning the matter over like a prudent man, considered that none of his sons was yet twelve. Nor could such an untamed people be ruled without a master who would stick to them constantly. Since it was not always possible for him to be with them, and fearing that some other misfortunes might befall the people of Flanders because of this, he took refuge in the higher counsel of choosing someone from among those of the land.

33. Count Baldwin of Hainaut Jilts the Niece of Countess Clemence

At the time, Count Baldwin of Hainaut was known to be as greatly skilled in arms as anyone his age. His ancestor was the Baldwin who built the monastery of Hasnon and who was mentioned above. Taking Countess Richeldis of Hainaut as his wife, he [Baldwin of Hasnon] had ruled both counties, Flanders and Hainaut, and had two sons by Richeldis. Arnold succeeded his father and was killed by his father's brother, Robert, at Kassel. Baldwin, who held the country of Hainaut with his mother, fathered one son, Baldwin by name. He took the road to Jerusalem with the other nobles at the beginning and never returned. Whether he was killed or captured no one knows to this day. His son, Baldwin, became count.[1]

Clemence, countess of Flanders, urged Count Baldwin to marry one of her nieces and promised that she would give him a thousand marks of silver along with her. The young man consented and swore to marry her on a stated day. In like manner, he accepted from her an oath of betrothal made publicly in the presence of many witnesses. Before the stated day, however, the young man broke the oath he had made and took Yolanda, daughter of Count Gerard of Bamberg,[2] as wife. The countess gnashed her teeth at this, most of all because she saw that her brother, Archbishop Guy of Vienne, had now been made pope, with the name of Calixtus.[3] She complained to him that his family had been shortchanged by this petty count. He immediately sent letters directly to Ralph, archbishop of Reims, that he should not defer punishing this perjury.

The archbishop convened bishops, abbots, and many other ecclesiastics, and commanded the count to be present and answer regarding the agreement of marriage. Clemence complained loudly that he had promised by oath that he would take her niece as his wife on an agreed-upon day, adding that she had the testimony of three hundred knights concerning this if he should deny it. Baldwin answered that he did not wish to deny what she had said, nor could he do so, since what she had said was the truth. Nevertheless, he had already married someone else and he had been bound to her by solemn nuptial rites. He then added that he would accept whatever the judgment might be concerning the matter. One after the other the judges discussed the matter. Finally, in reverence for the lord pope, they asked for a recess and requested that a matter so great should deferred to Rome for the pope's judgment.

This was done; the case was referred to Rome. The cardinals met and, supporting the will of the pope, decided that the first promise made according to the apostle could not be set aside without condemnation and that the one whom he had promised first ought to be his wife. Meanwhile, a man named Bruno, of great authority among the cardinals, remained completely silent while the others were speaking. When he was asked by the pope to give his opinion, he answered that he would not refute the words of the others. Whereupon the pope ordered him by obedience that if in truth he held an opinion on this matter, he should reveal it. Bruno then carefully discussed each point in turn. First, indeed, a marriage is not made through a promise alone. In the second place, a marriage is made complete by a promise, a betrothal, a blessing by a priest, solemn nuptials, and then copulation with each other. He adduced different chapters of the canon and concluded that the second of the marriages could not be dissolved since it was the more advanced. He added that punishment ought to be imposed on the count for foreswearing his earlier promise. The pope and the cardinals assented to his opinion, and messengers were sent back to France with apostolic letters.

Count Baldwin was indeed overjoyed that Yolanda would remain with him. The girl grieved because she had been deprived of her marriage to the count. But, by a sudden marvelous stroke of fortune that made God's mercy manifest, that same girl was joined in marriage to King Louis of France and became the mother of him who is now King Louis and of other kings. Since she had grieved earlier for what had not befallen her, she later rejoiced even more, since she preferred being, and being called, queen of France rather than countess of Hainaut.[4]

Baldwin fathered by Yolanda another Baldwin and Richeldis, wife of Everard, castellan of Tournai. Since Richeldis married Everard, the leading man of his province, one may speak a little of her by way of a digression.[5]

34. Everard, Castellan of Tournai (1159–1189)[1]

This Richeldis was just as noble by lineage and beautiful in appearance as she was turbulent and worthless in worldly deeds. She bore Baldwin, a most beautiful and noble lad, but alas! he was overcome by a fever in the flower of his youth. He entered into a covenant with death and was buried in the cloister of the cathedral of St. Mary, Mother of God. When she died, Richeldis left two handsome sons, Everard and Godfrey, and a daughter, Yolanda. When he was still of a tender age, Everard gnashed his teeth and grieved exceedingly to see his paternal land overflowing with lawbreakers. Indignant and exasperated, exasperated by sights of fierceness, pride, and savagery, he unsheathed his sword and fell upon the evil-doers with a strong hand and swift attack. In short, he drove them all out. He returned his land to peace and returned peace to his land. He later married Gertrude, the daughter of Count Lambert of Liege, from whom he fathered a son, Baldwin. His sister, Yolanda, married Roger, seneschal of Flanders.

35. Count Baldwin of Hainaut Denied the County of Flanders; the Re-Burial of Count Charles the Good (1127)

Now we shall explain a bit of Count Baldwin of Hainaut. He was a lad when he succeeded his dead father, Baldwin, and married the sister of the count of Namur. When Flanders was deprived of Lord Charles, he was a young man and an able knight.

When Baldwin heard that the king of France had come in order to call a council to appoint a count of Flanders, he went to the king, taking with him the principal nobles and wise men of his land. He complained openly in the presence of the king's nobles that his grandfather, Baldwin, had been unjustly dispossessed and driven out of Flanders by his great-uncle, Robert, at the time that he went to Jerusalem. He humbly proposed that the king restore his grandfather's land and property to him and that the king should set a time and a place anywhere in his entire kingdom for him to come prepared to subject his body to the ordeal of arms and battle to prove that no one was more closely connected by kinship, or was more suitable, or had a greater right than he to be heir to Flanders. The knights who had come with him acclaimed his request. They told the king that this would bring a great peace to the entire province and added many other expressions of their wishes in the business at hand.

This most prudent king answered everyone gently, calling the count his kinsman and raising great hopes in the young man's heart that he would obtain what he had asked for. But, according to Solomon, "The heart of the king is in the hand of the Lord, and whatever He wishes, to that shall it turn."[1] The king's pleasure turned in a direction other than that the count would have wished. At a time when many considered it to be certain that Flanders would be given to the count, suddenly, blown by the blast of I know not what wind,[2] it was heard that it had been given to a certain young man by the name of William Clito. William was the son of Count Robert of Normandy, who was still being kept in custody as a prisoner by his brother, King Henry of England, and who had been born of the daughter of Count Robert the Elder of Flanders, as was mentioned some time ago.[3]

Young Baldwin was frustrated in his hopes and left the presence of the king an angry man. He entered Flanders under arms and, after a few days had passed, he attacked a fortified town called Audenarde and burned the entire place to ashes. More than a hundred people of all ages and of both sexes were burned to death in the church of St. Walburg. The king entered Flanders with the new count and came to Bruges. He then sent word to the Lord Bishop Simon of Tournai [1123–1146] that he should gather the abbots of his diocese and come as quickly as possible to bury the body of the most glorious Count Charles. I shall faithfully report what I saw of the body at that time.

The Lord Bishop called upon my humble self together with Lord Abbot Absalom of St. Amand.[4] The tomb that Prior Bertulf had had constructed out of marble columns, as we said a short while ago, was overturned. The body of the count was lifted out of it and was carried by the king and a great procession down to the church of St. Christopher the Martyr,[5] which was located in the same town. On a prearranged day, when the nobles and all the populace were gathered, the church of St. Donatian would be reconsecrated, and the body carried back to it and buried decently in the earth.[6]

We feared that the stench of the body might trouble the men carrying it, since more than fifty days had now passed since his death, but the mercy of God showed us that we had feared everything for nothing.[7] We could smell no noxious odor at all emanating from it, but quite the contrary. What was even more marvelous was that we saw that the linen in which the body was wrapped was clean and whole, and we could discern no stain at all on it, except that of fresh blood. I will pass over how great the sobbing may have been that flowed from all the populace, how great the grief, what cries and moans, and what sort of flood of tears may have poured from the king and all the nobles. The exertion of reading about pious things may be easily avoided by my remaining silent about these subjects.[8]

The church was restored after five days, and the body of the count was properly interred after the celebration of a mass.[9] The king then appointed Lord Roger, a young cleric, to the post of prior, since Bertulf had now abandoned it. When this had been done, the king attacked the tower in which the betrayers were still shut up and besieged. But he was not able to take it so easily, because it was very strong and the besieged stoutly resisted. The following night, Burcard and his uncle Bertulf left the tower by stealth and fled, abandoning all the others in danger of their lives. When these men finally realized that they were resisting for no reason, they surrendered to the king and allowed him to enter. The king ordered them first to be kept imprisoned in the tower for three days, then to be taken out and led up to the rampart of that high tower. There they were to be forced to jump off, one after the other.[10] He executed thirty men in this fashion. Although they had already left the province of Flanders and had reached Tournai, Bertulf and Burcard were unable to escape divine judgment. Back in Flanders again, they were seized and hanged most dishonorably.[11] They ended their unworthy lives with miserable deaths.

36. Rebellion and Civil War in Flanders; the Prophecy of the Respectable Woman at Last Shown to Have Been True (ca. 1130)

Meanwhile, the king had gone back to France and left Count William in Flanders. When he had first entered Flanders in the company of the king, William had promised wealth and independence to both the knights and burgesses, and he had confirmed by a public oath that he would keep his laws in the fashion of his predecessors. When he saw that everyone was subject to him, he quickly became puffed up and snatched away their goods and substance. Then he began to compel them with fetters to commit themselves to spending their money, and by prison to selling their goods, for their ransom.

The Flemish were soon terror-stricken since they were not accustomed to such behavior and expected worse evils. They prepared to rebel and, to a man, chose to suffer death rather than endure such things. The inhabitants of Lille, whom he was injuring the most, were the first who dared to resist him openly.[1]

At that time there was a young knight named Thierry in the province of Lorraine called Alsace. He was the son of Duke Simon of Alsace [1115–1139], who had fathered him from the daughter of lord Count Robert of Flanders. She had Count Henry of Brabant as her first husband but, when he was killed at Tournai, she was wed by the aforesaid Duke Simon. Knowing that this lad was closely connected to Charles since he was the son of Charles's maternal aunt, the Flemings secretly sent an envoy to him and asked him to come to Flanders. With scarcely three knights in attendance, Thierry quickly came to Flanders and was accepted with joy when he arrived. Now Count William was resisted with greater confidence.

The king returned at the request of William and the archbishop of Arras. Thierry was ordered by the archbishop to come to a hearing as if he were a lawless usurper. He was unwilling to attend while all of his supporters were publicly excommunicated; while the holy offices of Lille, where he was staying, were under interdict; and while he himself was commanded to leave Flanders as soon as possible and return to his own land. He turned a deaf ear and waited for the outcome of things. Having collected an army, the king and William besieged Thierry inside Lille and assaulted the town three times, in three different spots, in a single day. The king attempted to force the gates and overcome the besieged, but he made no progress and returned to France on the sixth day.

Thierry left Lille and travelled through Flanders. Sometimes his band appeared to be superior to William's force, sometimes inferior. Everyone was waiting fearfully to see which of them would be the victor and which the vanquished. William and a troop of cavalry again besieged Thierry, who had shut himself up in a castle called Aalst. In the month of August, when he was at his peak and bravely fighting to take the castle, William Clito was wounded in the hand under the thumb by a foot soldier and was also greatly oppressed by the heat. Feeling his arm swelling, he secretly called for Duke Godfrey, who was accompanying him at the time, and predicted that he would soon die. He advised him to try cautiously to lead the cavalry away from that place. Realizing that fortune was against them, the duke cleverly diverted Thierry by exchanging messengers and pretending that he wished to arrange a peace between him and William. Meanwhile, he carefully withdrew the army. Only when he was far away did he sent word to Thierry that William was dead. So William died from a slight wound and was buried at St. Bertin, next to Count Baldwin.

Thierry obtained the lordship of all Flanders [1128–1168], with the concession of the king of France. His wife had died, so Thierry married the sister of the count of Anjou and the daughter of King Fulk of Jerusalem. And so the prophecy of that woman who had foretold the future many years before to the emissaries of Count Robert, advocate Baldwin of Tournai and his companions, was finally shown not to have been false. For Baldwin, the younger son of Count Robert, had died without an heir. The handsome youth whom she predicted would come from Dacia without any doubt at all will have been Charles.[2] The two counts who would come after him and would quarrel over Flanders, and of whom one would kill the other, were William and Thierry. That which she finally added, that the victor and his descendants would possess Flanders until the time of the Antichrist, we will leave to the knowledge of God and the experience of future generations.

We see that Thierry is now secure in his county and that he is gladdened by many children. The king of France was able to dissolve the union of Thierry's daughter, who was already promised to Henry, son of Count Theobald,[3] by pointing out that they were closely related to each other, being in the third grade of consanguinity. It is true that we have made an exceedingly long digression through kings and counts, so now let us return to Lord Odo and his clerics as if along a wide and perfect road, lest they should be dying of hunger while we are wandering around through various matters.

37. The First Year of the Pauper Abbey of St. Martin's of Tournai (March 1092–March 1093)

And so lord Bishop Radbod and the procession withdrew, and five indigent clerics were left in penniless St. Martin's. With the aid of the townspeople, however, they soon bought a wooden house from a monk who was the agent for the court of St. Amand of Willemeau. They erected it next to the little church and bit by bit they began to grow, so that there were eighteen brothers found there at the beginning of their second year. Since they had nothing on which to live, they suffered no little want in those early days. Some pious laymen went through the city each day, carrying donation baskets and shouting that the townspeople should assist the paupers of St. Martin's. They passed an entire year with this sort of support.[1]

38. Canon Siger Drags His Son Off by the Hair, so the Congregation of St. Martin's Become Monks (1094)

Meanwhile, a young cleric named Alulf, the son of Siger, precentor of the canons of St. Mary's,[1] abandoned secular wealth

and joined the congregation of St. Martin's. When this was announced to his father, he immediately gathered his kinsmen and
went to St. Martin's full of fury. After he had beaten him severely
and the boy was lying on the ground, he grabbed the lad by the
hair and dragged him home. On the following day, when they
thought that he had gone to the cathedral of St. Mary's, the lad
stealthily returned to St. Martin's. But he was immediately led
back once again by his father and placed in shackles. After this
had happened several times, the lad fleeing to St. Martin's whenever he could and his father quickly dragging him back home, it
happened that Abbot Emory of Anchin came to Tournai to visit
and comfort those paupers.[2]

Master Odo discussed with Abbot Emory what he should do
about the lad who was violently dragged home every day by his
father. The abbot responded like a wise man who sees an opportunity to advance his cause. He replied without hesitation:

> Truly, good Master, this sort of thing may happen not only to the
> boy, but frequently to your other brothers unless they are made monks.
> Living near the city, your younger brothers may easily be influenced by
> their fellow secular clerics and led back into the secular world. Your
> habits and theirs are one and the same. If you were to become monks,
> however, they would not tempt any of your flock to return to secular
> life. Since the habit of the monks is black and that of the clerics is white,
> the clerics have such great horror of the habit of the monks that if one of
> them sees a monk even once, he is never afterwards considered worthy
> to have as a companion.
>
> Consider also how much softer and permissive the life of the clerics
> is; even those living under a rule dress in linen, frequently eat meat, and
> only on feast days do they read nine lessons. Since you are famous every-
> where and will be influential and give notice to the world, if you were to
> ask me, I would advise you and your clerics that it would be better to
> seek out a stricter, rather than a more permissive, order.[3]

The persuasion of the abbot of Anchin decided Master Odo.
He called out his associates, recounted the advice of the abbot,
and earnestly requested their agreement on the matter. They immediately consented to his words and asked the abbot to remain
there for the night so that the news would not get out, and they

might somehow be prevented.[4] They promised that on the following day they would become monks. The next morning at daybreak, when the chapter meeting was over, twelve clerics went to the altar of St. Martin's, took off their clerical garb, and donned monastic habits with a blessing and three days' silence from the hand of Abbot Amaury. So they had sung matins and prime according to the clerical rite, but now terce and all the succeeding hours up to the present day would be sung in the monastic manner.[5]

The master was not misled in accepting Abbot Emory's good advice. When Siger, the precentor of the canons, saw that his young son had become a monk, he never again tried to take him away. As a matter of fact, he himself was strongly inclined to a life of perseverance. Later, obedient to the will of God, he abandoned worldly riches and, together with his brother, Herman, the cathedral archdeacon whom we mentioned far above, became a monk in our monastery. He requested that five altars that he had acquired for his other son, the canon Adam, be given to us. These paid us more than thirty pounds of money each year.[6]

To return to our account, when the three days of silence were completed, Abbot Emory advised those whom he made monks to choose an abbot. When Master Odo attempted to select one of his associates, everyone rushed upon him and unanimously chose him. When he was chosen, they presented him to Bishop Radbod for confirmation.

Odo was consecrated in the cathedral of St. Mary in Tournai on the following Sunday, the fourth of the nones of March [4 March 1094], in the third year of his conversion.[7] The young man of whom we spoke above became the monk Alulf and held the offices of treasurer and cantor in our monastery for forty-seven years. He frequently re-read all of the books of St. Gregory portraying the Fathers and both the Old and the New Testaments.[8] He excerpted from the latter all of the passages that are explained by Gregory and composed three volumes out of them, to which he added a fourth, filled with various and extremely useful passages. He entitled these volumes "Gregorialis." And so he ended his life in a good fashion in the forty-eighth year of his conversion.[9]

When his father, Siger, first became a monk, he was sleeping one afternoon on his cot and saw in his sleep one of the canons of St. Mary's who had died many years before. The canon appeared to him, and they talked about various things. Siger had not forgotten that he had died, and asked him to reveal what sort of a life souls had in the other world. The canon immediately replied, "Lord Siger, why do you ask of the afterworld? I will tell you in truth that he who will have been a pauper here for God, will be wealthy there." Siger awoke immediately and, to his consolation, he understood what he had seen. Glorifying God for this, he immediately told us about it.[10]

39. The Monks of St. Martin's Decide to Go Live in the Desert and Sneak Away from Tournai, but Are Returned (14 September 1094)

Now then, Odo had become abbot and began to read continuously with his monks from the *Institutes, Collations,* and *Lives of the Fathers;*[1] and they were eager to put into immediate action whatever they had just read. They had God's gift of enthusiasm but certainly not much knowledge. It was because of this that, at the beginning of their third year, they began to complain that they ought not to stay in a pleasant place where they heard the shouting of lads and the songs of girls and where they saw the vestments of the seculars. Because of these things, many of them were hindered in their spiritual endeavors. A desert was a more desirable place, they said, where they might more freely devote themselves to divine meditation.[2]

They talked about these and similar matters every day, often heaving great sighs about them. Finally, they all agreed upon a

plan. One night when they had finished singing early matins, they
loaded their clothes and books in a wagon and, before midnight,
had left the church empty.[3] Led by the abbot, they had all they
could manage in getting out of the province as quickly as possible
without any of the citizens learning what was going on.

When morning came, people came from the city to pray at St.
Martin's according to their custom. When they discovered what
had happened, they began to wail as if the city were about to fall.
Some of them listened to others cry out with grief and to pro-
claim that they had not been worthy of the monks' fellowship.
They then ran in swarms over to the church and tearfully circu-
lated about where the monks had slept and where they had eaten.
Loudly weeping, everybody began to announce that some new
calamity would strike the district.[4]

They were then told by some nuns who lived near the church
that the monks had gone to Noyon, where Bishop Radbod was
staying at the time, to ask him for leave to depart. Lord Everard,
the castellan, the most important lord in the district, quickly met
with all the leaders of the city. They accepted his advice and
swiftly sent a warning to the bishop that he should have no hope
of entering Tournai again if he gave the monks license to leave.[5]
The municipal emissary spurred his horse to exhaustion and arrived at Noyon before the monks. He told the bishop what had
been decided and then added the words of the noble and citizens.
The bishop burst into tears and answered immediately that it was
not necessary for the citizens to make such demands because,
even if they themselves were to beg him to permit the monks to
leave, there was no way that he would give permission for this.

The emissary then set out to explore the road along which he
expected Odo and his monks to come. He saw them and rode out
to meet them. When he saw that they were almost thirty men and
all coming on foot, he ordered his knights and clerics to dis-
mount their horses and have the monks ride. The monks were
unwilling to mount, however.[6] They reached the bishop and,

there in the middle of the city gate of Noyon, they threw themselves at his feet and pleaded for leave to depart. Bursting into tears, the bishop prostrated himself at their feet and declared by oath that there was no way that he would do so.[7] He took them to his palace and kept them with him for three days, feeding them well to restore them after such a great exertion. He finally required them by the bonds of obedience to return to Tournai.

As soon as the citizens of Tournai learned of this, it was as if they could see the sun returning after the dark. They exulted and hastened to meet the monks some distance from the city. It happened that they had returned on the day of the Exaltation of the Holy Cross [14 September], the day when the procession around the city was held.[8] As we mentioned above, this procession had been established by Bishop Radbod because of the fiery plague. And so when the canons, who had already left the city with the saints' reliquaries, heard that the monks had returned, they left their route along with the entire procession of almost sixty thousand people and joyously led the monks back to the church of St. Martin's.[9]

40. The Bishop Returns St. Martin's Ancient Endowments

From this time up to the present day, with the aid of God, our church began slowly to grow and to multiply. The citizens of Tournai were now for the first time assured of our stability and went to the bishop. They mentioned the ancient lands of St. Martin's, which had come into the power of the bishop from the earlier, ruined abbey, and which were held as a benefice by the advocate of Tournai. They then unanimously pleaded that they [the ancient lands] be returned to St. Martin's.

At this time, Baldwin, the advocate of Tournai whom I mentioned above, had just renounced the world and become a monk in the monastery of Bec, which is located in Normandy and was under the venerable abbot, Lord Anselm, who was later arch-bishop of Canterbury.[1] His brother, Ralph, a most energetic knight, had succeeded him in the advocacy and, with the advoca-cy, had received the lands of St. Martin's in benefice from the hand of the bishop.[2] So the bishop met with Ralph privately and began to influence him toward charity with honeyed words. Fi-nally, he asked Ralph to release these lands to the pauper monks for the benefit of his soul. Oh, inexplicable Spirit of Holy Mercy! The heart of the man suddenly caught fire; he responded gener-ously to everything and returned those lands to the bishop with-out delay.[3] The bishop then delivered them to St. Martin's, quit and clear, by the authority of his charter.

But other than this charter, we have no testimony in ancient writing that our church was an old abbey.[4] There was only a pas-sage contained in the *Life of Saint Eligius the Bishop*. When Eligius was dying, he called Baldred, abbot of Tournai, and ad-vised him not to return to his monks at "Turonis." We would claim with less confidence that St. Martin's had been an abbey were it not for this evidence. Lord Odo found nothing as to whether St. Martin's had been an abbey that would allow us to as-sert it with confidence. I will now tell you what happened to me when I was a young man.

41. The Mysterious Abbot and the Origins of St. Martin's (1117)

One of our monks was sent to Countess Clemence at Cour-trai.[1] He found an abbot there who had also come to the count-ess. He was asked by the abbot from where he came and, when he answered that he was from St. Martin's of Tournai, the abbot immediately began to question him where and what kind of place the monastery of St. Martin's of Tournai was. When the monk said that it was not far, nor was it old but new, and had been built twenty years earlier, the abbot immediately replied, "Truly, brother, it has been more than three hundred years since the monastery of St. Martin's of Tournai was established. Charters of St. Martin's of Tournai have been kept in our church up to the present day. Its monks were fleeing the persecution of the Vandals and brought them to us and left them. I have asked myself many times in what land the church of St. Martin's of Tournai might be, but I never found out until today."

The monk then asked the abbot where he was from, and he replied that he was the abbot of Ferrières. Begged many times to come to Tournai, he replied that he did not have the time. When the monk returned, he told us about this. He was immediately sent back to Courtrai with another monk who was skilled in letters, in order to inquire more fully. The abbot, who is now dead, was not to be found, however. We were greatly saddened, and the great question arose: where might the abbey of Ferrières be, we asked, but we did not know.

42. The Council of Reims; the Lost Village of Ferrières Found (1119)

Two years later, Pope Calixtus proclaimed a council at Reims. This pope was the brother of the Countess Clemence, had earlier been the archbishop of Vienne, and was called Guy. We had a reborn hope of finding out something there. The investigation of this matter was assigned to me when I was not yet a deacon, as I recall. I walked around the church of St. Mary's all day long, shoving and being shoved in that great assembly. I asked every monk I could get at where Ferrières might be and, after three days, I had found out nothing. From time to time I weakened, but this little verse restored my strength:

Persistent labor conquers all.

Finally, I heard that Ferrières was in the diocese of Paris. "Thanks be to God!" I cried. The abbot of Ferrières was pointed out to me by some Parisian clerics, and I immediately tried to go to him, but I was unable to make my way through the crowd.

The pope at last gave the longed-for permission to eat, and I joined the abbot. I recalled to him the words he had spoken to the monk from St. Martin's of Tournai a couple of years earlier at Courtrai, and was overjoyed that he remembered without difficulty. "What do these charters preserved at your church contain?" I asked. He replied that it was a charter of Charles the Great, confirmed by his seal, and that it was written in it that King Charles would give the village of Souppes,[1] with its mills and all its waters and appurtenances, to St. Martin of Tournai at the petition of Ingelran, count of Chateaudun. The witnesses and day and place of the donation were appended at the end. I begged that the charter be given to me since it was not of any use to them. He replied that he would not give it up for nothing. I promised him a hundred solidi, and he set a day on which I should come to him. He pointed out the way I would come, namely, from Paris to Chateaudun to Ferrières.

I went back to Tournai rejoicing, told what I heard and received the money. After passing through Paris, I came to Ferrières. I showed the abbot the coins and asked to be given the charter. But the abbot, as one of his monks told me, was afraid to offend the knight who held the village and said that he had not been able to find that charter after the council. He did accept an expensive belt from me, however, and had me taken to the village in question, which is called Souppes and was two miles away.

When I saw the mills and other appurtenances, I did not know how to hold back my tears. I went into the church and found one very old book there, rotten and almost falling apart, in which I saw written "The Book of the Monastery of St. Martin's of Tournai." When I went outside, I met a decrepit and aged peasant, and I asked him to whom the village belonged. He replied that it belonged to Goswin the knight and some others. I to him: "Let me ask you, father," I said, "tell me if you ever heard that it belonged to some saint or another." "We all know," he said "that this village belonged to some monastery called St. Martin's of Tourney,[2] but we don't know where it could be, and we wonder what the cursed monks of that monastery are doing, that they don't take back such a village."[3] Then I spoke. "And, father," I said, "did you hear how such a village came to be given to such an unknown and distant monastery?" "I heard," he said, "that a knight of this region who owned this village went out into that province with some mercenary troops. He was wounded there and given up for dead. He was placed in that monastery of monks, and later, when he had recovered, he returned and, through King Charles, confirmed this village to the same monastery of St. Martin's." I heard this, but was unable to do anything further. I returned sadly but nevertheless glad that I was a little bit more certain of the antiquity of our monastery. I recall that, having become more certain, I became absolutely sure because of other things I read.

43. The First Foundation of St. Martin's by St. Eligius, Bishop of Noyon and Tournai (649–665)

St. Ouen, bishop of Rouen, clearly and faithfully describes the deeds of St. Eligius and relates, among other things, how the saint had at first been a goldsmith in the court of Lothar. Lothar was king of the Franks and the son of the King Chilperic who greatly enlarged the church of St. Mary's of Tournai and of whom we shall speak later. St. Eligius asked the king for all the materials needed to construct a tomb of gold and precious stones for St. Martin of Tours, and King Lothar provided them.[1] Given the means and favorable opportunity, he also pulled two teeth from the jaw of the saint to keep for himself as relics. As will become clear shortly, however, he did this in accordance with the will of God.

Not long afterwards, it was St. Eligius' lot to become the seventh occupant of the episcopal throne of the cathedral of Tournai. He undertook to rule the people of Tournai and Noyon with pastoral care in the year of our Lord 649 and governed them for seventeen years, until the year of our Lord 665. Within a few days of the start of Eligius' clerical office, it pleased God, who had suggested to him that he separate Saint Martin's teeth from his body, that the practice by which holy relics were held in veneration in France should be extended and, that there should be many objects of veneration for the worshipful visitor.[2]

Eligius was immediately inspired by the Divine Will and was moved by a fervent devotion toward St. Martin. He considered that the relics might be adored with great reverence and that it was not right that they should be hidden under a basket. He saw that they would receive the most visitors and the greatest honor if they were located in some place in which there was the least possible devotion to the memory of some other saint. But it had to be so excellent a place that it would always be visited. So he took one tooth to be kept in the church of St. Mary's of Noyon, and he turned the other over to St. Mary's of Tournai.

There was a quite prominent hill, covered with woods and planted with various kinds of fruit-bearing trees, on the southern approaches to the city of Tournai. An old man could rest his spirit there and congratulate himself as if he had gotten a head start on some of the comforts of paradise. It was said that, in olden times, St. Martin in the flesh had stayed there when he had passed through during his preaching in Gaul. He had raised a man from the dead there, and he had offered the great gift of health to countless sick people. A great crowd of pagans was converted to divine worship through these wonders.

If it should seem unbelievable to anyone that St. Martin should have come to these parts, even today one can see signs of his passage. There is a city in Lorraine called Bouvignies through which Saint Martin passed in those days. He wished to water the animal on which he was mounted at a spring where the water flowed down rather inconveniently. Saint Martin rode over an enormous rock while making his way down, and his horse imprinted its hoof in that rock as if in the softest wax. Just as a fact may be neglected and blotted out by the silence and forgetfulness of many people, so too it may be preserved by memory if it is known to a few people somewhere. For the only matters that survive from earlier times are those that exist in the memory of later generations.[3]

Eligius, the servant of God, decided to choose this place since it had already been favored by St. Martin and made sacred by his presence. After he had placed a tooth of the saint there, he built a baptistery in St. Martin's honor, a place in which it would be fitting for people to gather at Lauds to receive God's holy gifts during the ministry of the sacraments. He did not forget his ultimate goal and also built monastic quarters. Time passed, and the devotion of the faithful to this place slowly grew. Eligius saw that some of them were inclined toward something that he had been planning a long time. They were prepared to live a communal life, serving God under a rule of discipline.

He gathered as many men as he could, both slaves and freemen, so that the residence that had been prepared should not be without residents. Gathering them from various tribes, he presided over them as abbot so that they should be dependent upon his commands. He established such a strict standard that the life of these monks was almost unique among the monasteries of Gaul. Nobles came there from every direction and they left their possessions and properties to the monastery when they gave themselves over into the service of almighty God. Eligius himself enriched the place with even wider estates and a sufficiency of land rents. He carefully provided all the things that the monastery might need. It possessed, among other things, some episcopal renders that he had purchased for a price, some that it [the monastery] had obtained as a royal gift, and some others that had been given freely and generously by other nobles.

He donned his bishop's robes in the third year of the reign of

King Clovis. He was very close to the king and all of his nobles because of the bonds of brotherhood that had been established between them in the palace under Clovis's father, Dagobert, and his grandfather Lothar.[4] Eligius was held in such esteem that he would immediately obtain whatever he asked of the king; and he gave whatever he was able to acquire to this abbey that he had founded on the borders of France, the latest of a number of famous monasteries he had founded in various places. For this reason, it was only a short time until the property that he had set aside for the use of the monks serving God there was sufficient for all purposes. Records of the properties that were donated to the monastery at that time have survived down to the present day. We believe it worthwhile to interject at this point how they reached our notice.

44. Herman Deduces That the Canons of St. Mary's of Tournai Have the Ancient Documents of St. Martin's

There was a canon by the name of Erbald in the church of St. Mary's of Tournai who held the office of treasurer there for many years. After some years, however, he was stricken by a fatal illness and took refuge in St. Martin's. One day, we were tending to his infirmity and talking among ourselves about the antiquity of this church. The sick man suddenly spoke, as if our words had brought about such a response. He said, "Truly brothers, this place was an abbey a long time ago. I have quite often read descriptions of the ancient possessions and renders of this church in some very old parchments kept within the church of St. Mary's. The names of a substantial number of your serfs, both male and female, can be found there." These words and writings bore witness of the old abbey, but Erbald did not indicate by name any of the serfs or properties. Because of our long-time disinheritance it is not easy to declare what present lineages or families might be descended from them or for which of their successors tenancy may have developed into dominion.[1]

We referred Erbald's statement to the canons of St. Mary's and asked them to make the truth more fully clear to us. They responded that there was no writing dealing specifically with our possessions to be found in their entire library. They said that some descriptions of our boundaries might have become intermingled with documents of their own in the early days. By now, however, they would have been destroyed by the ravages of great age. If there were some that had remained whole for such a long time, however, they had been placed in the charge of Erbald. Since he was frequently reading the materials, he was easily able to find something that had not come to the attention of others. We listened, but grieved because none of this was of any help to us.

Nevertheless we hold most firmly to what we were told by local tradition: that some of the ornaments and properties of our abbey, as well as the tooth of St. Martin, in veneration of whom this church was founded by St. Eligius, came into the power of the canons of St. Mary's at the time of the Norman persecution. They accepted these things either to keep custody of them, or they were turned over to the canons as a loan because of the troubles of the times. They are said to have the tooth even now, a belief that is corroborated by the words written below.

We have no doubt that the words of Erbald were true because the practice used today in the writing of charters was already emerging in that era. We observe that two charters are drawn up for the properties and priories given by nobles and bishops to abbeys today. One is sealed with the actual seal of the donor and handed over to the church to which possession of the property is being transferred. The other one is unsealed and remains in the church that is the seat of the bishop. So it is crystal clear that the records of those properties that this church possessed in early times were turned over to the canons of St. Mary's in the same fashion.

45. How the Bishop and Canons of St. Mary's Acquired the Properties of St. Martin's and Other Monasteries and Should Admit It

In our own days, there were old men along the Scheldt around Helkijn and St. Genois who said that they had heard from their ancestors that in ancient times this monastery had possessed rents within boundaries that were well-defined and remembered clearly. They said that the boundaries of these possessions included the altars of villages, their meadows, woods, arable lands, male and female serfs, and other renders that the bishop, canons, and the bishop's knights now hold; also the altars of Courtrai and Hames. When the monks left during the Norman persecution, these altars were left under the care of the bishop and the canons. When the monks did not return, the bishop and canons made them theirs by right of allod.[1]

Since this congregation has been reestablished, however, the records of its antiquity should now be returned so that no disagreements or controversy should arise between the sons of either the abbey or the cathedral about the return of properties. In addition, the canons should confess most fully that they possess the documents of the churches of St. Quentin Outside the Walls and St. Peter's in the midst of the city, abbeys in which congregations of the servants of God formerly met and which have not yet been restored, and that they are holding the properties of these churches.

46. The Necrology of St. Amand of Elnon Proves the Ancient Existence of St. Martin's of Tournai

Furthermore, I declare that evidence of the antiquity of St. Martin's that has survived up to the present day should by no means be concealed by silence. There was an ancient custom kept in the monasteries of that time that the names of brothers of nearby abbeys, to whom they owed mutual prayers or whom they knew and had promised comradeship, were placed in writing upon the holy altar so that the priest singing mass might recite them name by name when he came to that place in which it is said, "Remember, O Lord, your servants and handmaidens, who have preceded us with the sign of faith and sleep in the slumber of peace." At that point one of the ministers of the altar would approach him and present the list to be recited. We have learned that the early monks of our house had this fraternal connection with the monks of St. Amand of Elnon. The document that contains the names of the brothers of St. Martin's along with the names of brothers of neighboring abbeys has remained in the monastery of Elnon up to our times, and we have even held the thing itself in our hands and inspected it with our eyes.

And so, from this evidence that we have gathered, that we have learned either from documents or descendants, we may confidently confirm that this abbey was an abbey in ancient times. Such excellent evidence as we have discussed above was not preserved up to the present in vain. Nevertheless, we are willing to state publicly that not everything came to our notice.

47. St. Eligius Established the Church of St. Piatus in Seclin and Enlarged Its Territory at the Expense of St. Martin's

One reads in the record of the deeds of St. Eligius, our founder, that he buried St. Piatus the martyr in a similar fashion in Medenant, a district of the city of Tournai that is now called Seclin. Relying upon the aid of almighty God, he constructed a church to the passion of this saint and enlarged the extent of its authority. He established a congregation of clerics for the holy offices, just as we see them even now. But let us leave the transfer through documents of these additions to the territory of Seclin, and let us direct our pen to the narration of the manner of the desolation of our early abbey!

48. The Conversion of Tournai by St. Piatus about the Year 300 and Its Desolation by the Normans in 881

The city of Tournai came to know the faith of our Lord Jesus Christ through St. Piatus about the 300th year after the Incarnation of the Lord. Falling before the savage persecution that Diocletian in the East and Maximianus Herculeus in the West were executing, he suffered martyrdom. The churches of St. Mary and St Martin were established and in godly peace progressed both spiritually and materially. The people of Tournai began to flourish by their power, to be multiplied by their progeny, to expand in their possessions, to think well of themselves through their vanity, to be made jokesters by their prosperity, to be feasted luxuriously, and to enjoy their own pleasures for six hundred years less nineteen, that is, up to the year of our Lord 881.

They did not happily enjoy these pleasures as much as they were unhappily seduced by them. They neglected true religion because of their vices and avarice, offended God, and brought His wrath down upon them. God suddenly raised up against the prosperity of their age, the hatred of the most uncouth of peoples, so that His anger against the people should be avenged by the blows of various tribes. A horde of Normans came swiftly and savagely, just as we read that the Vandals did in the year of the Incarnation of our Lord 453, in the era of the most holy Nicasius, when Merowech was ruling over the Franks.[1]

The Normans cast down the fortifications of many cities and they killed many people of both sexes, parents along with their children, with fire and by the sword. They continued to ravage Gaul for the next thirty years and, among their other villainies, they destroyed the walls and buildings of Tournai. The citizens and populace were pillaged, their properties and implements were left totally devastated, and the interiors of neighboring churches were rendered uninhabitable. In order to inform posterity of the manner in which this was done, we have decided to commit to writing as much as we have been able to gather from the writings of the chroniclers as well as the statements of modern authors.

49. The See of Tournai Mentioned in the Chronicle of Sigebert of Gembloux under the Year 881

In the *Chronicle* of Sigebert of Gembloux,[1] it is reported that the Normans, allying themselves with the Danes, wandered through France and Lorraine in the year of our Lord 881. With fire and sword, they devastated Arras, Amiens, Corbie, Cambrai, Thèrouanne, the district of the Menapiorum, Brabant, and all the land around the River Scheldt,[2] Tournai and its confines, Ghent, Courtrai, the abbey of St. Amand of Elnon, Condé above the Scheldt, where they established a seat for themselves in the first year of the episcopacy of Bishop Heidilo of Tournai, the monasteries of St. Walaric and St. Riquier, Liège, Maastricht, Tongres, Cologne, Buneville with its adjacent castles, Aachen both town and castle, the monastery of Stavelot, Malmedy, Cornelismünster, Prums, Triers, and Metz.[3] Tournai was the seat of a bishop at this time, and it is a certain fact that it had maintained this dignity for the previous 284 years. Saint Eleutherius had ruled as its bishop from the year of our Lord 484, and Theodoric had presided until a few days before. Nothing is known either of his origin or his management of affairs, or how long he ruled. It is remembered that he was killed by a divine dart; that is, by a bolt of lightning.

50. There Is a Description of the Devastation by the Normans in a Chronicle by a Monk of Marchiennes

There is another chronicle dealing with this Norman invasion and composed entirely by a monk of Marchiennes that provided the information given above.[1] He wrote that Tournai had been devastated at that time and reduced to nothing. He adds that Bishop Emmo of Tournai was killed by the Normans in the year of our Lord 860, twenty-one years before this devastation. This arranger of ages in this work describes in fine style the wars and battles that the Normans, with their insatiable lust to spill human blood, waged against the men of Reims, Paris, Orleans, and Compiègne, who bravely fought to the finish.

51. A Reconstruction of the Flight of the Monks of St. Martin's of Tournai and the Settlement of a Group of Them in Ferrières

The monks of St. Martin's of Tournai scattered at this time, each one to some suitable abbey in which they hoped that they would live more easily and be more useful. They abandoned their own monastery as well as the citizens by whose defense they had long been protected, by whose assistance they had been strengthened, and by whose good deeds they had been enriched. When they had dispersed over a very wide area and were happy with whatever lot had befallen them and were content with the customs of the abbeys they had found, many of them would recall in words the desirable qualities of their previous monastery, now razed to the ground. They did not wish to do more than talk, however. They did not undertake the labor of rebuilding its ruins, but ended their present life in the abbeys to which they had fled. They yielded up their hereditary properties as perpetual donations to those same abbeys in exchange for the benefits they had received. Indeed, because of their lack of funds and pressing needs, some sold their properties for a price.[1] Some lands lacked protection and defense and passed under the dominion of lay lords.

A group of the monks, in whom there was a greater devotion to God and a more reasoned attitude, turned aside toward the abbey which was in the diocese of Paris and was located in the fortress town named Ferrières. They carried off with them a few small items from the furnishings of their monastery and whatever they thought might be useful to them. Prominent among these things was the charter of their village, called Souppes, in that region, the evidence of which we discovered in about the twentieth year of the restoration. This village was close by, about two leagues away; its lands were extensive and returned abundant rents and renders. For this reason, they turned to that village, where they might be suitably maintained by its renders and might continue keeping their vigils as long as the stronger of their number might endure in this way of life.

We have already discussed above how they came to possess the village, and it would be superfluous to recapitulate the account. They organized themselves into a community so that they might renew the observance of the rule in which they had devoted themselves to God and His most holy confessor, Martin. If they could not fulfill the promises they had made with their own lips in that abbey from which they had been able to flee, at least they could discharge their obligation by the perfect observance of the precepts of the rule in another monastery.[2]

52. Brother Bernard Tells of His Vision of the Buried Treasure of St. Martin's and Dies as a Result; the Treasure Not Yet Found

We believe that it was then that the canons of the church of St. Mary's seized St. Martin's tooth, the papers we discussed above, and certain of the abbey's sacred vessels. Even up to the present day it is said that they buried beneath the earth somewhere within the monastery precincts the things that they were not able to carry away. For this reason, one may conclude that the treasure in the main chapel of the cathedral that was shown in a dream to a cleric named Bernard, son of the Vitalis mentioned above and whom many of us knew, belonged to this abbey. Bernard saw himself being met by a girl with a beautiful face, her long tresses tied up with a hairband, and dressed in matching clothes. She said, "Gaze upon the biers, crosses, books, phylacteries, and other ornaments of the church that I am carrying into the light of day." The girl said that all of the things with her might be inspected longer, but she added, "Understand that you may tell no one about what was shown to you. If you should ignore my command and talk, you will die within thirty days." Bernard immediately awoke and was joyous in his heart. He was not able to conceal what he had seen in silence but told all about it. In accordance with the words of the girl, he died within thirty days. He was well when he went to sleep in the evening and was found dead at dawn.[1]

Since we have not yet seen the treasure revealed, however, we cannot confirm the truth of his dream. Nevertheless, from the fact that he did not live to the thirtieth day, it would seem that what he dreamed had not been completely false. Perhaps the time has not yet come for the treasure to be revealed or for its hiding place to be found. Whether or not it is the treasure revealed to Bernard, we were often told by our predecessors that rich treasures lay in the vicinity of the abbey. In our own day, some people were shown in their dreams the places where these may perhaps lie. One of these people was a woman named Hersendis who indicated two places to us, saying that she had been shown that there was a well in one place and treasure in the other. We searched for the well in the indicated spot and found it to have a great amount of clear water. We also found in it a bronze vessel, quite similar to those used in churches. The next spot, indicated for the treasure, is over toward the western side of our grounds. We have not yet dug up the spot and, therefore, we do not know if it truly contains something.[2]

53. St. Martin's of Tournai Acquires a Tooth of St. Piatus

During the persecution we have already discussed, the body of St. Piatus of Seclin was carried off to Chartres where he had preached the name of Christ before he came to Tournai. They had not accepted his preaching, however, so he had gone to Tournai and spread the word of our Lord here. There has been a great dispute over his body up to our own times. We held that he should be taken back to Seclin, the scene of his martyrdom, and the clerics of Chartres affirmed the contrary. And so he has been kept in Chartres until the present day.

It is necessary to speak of the settlement of this dispute since a majority of us agreed that, when the body had been brought back to us, some part of should remain in Chartres. In the year of the Incarnation of our Lord 1143, the chest that contained the body of the martyr was uncovered and shown to the people. The monks of St. Martin's of Tournai were entitled to receive a tooth from his body. Then the body was restored to its original place, where it is watched over with great care. The church of Seclin rejoices that it is not destitute of the presence of its martyr.[1]

54. Miracles at the Church of St. Piatus of Seclin during the Plague of the Fires of Hell (1090)

The pestilence popularly called "plague of fire" raged among the people of Seclin to such a degree that it not only took the limbs of some but their lives as well. At the basilica of the blessed martyr founded at Seclin, many of them were killed by the hands of others.[1] The church was thus thrown into disorder by cries, and everyone implored God for help and the martyr for support.

There were the ten virgins of Scripture, five wise and five foolish, sculpted on the bier that contained the relics of the blessed martyr. They all demonstrated the power of the martyr. Grieving for the agonies of the wretched and fulfilling the will of God, they cried so that they were believed to be feeling creatures in whom there were great powers of virtue and who declared the presence of the blessed martyr Piatus.

When Piatus lived in the body and urged the people to the Christian faith, he shed not only copious tears but finally shed his own blood for them. And now these images showed the greatness of his love for his people. Drops of bloods exuded from the eyes of the wise virgins, while tears like clear water flowed from the eyes of the others. After this miracle, the sufferers sensed Divine Aid and the solace of the martyr, and those who were believed to be dying regained their health. But, having said these things about the power of the body of Saint Piatus and the antiquity of our abbey, let us now return to those matters from which we have digressed.

55. Bishop Radbod Demands That St. Martin's Adopt Some Established Order; the Monks Take the Cluniac Order from Anchin (September 1094)

After Bishop Radbod had returned the ancient lands of our church, he came to the chapter and spoke to Abbot Odo and the other brothers. [He advised that] they should not think for themselves any further, or try immediately to do whatever they were reading in *The Lives of the Fathers*. It would be better if they were to select some monastery whose customs they would observe. They accepted the bishop's counsel and chose the monastery of Anchin, which had been built fifteen years before ours and was at the time the only one in our province that kept the religion and customs of the monastery of Cluny. And so Abbot Odo turned to Emory, the abbot of Anchin. Odo and all of the brothers considered themselves to be Emory's monks, inasmuch as he had made them monks and had blessed them. But Odo pleaded that he still should teach them how to conduct their lives.[1]

The zealous abbot agreed, immediately placed his own monks as priors in our monastery, and led ours away to Anchin with him. He worked generously with us, and both he and his brothers dealt with us in counsel as fathers, in aid as brothers, and in work as fellow servants. For this reason we have always had a greater brotherhood with Anchin than with the other monasteries of our province. It is as if everything we have, both outside the abbey and within, were common property. Whatever we do for our brothers, living or dead, we undertake to do the same for theirs; and we receive the same from them in reciprocal exchange.

56. Ida, Widow of the Advocate Fastrad and Sister of Theodoric of Avesnes, Joins the Convent of St. Martin's

Meanwhile, many people, both men and women, began to renounce the world and to come to our abbey on account of our conversion and to turn over part of their wealth to us. Ida, as I recall, was the first to come to convert. She was the noble woman whom I mentioned above [chapter 9]. She was the wife of the advocate Fastrad who greatly wished to see the restoration of our monastery but was prevented by death from ever seeing it. Among other things, she gave us a house in town and a mill down on the Maire. We still hold them today. Although she was the noblest of the nuns, she never wanted to hold any position but that of the last handmaiden.

She was the sister of the noble prince Theodoric of Avesnes. It was at this time that Theodoric established the monastery of Liessies on his own lands, from its foundations on up, overseeing every aspect of its construction, placing monks there and providing that they should have abundant food and clothing. Since I have happened to mention him, and there will not be another place of reference, I shall say a bit about him that could be useful to anyone willing to read and learn from it. Theodoric, a noble and very powerful man, was waging war against Count Baldwin of Hainaut. He gathered a sizeable force one day, violently invaded Baldwin's territory, and carried away a great deal of plunder. Among the other things he did in Hainaut was to burn two convents, Ste. Waldetrud of Mons and Ste. Aldegundis of Maubeuge.[1] He did this because the count opposing him had posted soldiers in those places.

57. A Hermit Sees a Vision of Mary; the Family of the Hereditary Advocates of Tournai

There was a hermit living alone in a nearby woods called Bro-qeuroy. As he himself reported, it was not while he was sleeping but while standing vigil at midday that he saw Mary, the Holy Mother of God, appear in the sky as a queen seated on a very high throne. Those two saints were prostrating themselves at her feet and asking for the punishment of Theodoric of Avesnes, who had burned their abbeys. As they were bitterly complaining and asking for justice, the Holy Virgin answered them in the following manner:

Be quiet, I pray you, and stop annoying me, for I do not wish to grieve him at present. His wife, Ida, is doing me a certain service by which she is commending herself to me. I will not suffer anyone to punish either her or her husband.

And when they asked her what that service might be, she answered:

Every day she repeats sixty times that angelic salutation which first told me on Earth of my joy. Twenty times while prostrate, twenty times while kneeling, and twenty times standing in church or her room or in some private place, she remembers me with the words, *Ave Maria gratia plena, Dominus tecum, benedicta tu in mulieribus, et benedictus fructus ventris tuis.*[1]

When they made many even more urgent pleas to Mary, tiresomely demanding that they be avenged, the Holy Virgin finally said:

I beg that you will leave the decision about this punishment to me for the present. I promise that there will come a time when I will do justice on your behalf in this matter, and I will do no harm to Lady Ida.

Hearing this tale in my youth, I believed it to be false, but later I did not doubt too much that it may have been true. After about the twelfth year of his renunciation of the world, Lord Odo, our abbot, was elevated to the bishopric of Cambrai and was saddened because his kinsman, Theodoric, had had no children from his wife. They were relatives in the fourth line of consanguinity,[2] declared the same in the bishop's court, and confirmed it by oath on the statutory day. And so, by ecclesiastical judgment, they had their ties of marriage dissolved after they had already lived together for more than twenty years. Scarcely half a year had passed when Theodoric went into the woods to hunt, was treacherously attacked by Isaac of Berlaimont,[3] killed, carried to the monastery of Liesses which he had built, and buried behind the abbot's seat in the chapter-house.

And then it became known that what the hermit said that he had heard, Holy Mary's promise, might have been true, for she gained vengeance for the two abbeys and did no harm to Lady Ida now that she was separated from Theodoric. When Lady Ida was parted from her husband, she gave up the pomp of the world and retired to the same monastery that she had built with her husband. She did not give up all her property, but had a stone house built for herself next to the church. Not wishing to burden the abbey, she lived from her own renders to the end of her life, frequently giving necessities to the monks.

And she told many people that the tale we have recounted was true. Indeed, it was so widely spread that Goswin, son of Lady Ida, our first nun, who had succeeded his uncle, the aforesaid Theodoric, would repeat the same salutations to Saint Mary every day and urged his knights to say them. For this reason, although he may have committed many evils, Goswin nevertheless ended his life in a good fashion. Feeling himself to be suffering from a severe illness, he became a monk in the same monastery and was buried next to his uncle in the chapter-house. Since he had no son by his wife, Agnes, the daughter of Anselm of Ribomont, he established Walter, the son of his brother Fastrad and an excellent young man, during his own lifetime as his successor. His wife Agnes, imitating Lady Ida, gave up the pomp of the world, retired to that same monastery, and, living from her own renders, she had gold cups, candelabra, and many other precious ornaments made for the church.[4]

I have already mentioned Fastrad as the father of Walter and the son of our first nun, Ida. When Fastrad had lived many years as advocate of Tournai, he grew weak from illness, was made a monk in our monastery, and so died. His wife Richeldis imitated Ida, the mother of her husband. Abandoning the world, she put on the nun's habit with us. Although she may have been the richest and most noble, throughout twenty years she showed no sign of pride toward the others. She carried herself with humility and went to her rest in a good fashion. Since Walter saw that his mother and father were buried with us, he gave us a mill on the river Ries for their souls and his, and he was always like a father to our abbey as long as he lived.[5]

He took as his wife Ida, daughter of Everard, the castellan of Tournai,[6] from whom he fathered many sons and daughters, and he surpassed all of his predecessors in power and wealth. He was the son-in-law of the castellan of Tournai, later succeeded his father-in-law, held the fortress of Avesnes and almost the entire region called Brabant. Since he repented the many evil deeds he had done and wished to live in peace, he attempted to bring about an end to the war that had lasted many years between the counts of Hainaut and the lords of Avesnes. He joined the sister of Count Baldwin of Hainaut to his son, Theodoric, a young knight, as his wife. By doing so, he brought peace to the whole province.

But the Enemy of humankind did not tolerate that peace for long. Young Theodoric was unwilling to be content with his father's wealth, but ran around, not always in nearby but sometimes distant provinces, like an untamed horse. He undertook frequent raids for captives and booty in the lands of the duke of Louvain and the bishop of Liège until one day, puffed up with his frequent victories, he took a hundred knights and went even further and was unable to retreat. He was killed by footsoldiers rushing in from all sides and was carried on horseback through great perils to the monastery of Liessies, causing deep sorrow among all his friends.[7]

His father was grief-stricken and began to fear the vagaries of fortune. So he gave Brabant and the fortress of Avesnes to his second son, Nicholas, in lifetime tenure, and added to them the fortress that is called Walcourt. He gave the advocacy of Tournai to his third son.[8] He acquired two archdeaconries, Cambrai and Tournai, the priory of Nivelles, and many other ecclesiastical properties for his fourth son, Everard.[9] Also, he married his four daughters to rich husbands. As he told me many times, he would rather have been a monk, if he could have gotten permission from his wife.

In the present year, after the Feast of All Saints [1 November],[10] he was at the court of Count Baldwin in the fortress of Mons to plead his case against the count, who wanted to take the castle of Trélon away from him. He was struck by a sudden rage and lost the power of speech. The countess put him in the count's bed, and he died during the night. He was carried away by his sons to the monastery of Liessies and buried with his predecessors. The whole province was filled with great grief, since everyone was accustomed to call him "father of the poor and of churches."

But enough of these matters. It is now time to come to those two knights, Walter and Ralph, of whom I made mention a long way above [chapter 10], and to show briefly how true that dream was in which they were seen standing in the church of St. Martin's, rebuilding its walls.[11]

58. Walter, Son of Hubert, Joins St. Martin's; His Donations and His Humility

As I mentioned before, Walter was called fitz Hubert and was one of the richest and most powerful men of the province of Tournai. When he and Oda, his wife, came to enter into the monastic life, he gave us a mill on the river Maire where they grind all of the grain that is made into loaves of bread and eaten in the monastery. He also had a tract of land in the forest of Pévèle next to Templeuve that he wished to give to us, but could not because he held it as a benefice from the younger Robert, count of Flanders [1087–1111] at the time. The count was unwilling to give such a great tract of land that was his to grant as benefice or fief to the church without a price. When they were urging the count to donate this tract, Ralph, the knight I mentioned previously, happened to have a valuable horse that the count wanted to buy for forty marks. Ralph asked the count to accept the horse and to give the land in charity and for the remedy of his soul to Saint Martin's. The count agreed and confirmed that same tract of land by the authority of his charter to our monastery.[1] In time, the mill together with the land rendered us more than a thousand pounds.

One cannot easily describe how Walter carried himself once he had become a monk. Although he was in no way inferior to any of the high nobles of the region, he behaved as if he were more common than any peasant. He was never ashamed to carry the cooking water, to wash the pots and pans, to sift the flour, to tend the fire under the oven, to clean out the horse stables, or to haul dung, all in full view of his knights and kinsmen, who sobbed as they watched.[2] He converted many by his example and established this new abbey with the donations of the faithful. As we can see today, with the aid of God, he amassed enough to provide for a hundred monks.

59. The Advocate Fastrad Murders Prior Tetbert and Flees to Avesnes; the Advocacy Given to Ralph of Noyon.[1]

Ralph had two brothers, knights in the city, the elder called Tetbert and the other Theodoric the Minter.[2] Tetbert was the prior of Bishop Radbod and showed himself faithful to him as if to his lord.[3] Fastrad, the advocate, was angry with him for this reason, since he defended and protected the bishop's poor peasants everywhere. Fastrad first deceitfully struck up a friendship with Tetbert, accepting his son in baptism and becoming his compère.[4] A few days later on the Feast of St. Bartholomew, Tetbert suspected no evil but was shadowed as he went to visit the lepers. As soon as he was treacherously kissed by his compère, he was killed without any means of defending himself.[5] Fastrad immediately fled from the province and reached his uncle, Theodoric of Avesnes, and remained with him for almost three years.

Bishop Radbod gave the advocacy to Ralph, a knight of Noyon, and disinherited Fastrad completely for this crime. Some said that this had happened by the will of God, because when the bishop asked Ralph, the new advocate, he easily gave up the lands of St. Martin's that he held. Fastrad, on the other hand, later asserted many times that there was no way that he would have given them up if he had held them at the time.

After two of Fastrad's knights had been killed in revenge for his crime, Tetbert appeared to a priest of the city of Tournai, named Ranier, not while he was sleeping, but when he was keeping vigil. Since Ranier was greatly frightened, he asked if he were not Lord Tetbert and how he was. The figure answered that he was Tetbert and told him not to be afraid. He then added:

Indeed, I am in torment for my sins, mostly because I kept a concubine after the death of my wife. But I shall receive mercy because I was unjustly murdered for being faithful to my lord bishop. Saint Bartholomew, on whose feast I was killed, is my intercessor because I called upon him in the hour of my death. I pray you to go to my brothers and sons, and, for the good of my soul, to ask them on my behalf to forgive Fastrad my death and not to seek further vengeance for me. If they do this, my soul will gain great merit.[6]

Ranier replied that he would tell them what he had been commanded to say but that they would put little credit in his words.

The dead man then gave him the words of recognition that he should say to each one of them. And so he vanished.

Ranier then went to the brothers and sons of the dead man, and revealed his mission to them. When he added the secret signs, he easily restored them to harmony with their enemies. Several years later, a bare-foot Fastrad and his friends abased themselves at their feet, and he received their friendship and his properties from the bishop. In confirmation of this friendship, Fastrad joined his daughter Sarra in marriage to Goswin, son of Theodoric the Minter, who was the brother of Tetbert. The brothers of the dead man immediately gave the twenty pounds in money that they had accepted from Fastrad for the concord to St. Martin's. Moreover, they added six bonarios of land at Salimgotum and a vat in which they brew beer. They gave this for the soul of the dead man and arranged that our work be done without charge no matter how much we might have.[7]

60. Young Theodoric Refuses His Father's Purchase of a Prebend

Tetbert's brother, Ralph, then married a young woman by the name of Mainsendis. She was born of the knightly class of the province, the daughter of Herman, prior of St. Amand of Elnon.[1] Ralph had three sons by her, Theodoric, Walter, and Herman. Theodoric was the oldest, and Ralph turned him to the study of letters at the age of five. Upon the advice of the canons, he petitioned and requested of Bishop Radbod that a prebend in the cathedral of St. Mary's be given to Theodoric and promised the bishop thirty marks of silver for it. This was announced by the canons, who came to offer their congratulations to the boy while he was still in class. When he returned home that evening, Theodoric did not want to eat but sat gloomily at the table. His father thought that he had been beaten by the teacher for some boyish behavior. When supper was over, he took his son aside and asked him what he had to be sad about. The boy quickly an-

swered him, "In the name of God," he said, "don't I have reason
to be sad, when I know that you sank yourself into Hell for me
today? Haven't you heard that those who buy or sell prebends
are excommunicate? Think carefully about what you are doing
to your soul. And understand that I would sooner leave this
province than be maintained at the expense of your soul." His father was amazed at this. "Son," he said, "don't be sad about the
prebend any more, since I swear to God you will not have it any
longer." He spoke and straightaway sent word to the bishop that
he might do whatever he wished with his prebend, because his
son did not want it.[2]

61. Ralph and Mainsendis Decide to Renounce the World (1092)

Ralph was stricken by a severe fever in that same year and almost died. When, God willing, he recovered, he secretly went to
a monk named Walter, his wife's brother and a very wise man.
He began to confer with him about the state of his soul with
these words:

Since you owe faith to God as a monk and to me as the husband of your
sister, I implore you by that faith that you owe to God and to me, to tell
me how I may be saved. I was sick not long ago and I was afraid that I
would die. I asked the advice of the canons of St. Mary's. They told me
to confess my sins truthfully, take the body of the Lord, be anointed
with holy oil, and I would be secure in my future salvation. I did what
they advised, but when I recovered, I once again felt myself under the
weight of my sins. This doesn't seem to me to be truly confession, to
confess my sins when sick and to be once again soiled with sin when I
recover.[1] I beg you, for God's sake, give me some advice. What should I
do?

The monk answered, "What good would it do you to hear my
advice, when you're unwilling to take it?" "Give me your advice," said the knight, "and if I don't follow it, it won't be your
fault." Then the monk spoke, "I will tell you truthfully," he said,
"that as long as you live in the world as you have been living up

to now, I don't see how you can be saved. But, if you truly want to be saved, give up the world and embrace the monastic life." The knight said, "And how shall I do that without the permission of your sister, my wife?" "Since the Lord said in the Gospel, 'If anyone comes to me and he does not hate his father and mother, and wife and children for my name, he cannot be my disciple,' [Mark 14:26] I would never advise you to lose your soul for the sake of my sister. Ask her for permission. If she is unwilling to give it, I advise you to leave her part of your wealth and to abandon her and flee to God."

When he had heard these things, the knight thanked him and returned home. He entered his bedroom, sat down upon the bed, and began to weep most bitterly. Mainsendis came upon him and saw him crying. She asked him what had happened now that he should be so pained. He wanted to keep it secret, but she urged him so that he went over all that her brother, Lord Walter, monk and prior of St. Amand had said to him. And then she said, "And why are you so pained because of this?" Ralph replied, "Because I would like to be truly and completely a monk, except for the fact that I would have to abandon you." She quickly said, "In order to treat me well, you don't leave me. Well, I fear for my soul just as you are afraid for yours. Any day that you abandon the world, I will abandon it too. Right now, if you like. I give you license and I promise that I shall live without blame." The knight then asked, "But what shall we do with our three sons?" His wife answered, "We shall not leave them in the hands of the devil; it would be better to offer them to God along with ourselves. We are rich, and any place we chose would be happy to rear them." Ralph was overjoyed at these words, and said, "Where does it seem to you that it would be appropriate for us to put on the religious habit with them?"

At that time Master Odo was still running the school of Tournai, and there was no mention of his renunciation of the world.

For this reason, the woman did not know where she should turn. "It seems to me that we could properly go to St. Amand, since my father was prior there and my brother succeeded him. Also, I was born and reared there." Ralph agreed and immediately sent word of this to Lord Walter, the monk, by means of a special messenger and by his hand gave St. Amand a mill located near Tournai on the stream called the Marvis. Ralph then summoned his wife and said, "Whoever wants to do something well ought not to delay, because the devil is clever and always seeks circumstances in which he can prevent the servants of God from carrying out a good project. It seems to me that we should renounce the world tomorrow morning without delay." She then answered, "My Lord, this can't be done so quickly. I haven't yet told you of a certain secret. It has been two months now since I felt that I had conceived, and it certainly would not be reasonable for me to depart from the world while I was pregnant. In the meantime, let's make all the necessary preparations so that we may renounce the world immediately after I have given birth. Since I have already given you permission, however, which no one may alter after God's witness, you are free at any rate. Now let us do none of the things of marriage and matrimony with each other, but live continent from now on." After this, as they told me many times, they lived a secular life for an entire year and a half, lying in one undivided bed. But, for all that, they did nothing carnal, not through their own moral strength, but because they were protected by the grace of Christ. Mainsendis was still a young woman, so that she was only twenty-four years old when she abandoned the world. A fourth son was born to them, and he was christened Ralph at baptism.

62. Seven-Year Old Theodoric Runs Away and Becomes a Monk of St Martin's; Ralph, His Father, Decides to Help Saint Martin's (1092)

In that same year, Master Odo renounced the world and, as we recounted above, entered the church of St. Martin's with his clerics. Mainsendis visited them, many times giving her alms to them,[1] but no one in the city yet knew what she and her husband were preparing to do. One Sunday, she went to the church of St. Martin's with her son, Theodoric, by now a little cleric almost seven years old, to listen to their mass and watch their procession. She watched while the mass was being sung, but the boy paid no attention to her and joined the clerics and stayed with them. When the mass was over, the woman searched for her son among her but did not find him. Believing that he had gone to play with the boys,[2] she returned home. They called the boy when lunch was ready, and his mother said that he had gone with her to St. Martin's. Neither had any suspicion of his having entered the monastic life.

When they had finished lunch, the knight mounted his horse and went to the house of his brother, Theodoric. He asked after his son both there and in the houses nearby, but he heard no word of him. Then he went to St. Martin's. He found the boy sitting in the presence of Abbot Emory of Anchin and Abbot Odo, and he beheld him listening to them. The abbots had the knight sit with them and gladly instructed him in the mandates of God. As evening drew near, the knight begged leave of the abbots to depart. He turned to his son to tell him to come home with him. Then the boy disclosed his wishes for the first time. "If you wish, you return home, salute my mother and brothers, and tell them that they should pray for me. For I shall never again enter your house, but I shall remain here with these paupers. I recognize no mother or father but God and Saint Martin." His father was struck by this and thought that the boy was just playing by saying these things. "Come," he said, "you don't have anything here to eat tonight or a bed to sleep in." The boy answered him by saying, "And if I don't have anything to eat, I shall go through the city asking them for alms and at night, indeed, I shall sleep on the bare ground." The father laughed and, saying that this was mere childishness, wanted to lead the boy home by force.

Finally Abbot Emory, a very wise man, spoke, "Lord Ralph, if you would trust me, do not use violence with the boy but leave him with us. In one night we will give him a foretaste of what would be necessary for him to do. If indeed this desire comes from God, it will soon become apparent; if it is in fact from childishness, do not compel him, for he will return home of his own accord." Having listened to these words, the knight agreed, returned home and told his wife about the matter. She immediately kneeled and lifted her eyes and hands to heaven. "I give thanks to God," she said, "for having taken my first-born son into His service. It seems to me, then, my Lord, that God wants us to build this little church with our wealth. And we shall have this sign of Divine will: if the child perseveres in what he has begun, we should then be certain that I have spoken the truth. If he should return, then God wishes something different from us."[3]

At dawn, the knight remounted his horse and returned to St. Martin's. He was told that the boy was most constantly persevering in what he had begun. Ralph then summoned his brother Theodoric and others of his neighbors and offered his son, a seven-year old boy and not yet of legal age, to the altar of St. Martin's in their presence, and he conferred with him four mills that he had on the stream called the Ries.[4] Although he was still remaining in the world, Ralph later took the little church completely under his care, providing nothing less than would have been necessary if he had already become a monk.

63. Ralph Commends His Wife and Sons to God, Renounces the World, and Catches Up with Odo (September 1094); Mainsendis Puts Her Children on the Altar of St Martin's and Renounces the World; Their Donations to the Abbey; Some Problems with Water Mills

In that same year, as we recounted above, the clerics donned the monastic habit in the presence of Abbot Emory, and the boy Theodoric became a monk along with them. Indeed, when the monks decided to abandon the church to go to the desert, they thought that they would leave Theodoric behind. But he refused to stay behind notwithstanding the fact that, being only an eight-year old boy, he was not able to sustain the labor of walking the road on foot. They put him on top of the wagon with their books and took him away with them.[1]

It was late in the morning and Ralph was still in bed when this was reported to him. He arose immediately, went to the cathedral of St. Mary's, and quickly called the community of canons together. He voluntarily returned their treasury to them, which he had kept by force up to then, and asked forgiveness for the violence he had brought upon them.[2] Then he disclosed his will, namely that he would renounce the world immediately and follow after the departed monks of St. Martin's. Having said these things, he returned to his house with a company of clerics and a great throng of citizens. He held his wife's hands, lifted his eyes to Heaven, and said "Lord God, You gave me this wife and You will witness that I have served her up to this very day with the proper faith. Now, for love of You, I relinquish her and commend her to You." After this, he took Walter and Herman, his two little boys, and, holding them up, he offered and commended them to God.

How great and very sweet was the mourning of all when they saw Ralph's fourth child, still a suckling, brought in a cradle, taken from the nest by his father, lifted up, and commended to God! Then he swiftly mounted his horse. He did not wish to leave behind the pauper cleric Ranier, whom he had kept with him for two years in honor of God. He gave him another horse, and together they swiftly followed the monks. They joined them before they reached Seclin. Prostrated at Abbot Odo's feet, Ralph asked that he be permitted to join his party of pilgrims.[3] The abbot was amazed at such great ardor in a man of wealth and called together the monks who were accompanying him on foot and chose Ralph's renunciation of the world for the opening of his exhortation. "Look!" he said, "We monks thought we were doing something, but we've been beaten by the layman, Zacheus the publican." It was for this reason that Odo disclosed his desires to Bishop Radbod when he reached Noyon with his followers.[4]

The bishop, shedding tears because of his great wonder, kissed [Ralph] and offered thanks to God. He took his hand and placed it in that of the abbot and said, "Now tell me, my good abbot, why do you want to leave Tournai? Do you think that you haven't gotten enough ahead, you who have stolen such a sinner from Satan and united him to God? Go back, then, with joy and haste, because, truly, even now God might reward someone else for this."[5]

After Odo had returned to Tournai, Ralph again prostrated himself at the feet of the abbot and begged to be admitted as a monk.[6] The abbot said, "I will not accept you until you prove yourself according to the second rule of Saint Benedict, which says, 'Test their spirits, if they be from God.' Go, then, and publicly and in the presence of the people, get your food by working: carrying water to the taverns, cutting wood, cleaning out the horse stables, and similar things wherever you find work to be done." Ralph gladly carried out the command of the abbot. Far from all shame, he undertook the most vile jobs.

Mainsendis, formerly his wife, saw this and was not moved by fear.[7] She sent for Theodoric the Minter, Ralph's brother and the richest man in the entire city, and went to Saint Martin's. There she gave her sons to God, putting the smallest one in his cradle on the altar, not without the tears of many bystanders. Theodoric, their godfather, moved by charity and with the abbot's permission, had the children taken to his house to be reared and kept them with him for a long time.[8] Mainsendis put two hundred marks of silver on the altar, and she turned over to St. Martin's two mills at Constantin on the Scheldt and the remainder of all the wealth that her husband had left for her.

And so she came to throw herself at the feet of the abbot, stripped of everything and praying to be admitted. The abbot said to her, "First it is necessary for you to prove yourself. So go through the city, earning your food by spinning, weaving, and carding wool. And if by chance someone, either a man or a woman, should wish to give you an entire loaf of bread,[9] do not accept it, but only the broken crusts of bread, according to the custom of beggars seeking alms." The woman exulted in such delightful forage and, blushing deeply, she publicly begged alms. The women who saw her were in tears and wanted to send a great deal of bread with her, through her attendants, to St. Martin's.[10]

And this was the way of the conversion of Ralph and Mainsendis, which I do not believe pious Jesus can have ignored. These are the things that Ralph conferred upon our church: four mills on the Ries closer to the Scheldt. We used to have a fifth upon the Scheldt, but because it was easily swept away by the flood when the waters of the Scheldt rose in the Autumn, it was completely destroyed after a while. Nevertheless, he ordered that the posts be left and preserved in witness of the old mill, if only so that no one in the future might be able to build a mill downstream from those four to the Scheldt. If one were built and remained firm, the four on the Ries might easily suffer substantial damage as a result. He gave us two mills on the Constantin, with adjacent lands that had come to him by paternal succession and upon which he had a court built which persists to the present day.[11] He also gave us a herd of horses, the descendants of which are kept in our meadows down to the present day, and from among which we frequently select four-horse teams for plowing our lands, and we feed and sell horses of great price.[12] And in various expenditures, by now we have had the use of more than a thousand pounds from them.

With the money that his wife gave us, we redeemed the lands located around the church and bought other tracts in the region. We did not have a yard of arable land up to the time that she came to renounce secular life.[13] Ralph had a mill upon the Maire but, when he first had the desire to renounce the world, as was discussed above, he gave the mill to St. Amand because he wanted to be a monk in the monastery called "Elnon." At that time there had not yet been any mention of our monastery among men.

64. The Monastery of St. Amand Shares a Donation with St. Martin's and the Two Abbeys Become Associates

The venerable Hugh was abbot of St. Amand at that time. Because of a fire a few years earlier,[1] he restored the church of St. Amand from the foundations up. He built it most fittingly, with cloister, towers, and workshops, as can be seen today. Full of sweet charity, he saw that Ralph and his wife and children had abandoned the church of St. Amand and had turned to the poor little church of St. Martin's. He called his monks into the chapter house and said, "See, most beloved brothers, this worldly knight Ralph prefers St. Martin's poverty to our riches and wishes to become a monk in the pauper church. Let us show ourselves to have charitable hearts and confer half of the mill that he gave us on the pauper church of St. Martin's. And so let us make Saint Martin a partner in this mill with our patron, St. Amand." They all agreed, and not one showed himself to be unlike the others in paternal charity.

And so Lord Hugh came to Tournai, prostrated his body before the entire chapter, begged [to be admitted], and was received into the society and brotherhood of the pauper monks. He gave them half of the mill and ever afterward he showed that he had a paternal heart concerning us. When the monks wished to go with Lord Odo to the desert, as was said above, and had left the church of St. Martin's, Lord Hugh, abbot of St. Amand, sent five of his monks there so that the church of St. Martin's should not lack the divine office. He sent food to them every day, and he instructed them to remain there until the return of the monks of St. Martin's.[2]

65. Following Ralph, Other Rich Citizens Convert to St. Martin's; Henry and His Family Join St. Martin's; Their Donations to the Abbey

On account of Ralph, many men from the city of Tournai began to come to convert and to live in emulation of his fervor. One of them, Henry, an extremely wealthy man, together with his wife, Bertha, his as-yet unweaned son, John, and two daughters, Trasberga and Iulitta, entered monastic life in almost the same fashion as Ralph. Henry gave the church a great sum of money, with which the dormitory and the other workrooms were built, and some tracts of land. He himself publicly begged alms at the order of the abbot, proving himself to be in truth a man of great fervor, and at length he became a monk. He lived in our monastery for many years as cellarer and as a good example for all. About twenty-two years after his conversion, concluding a praiseworthy life with a good end, he rendered up his spirit to God at Eastertide, 15 April.[1] His son, John, was reared in monastic habit along with Ralph's son, Ralph, and received all of the ecclesiastical orders along with him.[2] To this very day, he busies himself in the priestly office and shows himself to be the good fruit of a good tree.

His mother, Bertha, and sisters, Trasberga and Iulitta, lived for many years above reproach as nuns and they have now passed over from labor to rest.

66. Many Other People Join St. Martin's; Everard the Castellan Rebels against Count Robert (1093)

After Henry became a monk, you would have seen a real marvel: youths and maidens, old men and youngsters, abandoning the world and coming from all over the province to convert. It was like that which one reads in *The Acts of the Apostles,* selling what they had and giving the payment for their things to Lord Abbot Odo. If the abbot had wanted to retain the money and properties given to him at that time, according to the practice of the abbots of his time, and to expend them in embellishing the church, there would have been none to equal it. How greatly, and by how many people, it seemed to have grown!

But in those times, as we noted above,[1] Everard, the castellan of Tournai, rebelled against Count Robert of Flanders. He maintained a large military force and frequently seized great numbers of men, both rich and poor, from the count's land and held them for ransom. Shackled and hungry, they flocked to Abbot Odo and tearfully pleaded with him to relieve their miseries. Moved to pity by their tears, the abbot gave them abundantly of the money that had been given to him and so redeemed many men.[2]

67. The Monk Ralph Hears the Choir of the Dead Worshipping in St. Martin's

There was at that time a priest and religious monk by the name of Ralph, of the Norman race, who had been one of Abbot Odo's first five companions. At the command of the abbot, he performed the worrisome task of striking the hours.[1] Since this

office is by rule also that of the bailiff, he put his cot in the more
remote part of the church—not for the purpose of guarding the
treasury of the Church, because there was none as yet, since the
abbot did not wish to have a silver chalice or cross or cloth—but
only to attend more carefully to striking the hours of the vigil. A
most honest man, Ralph told us many times how he was lying on
his bed one night so that he might follow the psalms and prayers
through the vigil, when he heard in the choir something like some
great crowd approaching and singing in a restrained voice the response of the Holy Trinity, "Blessings be to the Father and to the
Son and to the Holy Spirit." When the response was finished, he
heard two approach the altar and, with the sweetest and most
sustained melody, add the verse of the response, "You are
blessed, O Lord, in the firmament of the heavens." When the
verse was finished, the whole chorus again repeated the close of
the response, and then were silent. When this religious monk had
heard this several times, he privately told Lord Abbot Odo and
some of the older spirituals. They all said that they believed that
it was the souls of the good men and women resting here, who
were giving thanks to God for the restoration of this little
church.[2]

68. Odo Refuses Gifts of Gold, Accepts All Who Apply, but Requires Tests of Humility and Obedience

The abbot read the institutes and doctrines of the ancient fathers tirelessly and pondered the little verse of the secular poet,
"Tell me, bishops, what does gold have to do with a sacred
thing?"[1] He did not wish to make golden crosses, but distributed
all the money he was given to the burdened and destitute. Nevertheless, he kept all who came to convert, saying that he was trying to imitate the words of the Lord, "I shall not drive away him
who comes to me."[2]

Odo did not wish to accept anyone without first testing them, and he placed so many burdens on them during these tests that he seemed to be asking more than any of the tests of ancient times. He told one man who wished to become a monk to take an enormous rock, that could hardly be budged by many men, and move it all be himself beyond the city of Tournai. You could see that man first with his hands and arms, then with his entire body, pressing himself against the rock with all his strength and pouring rivers of sweat from every pore, laboring to try to be obedient to the master.[3] Odo commanded others to remain motionless for many days and nights under the rainwater running off the eaves of houses and to endure the pelting showers of water. But, in a quite wonderful fashion, although he imposed such harsh and unbearable burdens on them, more people, both knights and clerics, then came to become monks in our church than you see coming today. Today, no one is tested. On the contrary, as soon as someone comes, he is caressed with blandishments and promises.

In those days, even some of the canons of St. Mary's became monks here.[4] Lord Amand, for instance, held the post of prior at Anchin for many years and then was made abbot of Marchiennes. He ruled and reformed this latter congregation, which was almost completely ruined both in internal discipline and in external wealth. Then there was Lord Walbert, who was prior in our church and after many years became abbot of the monastery of Mont-St.-Martin, in the diocese of Cambrai,[5] and died there. There was also Lord Gunther, who held the office of prior in our congregation for many years, and Lord Bernuin. These four were first rich clerics and then pauper monks. If you heard the tale of how they were tested by Abbot Odo, you would scarcely be able to keep from laughing at the enormous delight of it. Seeing that they were excessively proud, Odo ordered them to milk the cows and make cheese for several days. After they had been tested in this fashion, he gave them the monastic habit.[6]

If he had been willing to accept the altars they held, our brotherhood today might be richer as a result. He proposed, however,
not to accept altars or churches or tithes, but that the congregation should live solely by the labor of their hands from the agriculture of their plow-teams, and the nourishment of their cattle.[7]
He said that he did not wish to have any of the ecclesiastical
rents these rich brothers possessed because such things were not
for monks, but ought to be possessed only by clerics. This intent
of his was in harmony with the life and institutes of the monks of
old. He later learned from some monks living by the city, whom
some call "populars" or "seculars," that the ancient institutes
could not be observed in their entirety.

69. St. Martin's Establishes a Convent; Mainsendis Is Unjustly Expelled, but Then Restored

Since he wished to drag everyone along with him to God, he
took in such a great crowd of women, not just paupers but rich
ones too, that it appeared that a monastery would have to be
built just for them. For this reason, the abbot looked at the stone
house that had formerly belonged to the knight Ralph, and which
he had given to his wife when he became a monk. It was not
small and was divided by interior walls into an oratory, refectory,
and dormitory. Odo established almost sixty women monastics
there, and placed his sister, a nun named Eremburg, over them.[1]
Among the other women he ordered to live there was Mainsendis, Ralph's former wife. Nevertheless, he established just as
many converts in another part of the city under another mother
superior.[2]

Mainsendis was laid low by a grave illness after a few days
and was forced to lie on a cot in a house that had formerly been
her own. She felt herself growing sicker and sicker, and she asked
her superior, the lord abbot's sister, if she might be given commu-
nion. Since the house was far from the church of St. Martin's, the

lord abbot had conceded that, in urgent cases, sick converts might accept absolution and viaticum from a priest of St. Piatus who lived nearby. When the Lord Priest Hellinus received word from the mother superior that he should visit Mainsendis with the viaticum, he went most gladly, since in secular life she had been a woman of his parish, and he had received many donations from her.

Well, when the priest came, the mother superior ordered Mainsendis not speak to him of anything but her sins. Mainsendis was therefore confessed of her sins by the priest and received the body of the Lord. The mother superior stood by and listened to everything that was said.[3] As the priest was leaving, Mainsendis begged him to be mindful of her and to pray to God for her. The mother superior turned to Mainsendis as soon as the priest had left and said, "That does it! Since you spoke to the priest of things other than your sins in defiance of the obedience you owe to me, you are excommunicate."[4] Mainsendis replied, "Truly, my Lady, I didn't think that I was doing anything wrong. When I begged him to pray for me, I didn't mean for the health of my body, but for the remission of my sins."[5] Then the mother superior called the other sisters and said that Mainsendis was excommunicated. She ordered her to be thrown out. Everyone prostrated themselves at the feet of the mother superior but were unable to sway her. Since Mainsendis could not rise from her cot, the mother superior ordered her carried in her bed out of the house and placed beneath some wooden steps leading down into the courtyard, so that the water from the kitchen situated above would flow down upon her.[6]

She lay here in this fashion for three days, perhaps sick in her body but exulting in her soul, because she was now enduring tribulations for God in a house in which before she had been the mistress. But since a benign God brings consolation after tribulation: Behold! After three days, Henry, whom we have mentioned and who was now a monk, was carrying a great bundle of linen on his head, at the abbot's command, to be spun. He went to the sisters' house, passed through the gate of the courtyard, and saw Mainsendis lying in her cot under the step. He was amazed and asked one of the sisters (who was allowed to speak to him when receiving linen) why Mainsendis should be lying there so. Having heard the reason but not daring to speak to Mainsendis, he presumed to say as much as this, with everyone listening, to console her. "O Saint Alexis, you who lay a stranger in your father's house for seventeen years and thence acquired great glory with God, comfort this handmaid of God, who now sustains such tribulation in a house where she was formerly mistress."[7] Mainsendis was so exhilarated at hearing this, as she told me many times afterward, that she completely forgot her illness. Henry came back with the abbot because when Odo heard what Henry had to say, he immediately commanded that Mainsendis be carried back into the house with the others.[8]

70. The Great Famine of 1095; Odo Gives All of the Monastery's Food to Beggars; the Community Limits Odo's Authority; Ralph Becomes Prior, Walter His Associate, Henry Cellarer, and They Beg Food

In this year, a lack of foodstuffs and the horror of famine greatly distressed the entire province.[1] The abbot began to distribute in charity whatever he could get his hands on to all the paupers who sought his aid, so that nothing remained in either the cellar or the granary. He was at last compelled by necessity and anxiety to call together the brothers who had been secluded for the entire year while being tamed by the yoke of silence and were ignorant of what was happening outside.[2] In the chapter assembly, he revealed to them how matters stood. He had supported a great throng of men and women, and the abbey did not now have enough food for even a single day.

Everyone was stupefied. They were struck with amazement

that he should have taken such an important action without having discussed the matter with anyone. They then asked him to turn over the care of the monastery's external affairs to some prudent man, that he himself should follow true doctrine and the health of souls and not undertake anything from then on without the counsel of the brothers. Moreover, he should not test those whom he had received by imposing grievous and contrived tasks upon them according to the customs of the ancients. Instead, he should be content with the institutes and rules of the monastery of Cluny, since it was preeminent among the monasteries of all of France for its reputation and discipline, as well as for its charity, and was ruled by the venerable Abbot Hugh.[3]

The abbot agreed to the counsel of the brothers, and immediately ordained Henry cellarer. He turned the office of prior over to Ralph and gave him Walter Hubert as an associate.[4] Commending the oversight of the whole church in external matters to these three, he permitted them to go outside without leave; he announced to the others that they should devote themselves along with him to religion and silence.

The three men left the chapter house and went into the kitchen to look for whatever might have been prepared for the brothers, but they found nothing. They then entered the gate of the city. They looked as if they had just crawled outside after a long term in jail, and the citizens they met would ask them how they were. The three men would wish them joy and would answer that everything was going well. After a short while, however, the citizens noticed that the brothers were in need. They quickly discussed the matter, and gave grain to one, wheat to another, and beans to yet another, encouraging and comforting them, and sent them back to the brothers cheerful and gladdened.[5]

Ralph revealed the church's lack of means to his brother Theodoric and asked him to lend him the money to buy necessities for the brothers. Theodoric immediately loaned him forty marks of silver, which he never later asked to be returned but gave up to the church for his soul. He gave a garden on the Scheldt, near St. Medard, that is very useful to our church. He was always preeminent among the citizens in the many things he did for us. Later, when the abbot ordered Walter to begin to build the abbey from the donations of the faithful, Theodoric immediately gave one hundred shillings as a start, one hundred shillings towards building a refectory, and another one hundred shillings to the cellarer. He often sent a full meal of fish to the brothers' refectory. They gave up keeping accounts and trying to repay him for what he did.

71. The Hardships of the Famine Year; the Monks Survive on Water and Bread Made of Oats and Straw (1095)

It is hard to believe what a great shortage of bread the pauper community endured throughout that entire year. There was not even a mention of wheaten bread or wine, unless by chance some was sent over to them by someone of wealth. There was no wheat at all; only ground oats were brought to them from the mill.[1] It wasn't sieved or sifted but was immediately covered with hot water and made into bread. It was baked and, when it was put on the monks' table, it seemed as if it were mostly burnt straw. When it was cut with a knife in front of the monk, it seemed to be more of a mass of straw than of crumbs. But because bitter seems sweet to a hungry person, according to Solomon,[2] monks wasted by starvation ate that oaten bread with such greediness that not a crumb or a straw of it remained. A few of them still survive, of whom one is Lord Ascelin, who succeeded Lord Henry in the office and obedience of cellarer. He still maintains that he often wondered to himself back then whether he might ever see the day when the church of St. Martin's would be so rich that he could just get his fill of bread.

Whoever of our successors might read this, pray for the souls of your predecessors. While they ate bread made of oats and straw, not of wheat, through their patience and by the grace of God they acquired an abundance of wheaten bread for you.

One thing happened at that time, however, that still pains us. Since Lord Odo was not able to retain the great number of women whom he had accepted, he gave them leave to depart and search for food. They accepted his leave and disappeared, but he did not return the money that some of them had given to him because he had either given it to paupers or spent it on the congregation.[3]

72. Ralph Acquires Lands and Establishes Farms to Produce Food and Rents for St. Martin's (1096)

Ralph looked around and realized that a pauper church, lacking rents and renders, could not easily endure without agriculture. He therefore bent every effort to acquiring and buying land. First he put four teams of draft animals in the church grounds and fenced off sufficient land for them, part of which he acquired from the donations of the faithful and part of which he bought with money.

Two citizens of Tournai, Walter "Little-aid" and Letard "the Guard," came with their wives and children to join our community. They gave us the workshops they owned within Tournai and farmland in the vicinity of Tournai valued at two hundred marks. It was claimed that Letard's lands were old possessions of the church of St. Quentin, which had been destroyed by Bishop Fulcher. Fulcher later gave them to the knights of Noyon. The knights found that the lands were not very profitable to them and sold them to citizens of Tournai, reserving some rent for themselves. We held the lands that Letard gave us from the bishop for an annual payment of twenty-two shillings.[1]

Ralph then built three houses or manses, which we incorrectly call "courts," in the suburbs of Tournai within about a mile of the church. The first of these was called Varnave, the second

Duissenpierre,[2] the third Longue-Saulx, and the fourth Taintig-nies. He placed ten teams in these four courts and acquired suffi-cient land for them. He built a fifth court between Nomain and Templeuve on the land that he had convinced Count Robert to give to the church in exchange for his horse, as was mentioned above; a sixth at Camphin-en-Pévèle; and a seventh at Costenten on land that came to him from his paternal inheritance; an eighth at Audolmanse above the Scheldt; a ninth at Gaurain; a tenth at Domeries; an eleventh at Cataine.[3]

73. Bishop Radbod Is Accused of Simony; Anselm Resigns as His Attorney; Radbod Commits Perjury and Dies (1098)

Meanwhile, Lord Bishop Radbod was the uncle of Everard, the castellan who took the castle of Tournai and the castle of Mortain a few days earlier. He established his dominion over them and expelled their legitimate heirs, Gerulf of Tournai and Hugo of Mortain. Bishop Radbod was a noble man and of great probity. Among the other praiseworthy things he did was to take care to restore this monastery, as was said above. But, alas, as the blessed Job said, that God should find perversity in his angels. [Job 4:18] Well, this bishop of such great probity was accused at the see of Rome of having gained his episcopacy by giving money to the king. When he had been knocked about many times at the papal court, he pawned many ornaments of the church of Tour-nai and gave [the money] to those aiding him.[1] He sold several rents of the altar of the Holy Savior of Bruges to the canons of St. Donatian, and he sold out completely several rents both of other altars as well as episcopal lands.

It had been decided that he would have to compurgate himself of simony with two bishops.[2] Master Anselm was a distinguished teacher of the school of Laon at the time and was most famous throughout all of France for his knowledge. Through his advice, the aid of the bishops was withdrawn from Radbod, since

Anselm knew that surely neither could take an oath that he was innocent. When many people had intervened on Radbod's behalf and they conceded that he might compurgate himself by a single hand,[3] Archbishop Hugh of Lyon and legate of the apostolic see, perceiving that he was willing to swear, rose up in front of everyone. "What are you doing, you unhappy man," he said, "Do you want to kill your soul by swearing falsely? Desist from this oath, and we shall plead that you should not be deposed immediately, but that you should have two years' delay. Later, you can give up the bishopric respectably and of your own accord, as if because of religion or old age. But if you swear.... Well, I predict that you'll die without honor within a year."[4]

The bishop, just as he had started to do, placed his hand on the Gospel, swore that he was innocent of simony, left the council safely, and returned to Tournai. A few days after he left Bruges, he wished to be bled because of weakness. While waiting for the doctor, he went into an inner chamber because of nature's call. When he had stayed there for a long time, one of the attendants followed him, saw that he had fallen on his face in front of the seat, and cried out with great grief. Everyone quickly entered and found the bishop undone by paralysis, having lost the use of both his limbs and his tongue. Lifting him up with their hands, they carried him to his bed. After a few days, they wept for a man who died without confession.[5] He was carried to Tournai and buried in the church of St. Mary's. Lord Baldric, archdeacon of Noyon, succeeded him as bishop.

74. St. Martin's Accepts the Rents of Church Altars; Inventory of the Altars Given to St. Martin's and a Record of Their Donors; Ralph Increases St. Martin's Farmsteads to Twenty

Ralph persuaded Lord Abbot Odo that if someone wanted to give altars to our church for the good of their soul and without simony, he should not refuse to accept them but should follow the custom of the abbots of other religious communities. The abbot agreed, and a canon of St. Mary's named Weric gave us the first altar, that of Esplechin. Then Baldwin, the cantor, and his son, Tetbert, gave us the altar of Saméon.[1] The canon Letbert, father of Lord Walter, abbot of this monastery, gave us the altar of Passendale. The canon Gerric and the knight Wenemar donated some shares of the altar of Templeuve. Bishop Radbod, in whose time our monastery was restored, gave us the altar of Evregnies. Canon Adam gave us five altars—namely Haltra, Saraucourt, Isengain, Gudelengain, and Estaimpuis—at the request of his father, Precentor Siger, who became a monk among us along with his brother, Prior Herman, as was mentioned a long time ago. The cleric Erpulf donated the altars of Willebecca and Fivia. The monks of Ter Duyn gave us the two altars of Beveren and Lendeguin for a certain tract of land on the sea that we held from Lord Bishop Simon of Tournai.[2] Didier, archdeacon of Tournai and prior of Lille, gave us the altars of Guerna and Lieda. Bishop Gerald and the clerics of Ecourt-St.-Quentin exchanged the altar of Mouscron for the farmstead of Bruges. The monks of Lhos were required by Lord Bishop Gerald to give us the altars of Annoeulin and Alelne in exchange for our farmstead at Pevélè. We have all of these in the diocese of Tournai.

Canon Letbert gave us the altars of Zulte and Warchin; Bishop Bartholomew the altars of Fasti and Proisy, Thomas of Marly the altar of Froidmont. We have these three in the diocese of Laon.

In the diocese of Cambrai, these: Albert, the altar of Sirault; Deacon Wericus, the altar of Gaurain; Ubald, the altar of Hacquegnies; Lord Odo, the first abbot of this monastery, gave us the altar of Maulde when he became bishop of Cambrai; Odo, the priest of Bouvignies, the altars of Ostiolo and of Papignies; Deacon Walter of Tournai, who was later bishop,[3] the altar of Vais. When Tetbald, prior of the church of Rouen, father of Ralph, archdeacon of Cambrai, came to us to become a monk, he gave us the altars of Floresbech, Ormegnies, Bailleul, and of Lierde of St. Martin. A tract of land above the Dender river belongs to this last altar, where the above-mentioned prior Ralph built twelve farmsteads and constructed a first-rate mill. Then Mascelino, prior of the church of Leuze, together with his wife Mainsendis and their son, Alexander, came to enter monastic life and gave us two altars, Bouvignies and Brantenies. Prior Ralph gave another three farmsteads in these parishes so that he completed the number fifteen. Sixteenth at Vezon, seventeenth at Merbeies, eighteenth at Torelies, nineteenth at Froyennes. He built the twentieth near Bruges, in a little church which is called St. Trudo.

75. Ralph Restores the Abandoned Church of St. Amand of Noyon as a Priory of St. Martin's.

He [Prior Ralph] found a small church near the castle of Thourotte in the district of Noyon. It had been built in honor of St. Amand, but it was so empty and destitute that he did not find a yard of land, or a house, or anything for nourishment belonging to it. Well, he had fallen so in love with this solitary place, far removed from human habitation, that he went to Bishop Baldric of Noyon and asked that the little church be given to us, and he obtained it.[1] Against the wishes of many of the monks of our monastery, who said that he was mistaken to work so far away and in such great solitude, he successfully petitioned Lord Abbot Odo to allow Ralph, a monk priest of Norman birth, to go, since he could no longer tolerate the toil of the community because of a bodily infirmity. Well, he was sent there, but he was not expected to eradicate the forest by digging and chopping. Supplies and money were sent to him from our monastery, and so he was able to improve that place, by the grace of God. Within a short space of time, he took great delight in serving God in the place where he had at first found nothing but an empty church surrounded by thorns.

The canons of Noyon used to visit the place and saw that it

was suitable for those wishing to serve God in solitude. They began first to confer their goods on the place and then to come to renounce the world and become monks. [Although they resided at St. Amand's,] they received the blessing, gave their monastic oath, and were accepted by the abbot into the community of St. Martin's abbey. One of them was called Peter and was like a father to the other canons. When he relinquished the world and became a monk, he gave two of the finest vineyards in Noyon. He became such an excellent monk that not only clerics and knights, but even monks from other provinces regarded him as a model; and so he was visited by many people who came to listen to his counsel, which was almost as if it came from God. He was so watchful of his humility, however, that he would not enter the priestly order, even though he was begged to do so by the other brothers and was given permission by the abbot. Nor would he consent to speak with those who came [to be counseled by him] unless he had been given permission by the prior, and he often reminded the prior about alms for the paupers.

76. Canon Peter of Noyon Gives Abundant Charity during the Famine; Prior Ralph, the Norman, Continues This Generosity in St. Amand of Noyon

When famine was greatly afflicting the whole province, and Prior Ralph was worried about the want of the brothers and dared to beg alms in the manner used by paupers, Lord Peter advised that nothing should decrease the customary number of loaves of bread [given to the poor]. Soon after the paupers had arrived, his assistant told him that they had run out of loaves. Lord Peter said to him, "Go and see if by chance some crust of bread might still remain in the chest." When the assistant said that he had left an empty chest that very hour, Peter urged him to go and hunt. Because of his persistence, the harassed brother went back to the chest, and what he had left empty a short while before, he now found brim-full of bread.

Because of Peter's faith, Prior Ralph began to distribute bread so abundantly to all of the paupers who came that none was entirely denied bread. It seemed to him as if the more he expended, the more the meager wealth of this house increased through God's will.[1] So the little church of St. Amand is still much loved and visited by its neighbors. Many people, both men and matrons, not only from Noyon but from Compiégnes and other nearby places, come to renounce the world, and they confer many things on that place. The brothers of Tournai, who had earlier murmured against prior Ralph because he was sending money away from Tournai, were now joyful and full of praise because he had not acceded to their wishes.[2]

Lord Peter, who spoke familiarly with us many times, used to say that he had been born, had been baptized, and had come to renounce the world all on the day of the Chair of St. Peter [22 February], adding that he believed that he would die on the same feast. That is what happened. On the day of the Chair of St. Peter, he passed over from labor to rest, so we believe. He was buried in the cloister next to the porch of the church of St. Amand, with great mourning by his brothers and co-provincials.[3]

Ralph, the prior of St. Amand, whom we mentioned was of Norman extraction, had three brothers among our congregation, all priests and men of great religion, William, Godfrey, and Roger. They had abandoned the world in the company of Lord Abbot Odo in the first days, and endured the burdens of poverty together with him.[4]

77. The Works of Godfrey and William, Scribes and Authors of St. Martin's; Godfrey's Death

One of them, Godfrey, was a most accomplished scribe, and left many written books in our church, namely, the *Moralia of St. Gregory upon Job,* divided into six volumes; a first-rate history that begins with the parable of Solomon and contains all the prophets, acts of the apostles, and epistles; a missal that has both of the daily masses that are sung in assembly; a text of the Gospels; Augustine's *The City of God* and his *Enchiridion,* and many other books. One could easily see by the regularity of the script that he had written them. While still in his youth and after having written many books, Godfrey was healthy when he visited the ailing lord abbot to chat with him. He was suddenly seized by the same infirmity while we were looking on. He was carried to bed and was anointed with the holy oil after three day's time.

I was taking care of the lord abbot, and I stayed with Godfrey when the others withdrew. I asked him how he was, and he replied that he didn't feel at all bad or in pain.[1] I was persuaded that if he would allow himself to be placed upon the stones on the ground, he should soon feel the hardness and sharpness of the ground, according to the example of St. Martin. He immediately and willingly agreed. When he had been laid down, he asked me to read to him the Catholic faith, that is, "Whosoever wishes."[2] When I had done this, I asked him if he wanted the tablet to be beaten and the brotherhood to be called for his end.[3] He answered that he did not feel at all bad but that he would willingly wish to see the brothers. I immediately ran, beating the tablet. The brothers gathered and sang a litany around the sufferer. I kneeled, put my ear against his mouth, and asked him if he could see the brothers, if he could hear what they were saying. He answered that he saw the brothers and heard the names of the saints, that he was suffering no pain at all, but felt a great joy. When he had said this, he immediately gave up his spirit, to grief and loss of our whole community.

Lord Gilbert was his associate in writing books, reared in the school along with Theodoric, the son of the prior Ralph, by Lord Abbot Odo. He also wrote a history of the entire *Old Testament,* and two large and very useful books with a very large and clear script that contain the lessons for all of the Sundays and feast days of the whole year. One of these books is called *Of Summer* and the other *Of Winter*.[4] He died on the Purification of St. Mary [2 February], to the greatest grief of all of our congregation.

78. Ralph Purchases and Equips Four Farmsteads in the Outskirts of Laon; Thomas of Marly Sacks a Farmstead of St. Martin's and Must Pay Damages

When the Lord Prior Ralph had seen a bit of how his plans for the little church of St. Amand in the suburbs of Noyon had turned out, he headed for the region of Laon and learned that many villages and land here were lying vacant and desolate because of a war between Thomas of Marly and Roger of Pierrepont. He gave money to Roger and asked him to give our church for the health of his soul some of that land, where we could progress by working. With the assent of his wife, Ermengard, Roger immediately gave us vacant land in a place called Canteleux and confirmed it in the presence of Lord Ingelran, bishop of Laon at the time.[1] Ralph built a house here without delay. Seeing that the land was fertile and sufficient, he placed four plows there and replenished it with sheep and cows.

He then approached another noble, who was called Gerard of Chérisy. He gave him a sizeable amount of money and asked that he should imitate Roger and also give something for the good of his soul to the church of St. Martin.[2] He then gave us lands that he held at Livri and Brancourt, and because they were in fief of the king, he had them confirmed by Louis, king of the Franks. This was the first charter that our community had from a king. Ralph built one farmstead at Livri and another at Brancourt, and he repaired the mill which had been destroyed earlier. He built a fourth court not far from the others in a village called Montcellis. It did not consist of a single donation, but was formed from many donations and working fields.

After some time, Thomas of Marly saw that our farmstead was furnished with an abundance of stock. Led by avarice, he looted it. He was excommunicated for this reason and when he requested absolution, he gave us an altar in a village called Froidmont in recompense for the plunder. He had this confirmed by a privilege of the bishop of Laon from whom he held it in fief. In this manner he received absolution for his deed. Prior Ralph built these four courts in the suburbs of Laon and enlarged our congregation considerably through them.

79. Ralph and His Son, Walter, Build a Farmstead and a Stone Church in Honor of St. Mary in the Diocese of Soissons

He built another farmstead in the forest of Pinon in the diocese of Soissons and had it confirmed by a charter of Lord Lisiard, bishop of Soissons [1108–1126]. He appointed his son, Walter, to direct construction in this place, and, when a small stone church was built here with the donations of the faithful and in honor of St. Mary, Mother of God, he asked that it be consecrated by the bishop.

80. The Scriptorium and Library of St. Martin's of Tournai

Prior Ralph placed more than sixty plows in the houses or, let's say more familiarly, courts that he had built in various locations. In this fashion, with the aid of God, he provided the entire community of our abbey with food and clothing both from agriculture and stock-raising and from the renders of churches. Lord Abbot Odo rejoiced at this and gave thanks to God for having given him such a man who would make him completely free and safe from the worries and tumults of the outside world. Having turned the external concerns of the whole congregation over to Ralph, Odo concentrated on religion and silence so fervently that he would often not leave the cloister for a month at a time, but he would devote all his energy to the constant and intense reading and writing of books.[1]

He was quite delighted that God had given him such an abundance of scribes. If you were to go into the cloister, you would see more than twelve young monks sitting in chairs in front of small tables and silently writing careful and skillful compositions. One could find all of the books of Jerome in explanation of the prophets, all of the books of St. Gregory the Great, and various books of St. Augustine, Ambrose, Isidore, Bede, and also Lord Anselm, abbot of Bec at the time and later archbishop of Canterbury. He had them so carefully written that you would soon find similar ones in the libraries of the neighboring abbeys, and they all would ask for exemplars from our monastery for the correction of their own books.[2]

Our monastery then was great in name and great in religion, since in all the archdiocese of Reims you would find only three congregations at that time that kept the customs of Cluny: those of Anchin, Afflighem, and our own. Indeed, Cluny was then the monastery of the most excellent discipline in the entire kingdom of France because the rigor of the Cistercians had not yet blossomed nor was there yet any mention of Lord Norbert.[3]

81. Abbot Lambert Invites Hugh of Cluny to Rehabilitate St. Bertin; Cluniac Monks of St. Bertin Are Invited into Numerous Monasteries of Flanders and Northern France

At that time Lord Lambert was made abbot of St. Bertin. When he saw his church so destitute from profligate excess that only a few monks were able to live in it, he was compelled by the greatest necessity and went to Lord Hugh, then the most famous abbot of the monastery of Cluny, and committed himself and his whole congregation to Hugh's authority. He made his public profession in Cluny. When he had been accepted by Lord Hugh, he led twelve monks back with him and committed the governance of the church of St. Bertin to them. Under their direction and with the favor of God, it advanced so greatly that, a short time later, you would find the place crammed with one hundred and fifty and an abundance of all things where you would have found scarcely twelve monks before. Seeing this, the famous Count Robert of Flanders, who had now returned to his own land after the capture of Jerusalem, placed monks chosen from the monastery of St. Bertin in the church of St. Vaast of Arras and St. Peter's of Bruges and reformed them greatly. Lord Odo, the venerable abbot of St. Remigius of Reims, placed monks received from the abbot of the monastery of St. Bertin in his own monastery. Then Louis, king of France, seeing that other churches were profiting from these same customs, required them by force to be observed in the monastery of St. Medard of Soissons. And so, by God's grace, there is hardly to be found in France or Flanders now any monastery in which you do not see the customs of Cluny observed. But when our monastery blossomed in prosperity and great fame among neighboring abbeys, as we were saying, behold how quickly the crown fell from our heads and joy fled from our hearts![1]

82. Abbot Odo Elected Bishop of Cambrai (2 July 1105)

Lord Manasses, archbishop of Reims, issued a general call to some abbots to attend a council and summoned others by name. Among the latter was Odo, abbot of St. Martin's of Tours. We were amazed at that and waited, stunned and in suspense for what would be send back to us from the council. Well, we suddenly heard that Lord Odo had been elected to the see of the diocese of Cambrai and had been consecrated by the archbishop and the provincial bishops without delay.[1]

One would have been hard-pressed to describe what grief filled all our community on that day and what sobbing struck our breasts. But hardly eight days had passed when something was given to us in consolation. Since Bishop Walter was rebelling and resisting, Bishop Odo was not able to enter the city of Cambrai peacefully; he was sent back to us by the archbishop and would stay with us for the whole year. Since the cause of this particular rebellion appears to be clear to few people, we may be excused if we digress from our narrative.

83. The Tradition of Royal Investiture and the Investiture Controversy; Bishop Walter of Cambrai Had Been Invested by the Emperor and Had Been Excommunicated in 1095; Odo Is Expected to Depose and Replace Him (June 1105)

One reads in the Life of St. Gregory that, when he had been elected to the rule of the apostolic see and was reluctant to accept, the Romans asked for the approval of the Emperor Maurice, and they raised the chosen man to the pontifical throne by means of it. And we read that the Blessed Eligius and Saint Ouen were chosen and elevated to the pontificate by Dagobert, king of the Franks. And the same sort of thing may be read in many other places, that holy men were raised to the pontificate by kings. Consider how suddenly, in the time of Emperor Henry the elder, the Roman pope who was first called Hildebrand and later Gregory the seventh prohibited anyone from being chosen or elevated by the Emperor Henry, and all those who were promoted by him, or who had received the crozier or the ring from him, were excommunicated and deposed, and in all of his realm, at least in the German portions, the holy offices were interdicted.[1] This caused the greatest perturbation in Holy Church since many were then saying that the prophecy of King Hezekiah was being fulfilled: "Consider in peace the bitterness of my most bitter" (Ezek. 38:17). It was bitter in that bitter age when the martyrs of the Church were slain by pagans, more bitter when they were slain in the time of the heretics, and most bitter when they are slain in the era of the peace of the Christians.

The emperor Henry would not suffer the dignity of his predecessors to be taken from him and said that the pope was not doing this for the liberty of the church but was using the occasion and the pretext of justice so that he might amass more money. He selected another pope, by the name of Guibert,[2] and had him who had excommunicated him, excommunicated, and compelled the holy offices to be celebrated in his realm against the pope's command. Then he assembled an army, besieged Rome, and devastated the entire province. Pope Gregory died, and Urban succeeded him. He confirmed those things his predecessor had established. Among the other things that he decreed at the Council of Clermont[3] was that he was striking Bishop Walter of Cambrai with the sword of excommunication and deposing him from the episcopal office because he had obtained his episcopacy for money and had received his staff and ring from the hand of the emperor.

Supported by royal power, Walter had pridefully ruled his diocese for many years and ordered divine offices to be celebrated in the city of Cambrai contrary to the precept of the pope.[4] Pope Urban died, and Paschal succeeded him [1099].[5] Pained that Walter had stubbornly persevered in his long obstinacy, Paschal sent a letter to Manasses, archbishop of Reims, instructing him by apostolic authority that, when the provincial bishops were gathered, he should choose a bishop for the church of Cambrai without delay and consecrate him. So our Lord Abbot Odo was elected and consecrated. But our abbot, now consecrated, was returned to us because the authority of the archbishop was not sufficient to expel Walter. Although Lord Odo exercised some of the episcopal offices, he did not have entry to the city and royal renders.[6]

84. Pope Paschal II Stirs Up Civil War in the Holy Roman Empire; Henry V Defeated by the Men of Liège (22 March 1106)

Meanwhile, the pope sent letters to young Henry, son of the Emperor Henry, that cleverly aroused him against his father and admonished him to aid the Church of God. Young Henry coveted the realm and was happy that he had found, with papal authority, a suitable occasion to take up arms against his father and drive him from the country. [The elder Henry] found no one to support him, except Bishop Autbert of Liège.[1] The young man was furious. It was against his wishes that his father was given refuge in the city by the bishop, so he gathered an army and made ready to force his way into Liège on Good Friday. As Thursday was drawing to a close, when vespers were finished and the bishop was about to wash the feet of the canons according to ecclesiastical custom and to celebrate the Lord's supper, it was suddenly announced that soldiers of the young king had seized the fortress called Viset. The men of Liège sallied out in force and hastened to oppose those who were approaching under the command of the count of Namur. Meanwhile, the new king's army incautiously and impetuously started crossing the Meuse river bridge.[2] The bridge suddenly collapsed, and about five hundred of his men fell into the river, along with their armor, arms, and horses, and were killed.

And so the young king, because he had wanted to fight against his father on such a solemn day, later regretted it. He was compelled to retreat in great disarray and return to Mainz. Since he had now seized all of the realm except Liège, he replenished his forces and again took up arms against his father. His father had no support from any of the nobles and finally was besieged in a certain castle by his son. A letter survives addressed by the father to King Philip of France in which he complains bitterly about his son. Anyone who could read it without tears would seem to me to be hard of heart.[3]

85. Emperor Henry V (1106–1127) Deposes Bishop Walter; Odo Takes Up the Office of Bishop (1106); Prior Siger Chosen Abbot of St. Martin's; the Emperor's Conflict with the Papacy

Henry's father, Henry the elder, died, but because of sadness of heart rather than force of arms. His son, who had already been ruler by choice of the realm for some time, ordered the men of Cambrai to expel the excommunicate Walter from the city and to receive Lord Odo.[1] Lord Odo then peacefully entered his episcopal city for the first time and advised us to elect an abbot. With his counsel, we chose our prior, Lord Siger, a religious man given to fasting and prayer, who had already held the office of prior of our congregation for many years.

Henry had obtained the realm, but continued his father's policies and was not willing to lose the dignity of those monarchs of old who were accustomed to select bishops. He gathered an army and headed for Rome, saying that he wished to go there to receive his crown and be consecrated by the hands of the Lord Pope [1111]. He was met by the Romans with great rejoicing and a procession, and he made his way to the church of St. Peter's where the Pope was residing and waiting for him. At the moment when it is customary for the subordinate to be raised up to kiss the pope's feet, Henry made his long-premeditated betrayal and perfidy evident. With words spoken in German, he gave a signal to his armed knights and had the pope, who had been kissed by then, and all of the cardinals, who had surrounded him in such a festive procession, taken by force to his camp. He put them under guard as prisoners and slaughtered many Romans who decided to resist him, for he had come with a large army. The Romans had had no suspicion of a trap and were completely unprepared for battle. It should not be surprising, therefore, that they were easily overcome.

The pope saw the danger, not only for the cardinals and bishops who had been taken prisoner with him, but for the entire region, which Henry was maliciously devastating, not like an emperor, but like a tyrant. Because of the threat of coercion, the pope thought it better to change his way of thinking for a time than to ignore those whose necks were being threatened by the sword. So he yielded to the king and by his own authority confirmed the privilege that episcopal elections would be held with royal consent and that the king would invest the bishops-elect with staff and ring. When Henry asked for a suretor of his concession, the pope placed the body of the Lord in his mouth, and said, "I place this, the body of the Lord, here in lieu of a suretor that I shall not violate any of these things that I have promised you." Henry gleefully released the pope along with the others he had seized and returned to his own land of Lorraine.

In Liège, he married the daughter of Henry, king of England, who had been presented to him along with great riches, by her father.[2] Divine judgment, however, did not permit him to rejoice in his prosperity for long. He was soon deprived of his realm and his life, and left the queen a childless widow.[3] Various bishops came together after his departure from Rome and censured him for his betrayal of the pope, saying that he was the equal of Judas, who, after a kiss and through a kiss, betrayed the Lord. Calling the document that the pope had given him not a privilege but a crooked law [*pravilegium*],[4] they struck him with the sentence of anathema and decreed that whatever the pope had yielded while compelled by necessity was invalid.

86. St. Norbert and the Establishment of the Premonstratensian Order (1121)

A cleric by the name of Norbert, who had been the emperor's chaplain during the seizure of the pope, was led to such great repentance when he saw the wickedness of his lord, the king, that he prostrated himself at the feet of the pope. Having received absolution from him, Norbert abandoned secular life. He went to

France and found an isolated spot called Premonstrè in the diocese of Laon. He began to serve God there under the rule of St. Augustine, but much more rigorously and austerely.[1] With the grace of God, in a brief time he had made such progress that we can see no one since the apostles who has brought forth such fruits in the Church. It is not yet thirty years since he abandoned the world, and yet we have heard of about a hundred monasteries of his Order already having been built in various parts of the globe, so that their rule is observed even in Jerusalem.

Although I shall not discuss the other establishments, Lord Bishop Bartholomew gave Norbert a poor little church built in the city of Laon in honor of St. Martin. Norbert put a few of his brothers there and appointed a religious man by the name of Walter as their abbot. God conferred such grace upon him that today one may see five hundred monks living in that abbey, and already about ten other monasteries have been founded from there. Norbert himself was later made archbishop of Magdeburg, and he died in the time of the Emperor Lothar, who succeeded Henry.[2] But now let us return to our own monastery.[3]

87. The Canons of St. Mary's of Tournai Claim That St. Martin's Is Not a Monastery, but Their Chapel; Odo Petitions Pope Pascal on behalf of St. Martin's for Recognition, the Right to Bury Anyone, and Exemption from Tithes to St. Mary's; the Canons Resort to Violence

When Lord Odo had ruled our monastery for about thirteen years, he was made bishop and relinquished the governance of it to Lord Siger, our prior. At this time, the greatest tribulations came upon us. Now that Odo had become a bishop, the canons of Tournai began to prohibit us to bury anyone who was an outsider.[1] They said that our church was not an abbey but really by law their chapel, and that we might remain in it only as long as they wished.[2]

Two archdeacons of Cambrai, Anselm and Ralph, son of our brother-monk Tetbald,[3] who used to visit their bishop [Odo] when he was staying with us, were shaken by the contentiousness of the canons of Tournai. They had petitioned Rome with Bishop Odo's letters of intercession and had come away with a charter of Lord Pope Paschal for us. In this document, he granted us the privilege of burying, freely and without any argument, anyone (except excommunicates) who might wish to be buried with us. They had added something of which many of us were ignorant, that we would no longer pay tithes on the fields that we cultivated near the abbey, since they had been remitted to us by the Lord Pope.[4]

When this became known by the canons, they immediately rose up in opposition to us and stirred up the whole world against us, so that our community was greatly troubled by arson and theft. When Ralph, the prior of our monastery who has been frequently mentioned above, and Gunther, prior of the canons and son of his brother Tetbert, fought each other, uncle against nephew, with secular as well as ecclesiastical weapons, it was seen that this was not just a civil war, but that something worse was going on between the two churches.[5] Nevertheless, the Lord Pope never ceased to extend his aid to us, but looked to the interests of those frequently returning to his feet. It was for this reason that he send letters of the following sort, among many others, to our Bishop Baldric.

88. A Papal Privilege Is Granted to St. Martin's of Tournai; St. Martin's Is Given the Right of Burial and Exemption from Paying Tithes to St. Mary's; the Leaders of the Canons Are Called to Rome for Instruction

Bishop Paschal, servant of the servants of God, to his venerable brother Baldric, bishop of Noyon and Tournai, greetings and apostolic blessing. We have now sent a second letter to you [stating] that you should do justice to the monks of St. Martin's for the injuries they have suffered at the hands of the clerics of Tournai. But you have ignored your obligation to perform this equity for an excessively long time. For this reason, we have considered it proper to turn this affair over to Lambert of Arras and John of Thérouanne, your co-provincials. Just as one might have expected of religious men fighting fiercely for peace, they have handled the affair somewhat less than canonically.

Because of this, we called both parties to our presence. And we have demonstrated to these clerics on the authority of the Holy Fathers how improper it is that they should oppress monks by the exaction of tithes and the prohibition of burial. The Blessed Gregory, writing to Augustine, bishop of the English, said, "What is there left for us to say to those living a life in common about making portions, extending hospitality, and fulfilling the obligations of charity, when everything that is left over is spent in pious and religious causes." Leo IV decrees by conciliar constitution that tithes and first fruits and any oblations whatever of the living and dead ought to be given faithfully by the laity to the Church of God. It is to be noted here that he commands that tithes be rendered by the laity, not by monks. For monks, since many of them might be levites or priests, or employed in other ecclesiastical orders; and since, by the grace of God, they serve continuously as divine ministers, they are to be held exempt from any kind of exaction whatever. The same Leo, writing to the bishops of Britain, proclaimed that tithes are due those churches that are called "plebes," where holy baptisms are performed. It would appear evident from these words, that it is because of the baptisms, eucharists, penances, and other sacraments that the clerics provide for the people, that tithes are to be rendered by the people. In all of this, there is no mention of any service provided by clerics to communities of monks.

Further, the Blessed Gregory clearly demonstrated his belief that burial by monasteries was to be permitted. He restrained John, bishop of Civitta Vecchia, from prohibiting that the dead might be buried in a monastery with these words, "If it is so, I exhort you to turn back from such inhumanity, and allow the dead to be buried there, and masses to be celebrated without further argument, lest I be compelled to take up anew the quarrel about those things that were told to me by that venerable man, Agapitus."

Having a full knowledge of the authority of the Holy Fathers and cognizant of true doctrine, the aforesaid clerics of Tournai who came to me submitted to the bonds of humility, and they have promised that they would not cause the monks any further trouble concerning these complaints. Therefore, most beloved brother, we call most forcefully upon your concern lest you should permit the brothers of the said monastery to be attacked in this fashion any further, and that you not say anything from your episcopal throne or do anything else that might disturb the regular order.

Concerning the division of the alms that are left to churches by the dying, distribute yours between your diocese and your parishes, and, by the attentiveness of your oversight, let both clerics and monks be served by these gifts to God, and let the peace of the churches remain firm. Given in the Lateran, by the hand of Cardinal John, 29th of October.[1]

89. The Conflict Becomes Violent; the Canons' Men Plunder a Farmstead of St. Martin's and Beat the Monk Who Defends It; Eighteen Men Are Killed in a Battle between the Canons' Men and the Monk's Kindred; Abbot Siger of St. Martin's Orders a General Penance

The clerics returned to Tournai from Rome and ignored everything that the pope said that they had promised him. Again they began to devastate us with fire and to give money to knights to lay waste our lands and properties. One day toward evening, they sent their servants over to plunder our farmstead at St. Maur. When this was announced to Lord Abbot Siger, he sent one of our monks, named Garulf, who had been a vigorous knight in secular life and was related to the best men of the region, to reprimand the rashness of the thieves. They came in a large number and were armed; they pillaged the farmstead and they beat the monk, who had tried to resist them single-handedly, so badly that he had to be carried back to our abbey on a stretcher.

His kinsmen was greatly disturbed at this;[1] after a few days they assembled against the clerics and their partisans. A battle began, in which they killed eighteen of the clerics' servants, some by cutting off their feet, and turned them all equally to flight.[2] Some of the knights said that during the battle they had seen St. Martin in the sky seated on a white horse and with his sword thrust forward against the fleeing foe.[3] Since their number had been much greater than ours, he nevertheless granted the victory to us.[4] Lord Abbot Siger saw some of our young men exulting about the victory; he entered the church and, prostrating himself before the altar, began to weep most bitterly, both for the souls of the enemy who were dead and for the danger to the brothers who were rejoicing over this fact. When everyone had quickly assembled in the chapter, he commanded that the next day the entire community would fast on bread and water, on Friday they would rise and read the entire psalter and make a procession with bare feet, and then everyone would undergo instruction in chapter meeting. Events soon demonstrated that God was pleased by his piety.

90. Castellan Everard Speaks to the Chapter of St. Martin's and Sets the Terms of a Compromise; Peace Is Restored, and the Monks and Canons Live Together in Harmony

While we were still sitting in the chapter-house, Everard the castellan, the ruler of the whole district whom we mentioned a long time ago, suddenly and unexpectedly was knocking at the gate of the cloister and asking to be permitted to enter the chapter-house. He came in with certain wise men, and said, "My Lords, we are extremely pleased with the restoration of your congregation. We would be no less extremely saddened by its destruction now, when its twentieth year is not yet completed.[1] We know that the clerics would unjustly forbid your burial of anyone who is not your parishioner, and that no less unjustly you wish to take their tithes from them. Although we may give our lands to you for the remedy of our souls, we nevertheless cannot give the tithes of our Lady Saint Mary to you. You must therefore be content with what we give you, and you holy men must not take away from Saint Mary what we sinners have given to her. If, indeed, you do wish to take away from her that right which she has now held for five hundred years, I do not know what good it may have done you to have given up secular life. Saving your grace, I would say that you would appear to be greedier, more rapacious, and worse than we, were we to take their property away from the poor and still pay our tithes to God.[2]

"Wherefore I entreat you, my dearest Lords, that henceforth you desist from this obstinacy and not disturb the province with such strange and unaccustomed liberty, but that you follow the ways of neighboring abbeys, which are older and richer than you. And we shall have the clerics, whether or not they wish, concede to you the same right of burial that they enjoy. If you are unwilling to accede to our prayers, then indeed hold up your arms against the torrent, because there is no way that we will permit you to take her tithes away from Our Lady Saint Mary."

Our community agreed to the ruler's plea and submitted to his persuasion. And so, the abbots of nearby monasteries and the persons of many other churches assembled on a pre-arranged day, and both sides agreed and confirmed in a charter that we would give tithes according to customary practice and that we should be permitted to bury in the same manner as the abbey of

St. Amand and other neighboring monasteries.[3] When this peace was concluded, the clerics, who for so long had tried to overthrow us utterly, were again joined with us in such great friendship that Prior Gunther himself, a most turbulent man, made every effort to relieve our needs and endeavored through new services and assistance to amend and resolve the evils that he had done us during the time of discord.[4]

EPILOGUE[1]

In the same year as the final reconciliation between the monks and canons, Bishop-Elect Odo became ill and sought refuge in the monastery of Anchin. Hearing of this, Abbot Siger went to Anchin and asked that he be allowed to take Odo to St. Martin's, the abbey that he had restored and of which he had been the first new abbot. Abbot Alvisus of Anchin refused this request, saying that he would not send elsewhere anyone whom God had entrusted to him. Within a few days, Odo received word from Rome that, because he had accepted the crozier and ring from the emperor and had done homage to him, he had betrayed the position of the Church in the struggle underway against imperial investiture. The papacy would never allow him to become bishop. Odo's condition quickly worsened, and he died on 9 June 1113. Alvisus had him entombed with great pomp before the altar in the church of Anchin and a likeness carved in white marble was placed atop his tomb. He was soon recognized locally as a saint, and some pilgrimage traffic to his tomb developed over time.

It was true that the abbey of St. Martin and the cathedral of St. Mary worked together in the following years. Abbot Siger and Prior Gunther cooperated, although unsuccessfully for the most part, to foil the efforts of the canons of Noyon to elect new bishops without consulting the cathedral chapter of Tournai. Gunther shuttled back and forth between Rome and Tournai indefatigably. It was in the year 1121, on the road back from Rome, in fact, that he was overtaken by death. Carried back to Tournai, he was buried in the cathedral and was succeeded as prior by his nephew, Theodoric, son of Theodoric the Minter.

The years 1125–1126 saw another of those periodic famines that began to afflict Flanders more frequently as its population grew and its arable land did not. The poor suffered terribly during such times, and the monks struggled vainly to sustain them until the new harvest. Communities went on short rations themselves, and abbots, such as Siger of St. Martin's, sold the church ornaments and vessels to buy more grain for charity although prices rose so high that even extreme sacrifices seemed ineffectual. The monks had to balance the needs of the moment to feed the hungry against the equally pressing necessity of holding back sufficient seed grain to plant the new crops. It was not possible to strike a happy medium; paupers starved at the abbey door, and the monks inside were constantly haunted by the words of twenty-fifth chapter of Matthew.

Like as not, violence and disease accompanied famine. Violence and the threat of violence added to the monks' concerns, and the older and more heavily-burdened of them were vulnerable to whatever pestilence was making its rounds. The prior of St. Amand's of Noyon, Ralph the Norman, was the first casualty of St. Martin's community. One of Odo's original followers, Ralph could not have been much under sixty years of age and had been infirm when he had first taken up Ralph of Noyon's charge to establish a priory on the site of a ruined church. The constant admonitions of the saintly Peter of Noyon to remember the poor must have placed him under additional strain. At any rate, he died as the year 1126 was drawing to a close. Theodoric, abbot of St. Eligius of Noyon, had developed a special regard for him and had him buried in the cloister of his own abbey, near the door where the poor gathered daily to receive charity.

The news of his demise apparently struck Ralph of Noyon particularly hard, and Ralph soon fell ill himself. He was placed on the bare ground in remembrance of Saint Martin of Tours and lingered there for three or four days. It was perhaps characteristic that, when he felt himself to be dying, his last words were that the community should not let go of some land that he had just bought from Clerembald of Roseto in the diocese of Laon but that they should work it because it would be very profitable to them. He died in the middle of the night of the Sunday before Christmas Day of 1126. His loss was a great blow to St. Martin's. He had been its prior for almost thirty years, and no one could remember that he had ever called anyone silly or stupid.

The abbot proposed that he be buried in a place of great honor, before the abbot's chair in the chapter house, since everyone realized that the abbey owed its buildings, properties, and very existence largely to his work. His sons—Theodoric, Herman, Walter, and Ralph—asked that he be buried instead in the abbey's cemetery, among the paupers and his departed colleagues. Years before, the townspeople of Tournai had pressured Bishop Radbod to reestablish a monastic community on the site of Saint Martin's, proclaiming that they wished to be buried among the paupers who had been ejected from the cathedral and consumed by "The Fire of Hell" in the half-ruined church there. That wish was fulfilled for Ralph of Noyon almost forty years later.

His wife, Mainsendis, survived him for some twelve years and died in 1138 at the age of sixty-eight and after having spent some forty-four of those years as a nun. At her wish and that of her children, she was buried in the same cemetery as Ralph and, we may guess, not too distant from him. The chronicler of these events states that the brothers believed that it was much better to be buried in the company of so many good men and women than to be entombed alone in some church or cloister.

Herman was chosen to take his father's place as prior and assumed his duties during the Christmas season of 1126. Again according to the unknown chronicler, Ralph appeared to Herman in a dream at about Eastertide. Herman asked his father if his soul had found complete rest, and his father replied, "My son, if I had been allowed to live a cloistered life and the priorship had not fallen to me, without a doubt I would have found perfect rest." Herman settled up the abbey's accounts and asked to be relieved of the post of prior. His wish was granted, but his experience with the quiet cloistered life was soon ended. Abbot Siger's health began to fail soon after Ralph's departure, and he died Sunday, 30 January 1127. He was buried before the altar of the chapel of St. Mary, and the monks chose Herman to succeed him.

There are conflicting accounts of Herman's abbacy. One states that he tended to be lax in enforcing clerical discipline and, when he was admonished for this, abdicated the office. The narrative offered by his continuator states that he was struck with a weakness of the body called paralysis and gave up his position of abbot for the good of the community. In view of the active life he led after leaving St. Martin's and considering his indifference to the norms of established religion, one might be inclined to accept the former view of the matter. At any rate, he relinquished the abbacy in 1137 after a term of ten years.

Herman then became a man of both letters and ecclesiastical affairs, travelling to Rome and elsewhere. The diocese of Tournai gained its independence of Noyon in 1146, and the goal for which Herman had worked for much of his life was achieved. In 1147, at the pope's urging, Bernard of Clairvaux began to preach the crusade. Louis VII of France and Conrad III Hohenstaufen of Germany took the cross. Interestingly enough, since the count of Flanders accompanied Louis, Herman chose to join the emperor's ill-fated contingent. Conrad proceeded over land to Constantinople and crossed over in Asia Minor. The Germans suffered a disastrous defeat at the hands of the Turks, and scarcely a tenth of the original force managed to make its way back to the port of Nicaea. The remnant of this force continued to make its way to the Holy land by sea, and Conrad and Louis were finally united at Jerusalem. They quarrelled shortly afterwards, and Conrad and his men returned to Germany. Herman was not among them, and the author of the continuation of his narrative wrote somewhat plaintively, "We have nothing certain of what he might have done on the way or what achievements might have been his, for some reported that he was martyred for the love of Christ, and others said that he was led away a captive."

APPENDIXES

ENDNOTES

SELECTED BIBLIOGRAPHY

INDEX

APPENDIXES

APPENDIX I
READING HERMAN

The reader should not be misled by Herman's ingenuous style and dramatic flair into believing that his account is simply that of a storyteller. Herman fills his narrative with allusions, suppressions, inferences, and double meanings. One must always be ready to look beneath the surface of Herman's account, because what he wishes to say is not always apparent. It is not possible to comment fully on every such case, but Herman's first allusion may serve as an example of the potential complexity of his presentation.

When identifying himself in the salutation that begins *The Restoration,* Herman paraphrases Ps. 137:1: "By the rivers of Babylon we sat down and wept as we remembered Zion." The phrase suggests his homesickness and also refers to the fact that he was acquiescing to the requests of the monks of St. Martin's to write a history of the restoration of their abbey. The Psalm goes on, ". . . those who had carried us captive asked us to sing a song, our captors called upon us to be joyful: 'Sing us one of the songs of Zion.' How could we sing the Lord's song in a foreign land?" (Ps. 137:3-4). It is probable that Herman was part of a group from Tournai and that it had been members of that group who had importuned him to undertake the history of St. Martin's at that time. Since the Psalm states that the captors had asked for the song of Zion, there is an underlying inference that Herman found himself in Rome, a "foreign land," because the clerics of Tournai had required his services and not because he had chosen to be about such work. By inferring that the papal court was a strange land, Herman not only suggests that he was a small-town northerner in a big city of the South, but that a monk away from his monastery, his Zion, was always in a strange land.

Although not perfect, Herman's allusion would seem reasonably apt, unless one considers its further implications. He tells his audience that he was lodged in the Lateran Palace, which, as most ecclesiastics knew, overlooked the Tiber. "By the waters of Babylon...," Herman was equating Rome with Babylon, which may have startled his audience considerably. This image was common enough at the time, but it implied a criticism of the papacy or the Church in general, and this can hardly have been what Herman intended. Although Herman states that *The Restoration* was written during a few weeks in the summer of 1142, it is clear that he had continued revising it right up to 1147, the year in which he departed on the Second Crusade. When one realizes that he is referring both to the Rome of 1142 and that of 1147, the significance of his choice of Psalm 137 becomes clearer.

In 1143, the people of Rome seized power, drove Pope Eugenius and the curia from the city, and declared a Commune. Arnold of Brescia, a former student of Peter Abelard, soon became its leader, attacked the wealth of the Church, and demanded its return to apostolic poverty. The Roman populace seized Church property within the city and showed their contempt for the established clergy by threatening many of them and injuring more than a few. The Commune was not overthrown until 1153. Arnold was finally taken prisoner and executed by Frederick Barbarossa in 1154.[1] However, when Herman left off working on *The Restoration*, Arnold and an anti-clerical Roman populace still controlled the city. In equating Rome with Babylon, his reference most likely was toward the Commune of Rome, not the Church of Rome.

Once this is understood, Herman's choice of Psalm 137 to describe the city gains added meaning. "Zion" can refer to the Vatican, "the city on a hill," the seat of the papacy, and the Other Jerusalem. Herman's remembrance of Zion is also a prayer for the delivery of the papacy from the exile imposed upon it by Arnold of Brescia and the citizens of the Commune. One should note that Psalm 137 ends on a brutal note: "Remember, Lord, against the children of Edom the day when Jerusalem fell, how they shouted 'Down with it, down with it, down to its very foundations!' Babylon, Babylon the destroyer, happy is he who repays you for what you did to us. Happy is he who seizes your babes and dashes them against a rock" (Ps. 137:7–9).

Although Herman, like many other medieval authors, delighted in such intricacies, the reader should not conclude that Herman's work is inaccessible. It is possible to read and enjoy *The Restoration* without becoming enmeshed in these complexities. Herman was attempting to construct a work that would offer his audience both pleasure and profit on several different levels, and it was on the level of drama and story-telling that he excelled.

APPENDIX 2
THE NEW LEARNING

Herman lived through a revolution in western European thought. Much has been written of the new learning of the twelfth century, the challenge to authority, and the Realist-Nominalist controversy, and it is enlightening to learn how this intellectual upheaval appeared to a participant.

The intellectual developments of the period appeared to Herman in the guise of a sudden shift in the popularity of the standard textbooks and the emergence of new teaching methods. For centuries, the works of the sixth-century scholar, Boëthius, had been the most popular text for teaching the seven liberal arts, or *trivium* (grammar, rhetoric, and logic) and *quadrivium* (music, astronomy, arithmetic, and geometry). Other standard texts, such as those of Isidore of Seville, Martianus Capella, and Porphyry, were much less favored. Odo taught from Boëthius, and Herman had learned from Odo. With the rise of the Nominalists, however, the *Isagoge* of the third-century Greek scholar, Porphyry, gained greater popularity since it placed heavy emphasis upon the use of logic and dealt directly with many of the points raised in Aristotle's works. Dialectics began to overshadow the other subjects of the *trivium* and *quadrivium,* and up-to-date teachers, eager to attract students, adopted Porphyry as a text and rejected Boëthius as old-fashioned.

There was an accompanying change in teaching methods. The contemporary teachers regarded the categories of traditional dialectics—truth, justice, beauty, and the like—as intellectual constructs, the validity of which had to be established by disputation, and they taught in this fashion. They would offer a proposition to their students and present the arguments for and against it, or allow the students to debate the issue, or even uphold one side or another against the invited attacks of their charges. Establishing the nature of the category through rational debate would become fundamental to the scholastic method in time, but was distasteful to many when it first became an accepted practice.

Herman felt that the students of the "new learning" were searching for novelties and skill in persuasion in order to appear to be learned rather than actually being so. Far from being valued, the ready wit and a persuasive tongue of these younger scholars were viewed by many with suspicion. Herman shared this distrust and made a point, for instance, of showing that Bishop Radbod's gifts of persuasion concealed a sinful and immoral man.

There is a tendency to connect the Realist doctrine—that reality lies in the categories of existence and that individual sense objects derive their identity from the categories of which they are members—with the revival of Aristotelian logic, perhaps because the great Realists of the thirteenth century were also Aristotelians. This was not the case in the early twelfth century. Both Odo and Herman were Realists of the deepest hue, but they both drew their inspiration from the Platonic theory of forms as transmitted by Boëthius. Odo was the author of several Realist treatises, among them an elegant proof of Original Sin. All men and women belonged to the category of Humanity and partook of the essence of the category by descent from its original members. Adam and Eve had corrupted that essence through their disobedience toward God. Therefore all men and women were initially corrupt.

Herman believed that the tradition exemplified by the Roman Boëthius was truer to ancient doctrine and the "Hellenic" spirit than was that of the Greek Porphyry and Aristotle. Insofar as the "new learning" was supplanting Platonic Idealism and introducing a new professionalism to scholarship, he was correct. In many ways, the concept of a humanism based upon a broad knowledge of the seven liberal arts and in which the cathedral and monastery schools were beginning to excel, was already being overshadowed by a concentration on Philosophy, Theology, and Rhetoric, the art of argumentation.

APPENDIX 3

THE CLOISTER AND THE

CATHEDRAL SCHOOL

The activities of the cathedral school were located generally within the cathedral cloisters, and a general knowledge of the plan of cathedral cloisters is useful for visualizing some of the events that Herman describes.

The cloister of St. Mary's of Tournai was situated on the north side of the cathedral. It was centered on a small square garden and surrounded by a roofed walk. The wall of the church formed the south side of this rectangular space, and stairs at the corners of the cloister led to the interior of the cathedral. The main entry to the cloister pierced a wall on its south side, beyond which lay the cathedral cemetery. In the late eleventh century, the canons of St. Mary's were not living a communal life but lived separately in several buildings they owned within the cathedral close. The rear of a block of these houses, one of which may have served as Odo's residence, formed the north wall of the cloister. The east side was the center of considerable activity, since the canon's refectory (dining hall), its kitchen and its storehouse were located there alongside the cathedral school. The hospital and infirmary were located less than a hundred feet away, convenient to the cemetery. The canons' wine-cellar was located at the far end of the cemetery, and their daily rations had to be brought through the cloister to the refectory.

There was also a constant procession through the cloister of laymen from various walks of life. Some were workmen and provisioners, others were bringing their children to the school or collecting them, and still others were the friends and relatives of the canons themselves. The canons had not yet taken vows of poverty, chastity, and obedience, although there was already considerable pressure for them to do so, and many of them had wives and children to care for. The cloister was the most convenient route for the canons to follow when going from their residences to the cathedral, and there must have been a steady flow of canons and cathedral officials. The townsfolk too often used the cloister for meetings of the town council or municipal court, and many no doubt wandered in and out waiting for their meetings to begin. As was the case with most medieval cathedrals, the cloister of St. Mary's of Tournai was the crossroad of traffic and a center of daily activity in the cathedral. It was a bustling place, not the quiet island of repose that modern tourists usually view.

The cloister was also the place where the lectures of the cathedral school were delivered. If these lectures followed the normal pattern, Odo's assistant would place a tall straight-backed chair with a lectern on the steps leading from the cloister into the church, and Odo would deliver his lectures from this vantage point. There would be plenty of room for the students during good weather, but when it was raining or otherwise inclement, the students would crowd into the roofed aisles, and press as close to the lecturer as possible in order to be able to stay dry as well as to hear. It was particularly important that they be able to keep the parchment on which they were writing out of the snow and rain.

The cathedral school of Tournai, like the other schools of the day, was not free. The custom was for the master to announce that he would offer a certain number of "lectures," that is, he would read and discuss certain important books. Students would choose what books they wished to hear, go to the master's assistant, and pay the fee for that series of readings (*lecturae*). The assistant would put the money in his money-bag (*bursa*), write their names in the roll book (*regestum*), and they became members of that class (*schola*). It can be seen that the vocabulary of today's universities was already taking shape: "lecture," "bursar," "registrar," and "scholar."

The general procedure within a given course was for the lecturer to read a passage of text slowly, while his students, seated on benches or even on the ground or pavement, copied it down on a sheet of parchment. The lecturer then commented on the text, and the students would note his comments in their margins. Many of the manuscripts surviving from the Middle Ages are textbooks that were copied in this fashion. They are frequently filled with the errors of a sleepy, dull, bored, or simply confused student, but their most striking characteristics are the tiny writing and abundance of abbreviations. Parchment cost money, and so students wrote a small script. Upon completion of the course, the students would have their copy bound, and they would receive a certificate of completion issued by the bishop's secretary, the *cancellarius*, or chancellor.

APPENDIX 4

THE TREK TO NOYON

Odo's migration from Tournai seeking license from Bishop Radbod to depart with his congregation to some desert place was, by Herman's own observation, the turning point of the fortunes of St. Martin's abbey. It is the critical episode in his account and also the most puzzling. Herman presents two versions of the event, and one must combine them to see the difficulties that his narrative presents.

Herman portrays the monks of St. Martin's as growing excited by their reading of John Cassian's works on ascetic monasticism and chafing at their pleasant location and proximity to the laity. They finally yield to their impulsive enthusiasms and, heaping their belongings on a cart, steal off under the cover of night to begin a hundred-mile trek to Noyon to plead with Bishop Radbod for permission to remove their community to some distant and isolated place. Upon discovering that the monks have departed, the townspeople run frantically through the abbey's buildings, crying out as if some great calamity had befallen them. They apparently fail to notice that there are five monks from St. Amand present, continuing to sing the holy offices, but they do discover that some nuns living nearby not only know the full details of Odo's well-kept secret but are quite willing to discuss them.

Once learning that Odo and his followers are hoping to gain permission to leave the province, the leading citizens of the town immediately convene a council. Acting under the advice of Everard, castellan of the city and Bishop Radbod's nephew, the council dispatches a swift messenger, followed by horsemen of the municipal militia, to Noyon. The messenger is instructed to tell Radbod that the city gates will be closed to him and that he will be shut off from his cathedral if he grants Odo the permission he intends to request. This is nothing less than an act of rebellion on the part of the citizens and might earn them excommunication, interdict, or even worse. The bishop bursts into tears when the ultimatum is delivered to him, and he swears that he would not have given Odo permission to leave under any circumstances.

Ralph Osmond, meanwhile, has ridden over to St. Martin's to see the state of affairs for himself. Once convinced that the congregation has in fact departed, he rides home, collects his personal priest, gathers his neighbors and relatives, commends his wife and children to God, and speeds off to overtake Odo. When he reaches Odo's band, he immediately requests to be accepted as a monk, and Odo delivers a joyful sermon. Odo and his followers are escorted the last miles into Noyon by the Tournai militia, and he and the bishop enact a tearful and public scene of petition and rejection.

Once in private, however, the bishop congratulates Odo on his conversion of Ralph Osmond and tells him that there is now no reason for him to want to leave Tournai. The monks rest for three days and then set out for Tournai under armed escort. They arrive just at the beginning of the recently-instituted great procession, and the entire crowd—including the monks' enemies, the cathedral canons—joyously lead them back to their abbey. Shortly after, Bishop Radbod, who had only recently been so pleased with the matter, comes to Odo and the chapter in a foul mood, telling them that they should never again think for themselves but should adopt some established monastic rule and live by it.

Herman's account is full of detail, but he fails to present the causes and connections of this series of extraordinary developments, nor does he explain the apparent contradictions. If Odo and his followers had been so secretive, how did the nuns who were their neighbors come to know the entire matter? Why were the citizens so distraught at the departure of the monks of St. Martin's when they had so studiously neglected them previously? Why did they not take note of the monks of St. Amand's who were maintaining the offices of the abbey, and why did they so quickly adopt such drastic measures to have Odo and his followers returned?

Herman seems to have enjoyed posing this puzzle. His picture of the townsfolk searching the abbey and loudly wailing has more than a bit of fun about it, but this was in fact a serious business, and Herman provides enough information to allow one to solve his puzzle and learn what was actually going on.

The key to the matter occurs when Herman describes Odo and Abbot Emory watching Canon Siger Osmond thrash his son, who had tried to steal away to join Odo in St. Martin's, and drag the boy back to his home by his hair. Emory advises Odo that his followers will not be drawn back by their comrades or dragged back by their kinsmen if they are made monks. Emory's counsel proves to be correct; once the congregation of St. Martin's don their black robes, they prove to be safe from any attempts to drag them away. Siger's son manages to reach Odo and St. Martin's and is now allowed to stay.

But why was young Alulf so intent on entering St. Martin's, and why was it so important to protect new members from being lured away? The answer to this lies in the curious reaction of the five-year old Theodoric Osmond when the canons congratulated him on the prebend his father had purchased for him, thus ensuring him of a comfortable and respectable life. Herman portrays him as speaking with the vocabulary, knowledge, and passion of someone much older, and adamantly upholding the cause of ecclesiastical reform in defiance of his entire family. It is difficult to escape the conclusion that Odo and his assistants had coached the boy after the canons had left and that he had accepted without question what they had told him. Later, when the opportunity presented itself, he slipped away to Odo and rejected his father, again with language and emotion that he could have acquired only from Odo.

It is clear that Odo had won both the minds and the hearts of the two boys attending the grammar school. They stand out in Herman's account because they were both Osmonds, so there is no reason to suppose that Odo had not similarly captured the affections and aspirations of other boys from his school, the sons of the city's leading citizens. At its establishment in 1092, St. Martin's had five or six members; by 1093, the congregation had grown to eighteen; and, in 1095, thirty monks made the trek to Noyon. One would suppose that, if two of them were Osmond children, there were probably several others whom Odo had captivated and who had been drawn to him at St. Martin's. This explains a good deal, starting with the citizens' distraught behavior when they found the abbey "empty." The fact that monks of St. Amand's were maintaining the holy offices there was beside the point; Odo had stolen their sons.

The question occasionally arises of whether the men and women of medieval Europe "loved" their children. Whatever abstract answer one may care to offer, it is clear that the bonds between parents and children were quite powerful in Tournai during the closing years of the eleventh century. Established citizens rarely joined St. Martin's alone; they brought their wives and children with them. Often enough, fathers followed their sons into the monastic life as Siger eventually followed Alulf, or brother followed brother as Herman had followed Siger. One can only wonder what sort of family life they contrived to maintain under the Benedictine rule, but there was evidently some form of close contact. Herman mentions speaking frequently with both his mother and his father, and he revered them both. There was surely a bit of idealization in his equation of his mother with St. Alexander and his casting his father in the heroic mold of Erwig.[1]

This consideration of familial devotion does much to explain Herman's ambiguous portrayal of Odo. Odo had indeed succeeded in reestablishing the abbey of St. Martin's, but he had done so by raising up children to defy their fathers and proposing to separate them forever. There is no humor in his description of his older brother's rejection of their father, and it should be noted that, each time, Theodoric used the threat of leaving his parents forever as a weapon against which Ralph had no defense.

Although Herman leaves sufficient clues that Odo's trek to Noyon had been carefully planned, he explicitly presents it as the result of the monks' excessive enthusiasm. Because Odo's actions and intentions were reprehensible according to the standards of the time, Herman could not recount precisely what Odo had planned and why. The portrayal of Odo was probably the most difficult problem that Herman had to face in constructing what he considered to be a true account of the events surrounding the reestablishment of St. Martin's monastery. In order to understand the facts of the matter, Herman's readers had to realize how Odo had accomplished his goal and to learn of the trouble he had caused along the way. But Herman had little desire to vilify his old master, the founder of his abbey, and a departed brother widely regarded as sainted, and so he sought to provide Odo with some justification. His portrayal of Odo as impulsive and more than a bit thoughtless offers something of an explanation but hardly a justification of his old master. Perhaps Herman was content with his suggestion in chapter 69 that Odo's impulsiveness and his lack of concern for others was of a high moral order, that Odo "wished to drag everyone along with him to God." In his portrayal of Odo, Herman draws an acute characterization of a zealot, and religious zeal was more appreciated in Herman's day than in our own.

It is intriguing, if only as a reminder that much of the past has been lost to us, to consider that other factors may have existed to mitigate Odo's actions. Many readers have no doubt already been struck by the similarities between Odo's trek to Noyon and the old tale of the Pied Piper of Hamelin. Like the piper, Odo had been called upon by the citizens to do a job for them, to reestablish the abbey of St. Martin, but, again as in the story of the piper, the citizens had failed to keep their promises once the job was done. Finally, and again like the piper, Odo led their children away from the town. The moral of the story of the piper is that you deserve what you get when you fail to live up to your obligations. The story of the piper bears all of the earmarks of those folk tales that have persisted in various forms over the centuries. If a similar tale was current in twelfth-century Tournai, the reaction of Herman's audience when they realized what Odo had done might have been quite different from what we have supposed.

Whatever the case, the details of Odo's migration become clearer once one understands that children of the citizens of Tournai were among those who were being led away to the "desert." The citizens reacted quickly and, in their council, Everard advised that they send an ultimatum to his father-in-law. Ralph, meanwhile, did not wait for discussion but quickly set his affairs in order and left to be united with his son in the only permanent bond he could think of. Odo had perhaps been hoping that the prospect of losing their sons would lead the townsfolk to provide the abbey with the landed property that would establish it firmly, and he was surprised and delighted to find that the man who possessed those lands he craved had come to surrender himself completely.

Radbod, meanwhile, had heard the citizens' threat and had immediately acquiesced. He, too, was delighted when Ralph appeared following Odo, and he immediately transferred the lands that the abbey claimed. Radbod then arranged that Odo and his troop should appear at the precise moment of the public procession he had recently instituted. When Odo and the sons of the citizens appeared, as if in response to their act of penance, citizens and clerics alike reacted with a wave of enthusiasm and escorted the truants back to their abbey. It did not take Radbod long, however, to discover what Odo had done and why the citizens had been willing to rebel against him. Although he and Odo had won their point, Odo had used means that had put them both in disrepute. Radbod accordingly went into the abbey's chapter meeting to reproach Odo in front of his congregation and to demand that he never again dare to think for himself or act on his own.

Nevertheless, the thing was done, and the citizens and clerics who espoused religious reform, or whose children had followed Odo, began to enter St. Martin's. A third of the cathedral canons left their prebends for the more demanding life of a Cluniac monastery, and many of the wealthiest citizens of the city began to endow the abbey with themselves, their families, and their possessions. There were now two religious centers competing for the loyalties of the residents of Tournai, and not everyone agreed on which deserved their devotion. Both clerics and laity differed, and the competition between the two soon began to divide the town, a division that was nowhere more clear than in the ranks of the Osmond clan.

APPENDIX 5
HERMAN'S ACCOUNT AS
FAMILY HISTORY

Although Herman's work has traditionally been titled *The Restoration of the Monastery of Saint Martin of Tournai*, it is more than that. If the restoration of the abbey were all that Herman had in mind, he might have ended his account on 2 May 1092, when Odo and his companions took up residence at St. Martin's; or on 4 March 1094, when the congregation of St. Martin's entered the Benedictine Order and Odo was confirmed as the restored monastery's first abbot; or in the fall of 1095, when the bishop restored the monastery's ancient lands and issued them a foundation charter; or later in that same year, when Odo and his monks adopted the Rule of St. Benedict and entered the Cluniac Order. He chose to end it in 1108, however, when the cathedral canons and the monks of St. Martin's were finally reconciled and began to work together in harmony.

When one considers Herman's apparently wandering discourse, one is struck by the reiteration of two themes, the expulsion of the innocent and contention between kinsmen. The long treatise upon the history of Flanders between 1050 and 1130 is in fact an example of the latter, tracing the troubles brought upon his descent by Robert the Frisian in foreswearing himself, killing his brother's son, and seizing the boy's lands. Herman presents the price of these offenses as a family curse that manifests itself in deadly strife among Robert's kindred. Henry I seizes his brother's lands and imprisons him for life; Henry's nephew, Stephen of Blois, snatches the throne out from under his cousin, Mathilda; Baldwin VII encourages William Clito to rebel against Henry, his uncle; and Baldwin himself dies trying to take his father's cousin's lands. Thierry of Alsace and William Clito, second cousins, war against each other until William is killed.

Herman's other political digression deals with the Investiture Controversy and civil war in Germany. His stated objective is to clarify the origins of the struggle between Odo and Bishop Walter for control of Cambrai, and he begins with a defense of lay investiture and of Emperor Henry IV's struggle against the reforms pressed by Pope Gregory VII. This alone would have been sufficient for his purposes since it explained the imperial support that allowed Walter to retain control of his see, but Herman goes on to discuss how Paschal raised up Henry V in rebellion against his father, who finally died sick at heart. The connection between this digression and Herman's main account becomes clear when one remembers from chapter 13 that Robert had sent legates to Henry IV immediately after he had encompassed Arnulf's death and seized Flanders, and that Henry had supported him. In the end, the old emperor was forced to suffer the same sort of betrayal by kin that he had earlier condoned.

When we view the various themes upon which Herman plays throughout the work and the insistence with which they are presented, we may take it as given that expulsion of the innocent and contention among kinsmen are the primary and unifying motifs of his account. The episode with which the narrative closes is quite appropriate in these terms. The canons of the cathedral and the monks of the monastery had finally been reconciled, and Herman closes his tale with the note that Gunther, prior of the cathedral chapter, now worked as diligently to assist Saint Martin's as he had once striven to harm it. This passage gains its significance from the fact that Gunther was Herman's cousin and that several other members of the cathedral chapter were also his kinsmen. Several members of the abbey of St. Martin's were his relatives too, and so the contention between the canons and the monks, a contention that had led to a pitched battle and the death of several men, had long been a struggle among Herman's kinsmen. It seems appropriate, then, to retrace Herman's account from this point of view. There are other approaches that one might take, of course, but this particular thread of discourse not only explains many confusing passages of Herman's narrative, but it also offers a glimpse of the network of loyalties and animosities that underlay and charged the communal life in an eleventh-century Flemish town.

The circumstances of the Osmonds' arrival in Tournai and the extent of their power and wealth is discussed in the Introduction, but it is important at this point to identify the members of the family and their respective positions and concerns in 1090, when dissension began to arise among them.

Two Osmond brothers, Herman the archdeacon and Siger the

precentor, dominated the cathedral chapter, supported by their kinsmen Letbert, Baldwin, Walter, Gunther, and perhaps others.[1] The chapter was an independent corporate body with its own lands and buildings. In addition, it possessed the revenues of a number of endowed chapels throughout the diocese and its wealth was regularly increased by the substantial contributions expected of newly-admitted members. It also shared in the ecclesiastical and secular administration of the prince-bishopric of Tournai. Since the bishops were usually absent, the canons of the chapter were the effective rulers of both the diocese and the city, and they received a regular income from secular levies such as the tolls on the bridge over the River Scheldt. The chapter was able to maintain this position for the most part because, although Tournai was the larger and wealthier of the two bishoprics, the canons of the cathedral of Noyon generally controlled episcopal elections, and the bishops they chose were concerned primarily with the revenues they derived from the burgeoning commercial life of the Flemish city.

The canons of Tournai thus represented local interests over and against the "foreign" exploitation of the bishops whose attentions and interests were usually fixed on Noyon. This arrangement drew wealth out of Tournai, and there were economic factors fueling the canons' work to have Tournai granted independent episcopal status. Their championing of the interests of Tournai did not gain them a great deal of local support, however. The lay citizens of the commercial center were interested in their own autonomy and would perhaps have preferred to see the chapter's authority diminished in their own favor. A wave of urban revolts, primarily against ecclesiastical overlordship, was sweeping western Europe, and Tournai could not have been exempt from the tensions of the time.

Beyond this, the chapter faced a rising tide of popular enthusiasm for religious reform, reform that called for ecclesiastics to show a greater commitment to asceticism, morality, spirituality, and Christian ideals. The fact that such a commitment would necessarily entail a certain withdrawal by churchmen from secular affairs and lay interests lent the movement a social and economic dimension. Reform sentiment did not come only from outside, however; some of the canons themselves were dissatisfied with the state of affairs in the chapter.

It has been noted in the Introduction that the chapter did not maintain a high level of spiritual life, even under the relatively undemanding standards of the Augustinian Rule, but there were reasons for this. A fire in 1070 had destroyed or badly damaged a large portion of the cathedral complex. This was not an unmitigated disaster, however, since many of the newer churches in growing towns such as Bruges and Ghent had already surpassed the diocesan cathedral in size and adornment, and, as in many such cases, a desire to build a new cathedral arose from the ruins of the old. This was not a simple undertaking, however, since the bishop could not be expected to provide much leadership or resources to this endeavor; the matter would be up to the canons and whatever popular support they could muster. They repaired their chapter house and much of the cloister complex, but not their dormitory. Instead, they purchased the houses adjacent to the cathedral and, while they waited for them to be demolished as a prelude to the construction of a new and enlarged church, they used them as residences. Since a fully communal life was not possible, several canons continued to live in their own homes and to be caught up in family affairs.

The Osmonds who controlled the chapter were thus ever mindful of money. The chapter needed all it could amass if a new cathedral were ever to be built, and it was unlikely that even this would be enough unless the canons could secure the right to elect bishops whose interests and prestige would be bound up with Tournai. Conversely, however, the sad state of their cathedral made it less likely that they could convince Rome that they were ready to support an independent see. The reader of Herman's work must imagine the cathedral as being small and in disrepair, and the leaders of the chapter as being deeply concerned about maintaining the cathedral complex in a usable state while also building up the money reserves to begin construction of its replacement. It is common enough that spirituality wanes during fund drives, no matter how worthy the cause. There were reform-minded clerics who apparently found the cathedral chapter too secular for their needs, but, like Ohtfrid of Tournai and his associates, they chose to withdraw from the chapter and the city to pursue their lives of greater spirituality.

Another branch of the Osmond family had gained position and influence in the wake of Baldwin Osmond's acquisition of the post and properties of the episcopal advocate in about 1071. There is reason to suspect that the four brothers who formed this branch may have been late arrivals from Noyon. Herman never mentions his grandfather in any of his discussions of Tournai; he refers to his father more than once as "Ralph of Noyon;" and Ralph would later show a distinct predilection for the Noyon region. Whatever the case, Baldwin became the episcopal advocate; his brother Tetbert was appointed episcopal prior; Theodoric, a third brother, was give the post of coiner of the bishop's money; and Ralph, apparently the youngest, was presented with the not inconsiderable gift of the bishop's brewing monopoly.

Despite their blood relationship, the two groups of Osmonds were not in the same camp. The four brothers, at least nominally, were episcopal appointees serving the bishop's interests, but in addition, Ralph and Theodoric were also part of the commercial lay community of Tournai. Theodoric was in effect the city's most powerful banker, and Ralph was a tavern-owner and beer-seller in a society in which malt beverages were staples. Nevertheless, the turmoil attendant upon Robert the Frisian's seizure of Flanders had upset a delicate balance of power in Tournai. It would seem that secular power, in the person of the advocate, had been an hereditary possession of the Avesnes family, while ecclesiastical power had been wielded by the prior of the canons, a post usually held by a member of the Osmond family. Power had now shifted to the Osmonds, even if they belonged to different branches of the clan.

It is difficult to believe that this state of affairs was devised by Bishop Radbod, who was himself a member of the Avesnes family and would surely have preferred the support of his own kinsmen in key offices. It is possible that the arrangement was the doing of Count Robert. Flanders and Hainaut had been joined from 1051 until 1071 under the rule of Count Baldwin (VI of Flanders, I of Hainaut) and his son Arnulf, and it seems likely that the power of the Avesnes, vassals of the counts of Hainaut, had been fixed in Tournai during that period. After the battle of Kassel, however, Arnulf's mother and brother had fled to Hainaut, which his young nephew ruled as Count Baldwin II. Count Robert could not have appreciated seeing members of the Avesnes clan controlling the rich and strategically situated Flemish city of Tournai. The fact that the diocese of Tournai encompassed much of the county of Flanders, including Ghent and Bruges, would only have added to Count Robert's concern. Baldwin Osmond had been one of his trusted followers and had probably fought for his cause at Kassel, so it seems logical to conclude that the count may have required Bishop Radbod to endow the Osmond brothers with power and wealth as a means of maintaining his control over an important site. In any event, the bishop was soon at work to restore the power of the Avesnes in his city.

The arrival of Everard Ralph, the bishop's nephew, and his seizure of the authority of the count of Flanders in Tournai and its environs, strengthened Bishop Radbod's position considerably. Whether or not this was the direct cause, Baldwin relinquished his position as advocate in about 1082 and left the county to join the monastery of Bec in Normandy. The arrival of Fastrad Avesnes as the new advocate marked yet another step forward for the bishop, but it proved only a temporary advantage.

There was immediate friction between Fastrad and Prior Tetbert. Their overlapping functions of securing the bishop's revenues probably made this friction inevitable, and, given Herman's biases, one cannot expect to discover any more specific reasons for what followed. Whether deceitfully or not, Fastrad became so close to Tetbert that he was granted the honor of becoming godfather to Tetbert's son, whose mother had died in childbirth. Despite this close tie, Fastrad arranged the murder of Tetbert, and, on 24 August, probably in the year 1084, Tetbert was killed by Fastrad's men. If Fastrad had expected the support of his kinsmen, Bishop Radbod and Everard the castellan, he was disappointed; when the Osmonds sought vengeance and killed two of Fastrad's retinue, the advocate fled to the protection of Theodoric, head of the Avesnes clan and baron of Avesnes castle on the southern border of Hainaut.

Tetbert's brothers should perhaps have continued the feud against the Avesnes within their reach, but they did not. Herman tells a tale of Tetbert's ghost requesting a halt to the feud, but it is more likely that Bishop Radbod's appointment of Ralph Osmond as advocate and investing him with the fiefs of the office bought an armistice, although not an end to the brothers' blood-claim. It may well be that Tetbert's son, Gunther, felt betrayed by his uncles. At any rate, he later became their bitter enemy, at least for a time.

If the supposition is correct that the Osmond brothers were members of the Noyon branch of the family, there was now much to draw them and their kinsmen of Tournai closer together. The feud itself would have been sufficient to have affirmed their blood-ties, and a lingering hostility to the bishop and castellan as members of the Avesnes clan would have aligned the brothers more closely with the outlook of the cathedral chapter. Moreover, there were now only two of the Osmond brothers left, and it would have been natural for them to secure their position through strengthened family ties. Beyond this, there were important social occasions of the sort that brought families closer together. In about 1086, Ralph married Mainsendis, daughter of the prior of the prestigious and influential monastery of St. Amand, and the births of their sons, Theodoric, Herman, and Walter followed at regular intervals. By 1090, the Osmonds had every reason to feel relatively content with their position.

A balance of power between the Osmonds and the Avesnes seems to have been regained from the turmoil of the preceding years. Bishop Radbod was an Avesnes, but the lion's share of ecclesiastical power in Tournai lay with the cathedral canons who were led by Herman Osmond. Siger Osmond, the precentor, led the choir school, but Odo of Orléans, an Avesnes, presided over a successful cathedral school. If Baldwin, Letbert, Walter, and Adam—other Osmonds in the cathedral chapter—strengthened Prior Herman's hand, his power was limited by that of the chapter treasurer, Walter d'Oisy, a member of the Avesnes family. On the secular side, the military power of Castellan Everard was greater than that of Ralph Osmond, the advocate, but Everard's leadership of the citizens of Tournai was limited by Ralph's role as tax-gatherer and his control of the city's supply of beer. Added to that was the local banking function of Theodoric Osmond, the minter. Ralph and Theodoric were both wealthy, as was their kinsman, Walter fitz Hubert. The three were leading citizens and were doubtless influential among their fellow laymen.

It was at this point that the canons, most probably in the figure of their leader, Herman Osmond, committed a serious error of judgment and unleashed the antagonisms that had been pent up in this complex balance. A growing shortage of food in the region had led to the distribution of alms bread made from old and mouldy rye. The grain had in fact been infected with ergot and was carrying ergot toxin. The consumption of the bread led to a widespread outbreak of ergot poisoning among the indigent and itinerants. No longer able to work or to beg, and suffering the beginnings of terrible agony, the afflicted gravitated to the churches of the area for comfort and aid. A rumor spread that St. Mary had effected miraculous cures in her cathedral at Tournai, and an unusually large number of tormented paupers collected there. There seemed to have been no problem in providing them with food and drink, but the canons were faced with a problem of space. The old cathedral could not have been very large, and the effects of the fire of 1070 still lingered. There would have been no room left for the cathedral's parishioners to worship, and the crowding and the stink of gangrenous limbs was making it difficult, if not impossible, for the canons to serve the cathedral's chapels. An appreciable portion of the canons' incomes came from endowed masses and prayers, and the people of the times felt strongly about honoring one's obligations. In addition, the canons were concerned about continuing to collect funds towards the construction of a new cathedral complex, and they would not further that cause by neglecting their own congregation.

Their solution was to thin out the crowd of suppliants by having those who were beyond help removed to the abandoned abbey of St. Martin's just beyond the city walls. Herman's account suggests that they may have neglected to provide for feeding and sheltering the dying or for offering them last rites and a Christian burial, but he is presenting the citizens' view of what was happening at this point, and the reader cannot be sure of the actual state of affairs.

In its general outline, this episode is an epitome of what was occurring throughout western Europe during the waning years of the eleventh century. Increasing population, a decreasing need for full-time agricultural laborers, and the conversion of arable land to the production of raw materials for manufacturing all conspired to swell the ranks of the indigent. At the same time, commerce facilitated the spread of disease, and epidemics became increasingly common. The churches, long the sole source of charity, were no longer able to meet the demands of the time, and secular institutions, particularly municipal governments, began to assume a part of the burden. This was what had happened at Tournai. The church was unable to hold those who had flocked to it for aid, and the canons' failure in their mission was fully visible to the citizens. The laity reacted passionately in their zeal to aid the unfortunates and to condemn the canons for having failed to do so.

Whatever the facts of the matter may have been, the cathedral chapter came under attack by the citizens. The townspeople immediately began to call for the restoration of the abandoned abbey, pledging it their full support and expressing their ardent wish to be buried there among those paupers who had been purged of sin by their sufferings. This outcry carried many undertones. The citizens were expressing a belief that the paupers who had died at St. Martin's without benefit of clergy were in a holier state than those men and women who had been laid to rest in the cathedral cemetery with the full rites of the Church. Not only the canons were under attack but also the sacramental system that they administered. Moreover, the citizens were threatening to divert their donations and gifts from the cathedral to this new abbey, along with the substantial endowments that traditionally accompanied burial. The public outcry was in fact a revolt against the rule of the cathedral chapter and, indirectly, against the Osmonds who controlled that chapter.

Bishop Radbod intervened and increased his authority and prestige by doing so. After a thunderous sermon and public acts censuring luxury and excessive worldliness, he proclaimed a universal fast and fixed a day for a barefoot procession around the city by both clerics and laity. Although this liturgy was modelled upon the example of Gregory the Great, Bishop Radford's purpose for the procession may have been significantly different. Gregory's procession had been a general act of penance to gain an abatement of the plague that was afflicting Rome, but ergot poisoning was not a plague. Very few of the upper and middle classes of the city, who customarily ate wheaten bread, were affected, and the infection was not contagious. In any event, the effects of the poisoning should have been swiftly decreasing by this time. It seems more likely that the penance was intended to restore some community of feeling by chastising everyone and to reassert the bishop's supreme authority in both the city and cathedral. The fact that the canons led the procession both confirmed their local eminence and placed them in the position of chief penitents.

The political situation was more or less stabilized, but the entire episode had raised questions and quickened latent hostilities that eventually affected the Osmond clan directly.

Sometime in early 1092, his relatives among the canons convinced Ralph Osmond to buy a prebend from the bishop for his eldest son, the five-year old Theodoric. Ralph paid a substantial sum for this lifetime stipend, and he would not have done so without an assurance that the canons would admit his son to their chapter when he came of age. The arrangement was one that would closely unite the two branches of the Osmonds, that of the city and that of the chapter. When the arrangements were concluded, the canons displayed the importance they attached to this alliance by entering the schoolroom where the boy was at work and publicly congratulating him on their future fellowship. But Odo, the schoolmaster, and his assistants were quick to coach Theodoric on the illegality and general sinfulness of the buying and selling of prebends. That evening, Theodoric defied his father and threatened to run away forever rather than accept the arrangements that had been made for him. Ralph immediately capitulated and sent word to the bishop that they did not want the prebend and were returning it to him. By so doing, Ralph rebuffed his kinsmen in the chapter.

The estrangement grew when Ralph fell ill and asked the canons for advice on how he might avoid damnation. It may well have been Prior Herman who advised Ralph that confession, penance, and absolution would wash away his sins and ensure his salvation, and that burial rites would ensure his repose until the day of resurrection. When Ralph recovered, however, he still felt himself to be burdened down by his sins and concluded that the sacraments he had received had not accomplished what the canons said they would. It would be easy for the modern reader to underestimate the effect that this thought may have had on Ralph. The tortures of Hell were much more vivid for the men and women of the time than the present generation. The pains of Hell were not pictured as eternal remorse or the pain of being denied forever the sight of God, but as actual physical pain, the searing agony of being burnt alive with the knowledge that nothing would end the agony but that it would go on forever. Ralph had trusted in the assurance of his kinsmen and, he had concluded, had almost suffered the most horrible fate imaginable as a result.

He could no longer depend upon such kinsmen, and went to his brother-in-law, Prior Herman of St. Amand's, for guidance. Herman advised him that only the monastic life could guarantee salvation. After some discussion, Ralph and his wife agreed to abandon the secular world and enter the monastic life with their children and all of their goods. They kept the matter a secret as well as they could, presumably so that Ralph's kinsmen would not try to dissuade him.

While this was happening, the chapter canons were facing another problem. Odo Avesnes had undergone a public and highly dramatic inner conversion, and he and a few followers had begun searching for a community of regular clergy to join. A delegation of citizens, presumably not including the Osmonds, met with Bishop Radbod and suggested that he restore the abbey of St. Martin's with Odo as its head. The bishop quickly embraced the idea as a means of reducing the power and prestige of his overly-independent cathedral chapter while at the same time adding to the local power of his own family. He found it difficult to convince Odo, but Odo finally agreed on the condition that the abbey and its property would be free of all obligations and that these privileges would be confirmed by an episcopal charter. Radbod then had to fight out the matter with the chapter. He wanted the canons to be co-donors, presumably to free the abbey and its property of obligations due to the chapter. Whatever the legal reasons for the negotiations that took place, the canons agreed to be co-donors on the condition that St. Martin's would be allowed to accept laymen and women for burial only with the chapter's approval.

It would appear that the Osmonds succeeded in gaining the support of the citizens regarding St. Martin's. Herman mentions that some people claimed that Odo's new austerity owed more to pagan philosophy than Christian zeal. It may well be that a rumor campaign was mounted against Odo; whatever the case, he found that his exemption from ecclesiastical dues did him little good since no one gave him any property. His congregation grew very slowly, and, since it remained without means, it would appear that the new members were primarily poverty-stricken students of the type whom he was accustomed to befriend. He received the support of the entire city, as the citizens had promised, but in a fashion that made a mockery of the citizens' promises. A layman would go through the city daily, begging food for St. Martin's just as other volunteers gathered food for beggars who could not beg for themselves.

The manner in which this impasse was broken is fully discussed in appendix 4, "The Trek to Noyon," and need not be repeated here. The resolution resulted in the transfer of the advocate's land to the abbey and the admission of Ralph Osmond and his family, as well as other prominent citizens, to the congregation. The rift that thus developed in the Osmond clan diminished when the monks of St. Martin's rebelled against what they considered Odo's mismanagement during the famine of 1095–1096 and turned the management of the abbey over to Ralph Osmond and his friends and relatives. There was more to Odo's humbling than the fact that he had given away all of the monastery's food. He had set humiliating "tests" for those seeking admission, and one supposes that the monks saw these as a means by which a member of the Avesnes family was mortifying members of the Osmond and other kindreds. In any event, Odo was forbidden specifically to set any more "tests."

The abbey of St. Martin's was opened up to other members of the Osmond clan with these developments, and a number of canons soon joined its congregation. Some came to embrace a more spiritual life, and some, it would appear, came to be with their children and kinsmen. Whatever the reason, they came with their properties and wealth, and the endowments they brought were wealth taken from the chapter as well as from the Osmond clan generally. Moreover, the support that Ralph had called up in the emergency of the famine winter of 1096 continued into less urgent times, and many rich men of the city who had chosen to remain in secular life gave St. Martin's regular and generous assistance. Ralph began to use the wealth now available to the abbey to purchase farmlands over a wide area and to lay the basis for St. Martin's later position as the richest Benedictine house in the Low Countries.

The Avesnes family had been successful in maintaining their elevated position in Tournai largely because of the influence of the bishop and because of the fact that Everard, the castellan, had managed to maintain a precarious independence between Hainaut and Flanders. The situation altered in the closing years of the eleventh century. Bishop Radbod died in 1098 and was replaced by Balderic, who had been selected by the chapter of the cathedral of Noyon and whose interests tended to center on his southern seat. At about the same time, a long struggle between Everard and Count Robert of Flanders came to an end. Unable to dislodge Everard, Count Robert decided the situation. He confirmed Everard's position as castellan of Tournai and lord of Mortain, and recognized him as a peer of Flanders with the charge of defending Flanders' frontier with Hainaut. Tournai's ambivalent position came to an end with this arrangement, and the extraordinary power of the Avesnes within its region diminished for a time. The competition between the main families of Tournai was replaced by cooperation and consolidation.[2]

The abbey flourished under these conditions, at least until 1105. Herman suggests that the trouble that was to follow was in some way related to Odo's elevation to the bishopric of Cambrai in that year, but there were other factors in the renewed strife between the monastery and the cathedral chapter. Herman Osmond had left the chapter to join St. Martin's in 1103, and his post as prior was taken up by Gunther, son of the murdered Tetbert Osmond. It may be that Gunther harbored a resentment of Ralph and Theodoric, his uncles who had abandoned the blood feud to avenge his father, but that was not all. Gunther was an energetic man, determined to elevate the position of both the cathedral and its chapter. He embarked upon the reform of the cathedral's canons and soon managed to reinstate communal life. In addition, he pressed the building of a new cathedral. The completion of a new choir in 1105 may have been a small beginning, but it was the first new construction in St. Mary's cathedral in well over a generation.

In the same year that Odo was called to the episcopacy, Pope Paschal began to press the matter of monastic immunity from paying tithes. The Cluniac monastery of Afflighem, situated between Ghent and Brussels, received an initial confirmation of this exemption in 1105, and one presumes that other monasteries, including St. Martin's, did also.[3] Gunther reacted violently to this innovation. He and the chapter declared that St. Martin's was in fact their priory and that the resident monks lived there only at the sufferance of the chapter. Although Herman does not provide enough information to determine on what bases the canons rested their claim, there are several possibilities. Bishop Radbod's foundation charter, of which the chapter had been co-donors, gave St. Martin's to Odo to be a residence of Augustinian canons. Although the residents may have changed the order to which they belonged, the canons may have argued, they could not change the purpose for which the property had been given without the agreement of the donors. The grounds for the chapter's claim were unimportant; the abbey was now involved in what might be protracted and expensive litigation.[4]

Herman states that the canons aroused the whole world against St. Martin's, and it is quite likely that there was a general opposition to the exemptions and immunities being extended to the abbey. St. Martin's owned properties in many different parishes, and the churches of each stood to lose income, not only from tithes but from other rents and renders with which they had been endowed, if the abbey were exempted from all obligations on its property. The archdeacon for Tournai and its environs was responsible for the well-being of those churches, and so the cathedral chapter was the natural leader of what was probably a widespread protest. Despite repeated papal directives, Bishop Balderic did little to restrain the increasing violence. It may well have been that he encouraged the attacks on St. Martin's property since he too stood to lose income as a result of this new arrangement.[5] Ralph Osmond and Gunther Osmond had reached the point of personal confrontation when the pope called the canons to Rome and directed the bishops of Thérouanne and Arras to protect the abbey and its rights.

When the canons returned from Rome, the violence resumed. The chapter hired fighting men and, according to Herman, plundered, burned, and devastated St. Martin's properties. It may well be that they were taking by force the dues they felt were theirs by right, but whatever the rationale may have been for the canons' actions, it was soon swept under overshadowed by a new source of contention. Abbot Siger sent one of his monks to stand watch over a property that the canons' men intended to plunder. This particular monk was a member of a numerous and martial kindred, and Siger perhaps hoped that the possibility of raising a feud would restrain the chapter's men. If so, he was mistaken. They beat the monk badly, and his kinsmen gathered to avenge him. In the battle that ensued, some of the canons' men were killed by having their feet chopped off, a mutilation that was clearly intended to remind everyone of the dying paupers whose feet had rotted off and how the canons had set in motion the series of events that had finally led to this.

The matter was no longer purely an ecclesiastical dispute. The men who had been killed also had kinsmen, and Tournai found itself on the brink of civil war. The matter was now clearly within the purview of the castellan, and Everard took resolute action. He proposed that the cathedral chapter relinquish to St. Martin's the right to bury whomever sought that privilege, and suggested to the chapter meeting of the abbey that it honor the payments due on the properties it had acquired. His compromise was one that ignored the papal directives, but it was backed by the threat of a more decisive resolution of the conflict. Quite simply, he promised to destroy St. Martin's unless it agreed to his proposal.

It is likely that both the canons and the monks regretted the lengths to which their conflict had taken them and welcomed Everard's intervention. It had taken eighteen years to restore the balance that had been disturbed by the Osmonds' expulsion of the dying paupers, and their kindred had almost destroyed itself in the process, but matters were at last set right.

APPENDIX 6

A CHRONOLOGY OF IMPORTANT EVENTS

1035–1046	Odo II, count of Lower Alsace.
1036–1067	Baldwin V, count of Flanders.
1039 06 IV	Accession of Henry II of Bavaria, Holy Roman Emperor.
1050	Odo is born in Orlèans.
1052–1063	Henry I, count of Lower Alsace.
1056 10 V	Death of Henry III, Holy Roman Emperor.
1056 10 V	Accession of Henry IV of Bavaria, Holy Roman Emperor.
1060–1108	Philip I, king of France.
1065	Fastrad I, advocate of Tournai.
1066	Elnon abbey destroyed by fire.
1067–1070	Baldwin VI, count of Flanders and Hainaut; founder of St Peter's of Hasnon.
1068–1098	Radbod, bishop of Tournai.
1070–1099	Baldwin, count of Hainaut.
1070–1071	Arnulf III, count of Flanders.
1070	Fire badly damages the cathedral of St. Mary's of Tournai.
1071 20 II	Arnulf III killed in the battle of Kassel by Robert of Frisia.
1071 (ca.)	Mainsendis, mother of Herman, born.
1071–1092	Robert I of Frisia, count of Flanders.
1075/1080	Everard I Ralph captures Mortain.
1077–1092	Odo is master of the school of the cathedral of Tournai.
1078–1110 20 X	Everard I Ralph castellan of Tournai.
1078–1089	Odo II, count of Lower Alsace.
1079	Gregory VII issues a papal decree commanding all bishops to establish schools for the study of letters.
1082	Baldwin, advocate of Tournai, relinquishes his post and joins the monastery of Bec. Fastrad II becomes advocate of Tournai.

1084 24 VII	Probable year of the murder of Tetbert.
1086	Probable year of the marriage of Ralph and Mainsendis, perhaps in October. Mainsendis would have just turned sixteen.
1087 VI(ca.)	Probable birth date of Theodoric, son of Ralph and Mainsendis.
1089 XII(ca.)	Probable birth date of Walter, son of Ralph and Mainsendis.
1089–1122	Godfrey I, count of Lower Alsace.
1090 V/VI	Outbreak of ergot poisoning. The canons expel the dying paupers from the cathedral of Tournai.
1090 VII/VIII	The townspeople of Tournai demand the restoration of St Martin's church.
1090 14 IX	Bishop Radbod institutes the Grand Procession in imitation of the procession of Gregory the Great.
1091 VI	Probable birth of Herman, third son of Ralph of Noyon and Mainsendis.
1092	Odo receives the gift of a gold ring.
1092 I	Young Theodoric refuses to accept a prebend and automatic membership among the canons. His father returns the prebend to Bishop Radbod
1092 I	Ralph of Noyon falls ill, recovers, and is advised to embrace the monastic life
1092 II	Ralph of Noyon and Mainsendis decide to renounce the world.
1092 04 III	Odo renounces the world and begins to neglect his school duties.
1092 IV	A delegation from the town meets with Bishop Radbod and requests the restoration of St Martin's, recommending that Odo be its abbot.
1092 02 V	St. Martin's church is reconsecrated and given to Odo and five of his followers.
1092 IX	Birth of Ralph, fourth son of Ralph of Noyon and Mainsendis.
1092–1111	Robert II, count of Flanders.

1093	Struggle between Everard and Count Robert. Robert is unable to dislodge Everard. He allows Everard to keep Mortain as an allod to defend against Hainaut and makes him one of the twelve peers of Flanders.
1093 V	St. Martin's has now grown to eighteen members.
1094 VI (ca.)	Seven-year-old Theodoric Osmond joins St. Martin's.
1094 04 III	Twelve members of St. Martin's don monastic garb. Odo is consecrated as abbot by Bishop Radbod.
1095 VIII	Odo and his monks walk to Noyon in a migration.
1095 VIII	Ralph of Noyon renounces the world. Ralph informs Odo of this while Odo is on his way to Noyon.
1095 IX	An emissary of the townspeople of Tournai threatens to bar entry to Bishop Radbod if he allows Odo and his monks to depart.
1095 IX	Upon persuasion by Bishop Radbod, Ralph, the advocate of Tournai, relinquishes the lands of St. Martin's that had become the benefice of the advocates.
1095 IX (post)	Fastrad returns to his advocacy and makes peace with the brothers of Tetbert.
1095 14 IX	Odo and his monks escorted back to St. Martin's. Bishop Radbod gives St. Martin's its lands and tells them to accept a rule.
1095 IX	Ralph tested before being allowed to become a monk in St. Martin's. Mainsendis dedicates her children to St Martin's and renounces the world. Children taken in by their uncle Theodoric the Minter.
1095 IX	St. Martin's accepts Cluniac rule. The monastery of Anchin sends priors to instruct them, and the monks begin a year of silence and isolation.
1095 27 XI	Urban II preaches the crusade at Clermont.

1095	Odo starts giving away the monastery's golden objects. Starts subjecting newcomers to tests of humility and determination.
1095, Autumn	Severe famine during which Odo gives all the monastery's food to the poor.
1096, Winter	When the monks are told, they limit his authority to Benedictine and Cluniac norms (consultation, no testing, a full-time treasurer, and two full-time outside representatives).
1096	Prior Ralph begins acquiring farm properties for St. Martin's.
1097	Death of Canon Baldwin, Herman's uncle.
1098 7–13 I	Death of Radbod, bishop of Noyon-Tournai.
1099	Baldwin, count of Hainaut, dies on crusade.
1101	Siger Osmond, cathedral precentor, joins the abbey of St. Martin's. Gunther Osmond becomes chapter treasurer.
1103	Ralph founds the monastery of St. Amand at Noyon.
1103	Gunther Osmond becomes prior of the cathedral chapter replacing Herman Osmond, who joins St. Martin's abbey.
1104	Ralph purchases land in the diocese of Laon.
1105	New choir in St. Mary's cathedral completed.
1105 29 VI	Odo consecrated as bishop of Cambrai. St. Martin's has seventy monks resident.
1105	Odo exiled for refusing to accept his investiture from the emperor.
1105 31 XII	Death of Henry IV of Bavaria, Holy Roman Emperor.
1106	Theodoric, Lord of Avesnes, killed by the men of Isaac of Berlaimont while hunting. The Avesnes open a feud against the Berlaimonts.
1106 06 I	Henry V of Bavaria, Holy Roman Emperor. Odo placed in Cambrai by Henry V. Apparently accepts crozier from his hand.
1108–1137	Louis VI, king of France.
1108	Open fighting between the canons' men and

	supporters of St. Martin's. Conflict ended by Everard the castellan.
1111–1119	Baldwin VII, count of Flanders.
1113 19 VI	Death of Odo at the monastery of Anchin.
1114	Emperor Henry V marries Mathilda of England.
1114–1115	Heretical uprising of Tachelm.
1119	Herman attends the Council of Reims.
1119–1127	Charles I of Denmark, "the Good," count of Flanders.
1121	St. Norbert founds the monastery of Prémontré
1123–1148	Simon of Vermandois, bishop of Noyon-Tournai.
1123	Death of Prior Gunther, Herman's cousin.
1124	St. Norbert sent to preach at Bruges.
1125 23 IV	Death of Henry V, Holy Roman Emperor.
1125 13 IX	Election of Lothar II of Swabia, Holy Roman Emperor.
1126–1127	Famine in Flanders.
1126	Death of Ralph the Norman, prior of St. Amand's of Noyon.
1126 19 XII	Death of Prior Ralph of Noyon, Herman's father.
1126 25 XII	Herman serves as prior.
1127 30 I	Death of Abbot Siger
1127	Herman becomes abbot of St. Martin's.
1127	Murder of Count Charles the Good in Bruges.
1127 22 IV	Herman directs the disinterment of the body of Charles the Good.
1127 25 IV	Reinterment of Charles the Good.
1127–1128	William I Clito of Normandy, count of Flanders.
1128–1168	Thierry of Alsace, count of Flanders.
1137–1180	Louis VII, king of France.
1137	Herman resigns the abbacy of St. Martin's and is succeeded by Walter of Tournai.
1137 01 XII	Death of Lothar II, Holy Roman Emperor.
1138	Death of Herman's mother, Mainsendis.
1138 07 III	Election of Conrad II Hohenstaufen, Holy Roman Emperor.

1140	Herman in Rome; receives papal letters for the archbishop of Reims.
1141 30 XII	Herman in Tournai at election of new bishop. Departs again for Rome.
1142 26 IV–14 VI	Herman in Rome. Writes *The Restoration of the Monastery of Saint Martin of Tournai.*
1146	The diocese of Tournai separated from that of Noyon.
1147	Departure of Conrad's contingent on the Second Crusade. Possible time of the death of Herman of Tournai.
1149	Death of Walter Pulkans, castellan and advocate of Tournai, lord of Avesnes, and master of most of the lands of Brabant. Death of Theodoric, eldest son of Walter Pulkans. Goswin succeeds his father, Walter, as advocate of Tournai.
1152 15 II	Death of Conrad II Hohenstaufen, Holy Roman Emperor.

ENDNOTES

NOTES FOR PREFACE

1. Since Herman's account is concerned with the establishment and early growth of an abbey, some knowledge of contemporary monastic life would be useful. Benedict of Nursia, *The Rule of St. Benedict*, which appears in many editions and translations, is the fundamental document for the study of medieval monasticism. Alain Dierkens, *Abbayes et chapitres entre Sambre et Meuse: VIIe–XIe siècles: contribution a l'histoire religieuse des campagnes du haut Moyen Age* (Sigmaringen: J. Thorbecke, 1985), discusses the early monastic development of a region near Tournai, while Jacques Dubois, O.S.B., *Histoire monastique en France au XIIe siècle: les institutions monastiques et leur évolution* (London: Variorum Reprints, 1982), offers a series of studies of monasticism during the height of the reform movement.

2. *Herimanni liber de restauracione monasterii Sancti Martini Tornacensis*, ed. Georg Waitz. *MGH SS* 14: 274–317. Waitz's discussion of Herman's works and extant texts of those works may be found on pages 266–73.

NOTES FOR INTRODUCTION

1. D. Berthod, "Hériman de Tournai," *Histoire littéraire de la France* 12 (Paris, 1869): 279–88, and J. C. Didier, "Herman de Tournai (1095–1147)," *Catholicisme* 5 (1958): col. 661, provide a discussion of Herman's life and work, while Georg Waitz, "Hermann von Tournai und die Geschichtschreibung der Stadt," *Forschungen zur deutsche Geschichte* 21 (1881): 429–48, places Herman's historical works within the historiography of the times.

2. David Nicholas, *Medieval Flanders* (London and New York: Long-man, 1992), presents an excellent summary of Flemish history from Ro-

man times to 1492 and provides an extensive bibliography of the subject.

3. This period is the subject of Albert d'Haenens' work, *Les invasions normandes en Belgique au ixe siècle. Le phénomène et sa répercussions dans l'historiographie medievale* (Louvain: Bureaux du Recueil, Bibliothèque de l'Université & Publications Universitaires de Louvain, 1967).

4. The citizens of Tournai gained a degree of autonomy in the period following that of Herman, a process discussed in Paul Rolland, *Les origines de la commune de Tournai. Histoire interne de la seigneurie épiscopale tournasienne* (Brussels: Lamertin, 1931).

5. The rise of the Avesnes family is fully discussed in L. G. Genicot, *La maison d'Avesnes. Histoire généologique et sociale, des origines à Gautier II* (Louvain: Université Catholique de Louvain, Mémoire de license en histoire moderne, 1967).

NOTES FOR PROLOGUE

1. This statement is an indirect reference to the difficulties the monks of St. Martin's encountered in recovering the abbey's former possessions. The monks lacked information as to the extent and location of the lands that the monastery had possessed prior to its abandonment, and they had no written records corroborating their rights of ownership to properties that they suspected belonged by rights to them. Herman's attempts to find the truth of the matter form one of the major themes of his narrative.

2. Biographies of saints were a common and popular form of ecclesiastical literature in the Middle Ages, and the writing of the life of a saint was a meritorious act. It was not unusual for someone to keep notes of the deeds and reminiscences of a particularly holy person in order to be ready to write the story of his or her life and miracles soon after the holy person had died. Herman is suggesting that he was afraid that people would think that he was taking such notes just to flatter the abbey's leaders by having them believe that he considered them to be saints.

3. Herman's fiftieth year was also passing. He was one of the few people left who had known the founders of the abbey intimately, and he was at an age where his days were numbered.

4. Pope Innocent II, 23 February 1130–24 September 1143. Herman had gone to Rome at the request of his cousin, Theodoric, prior of the canons of St. Mary's of Tournai, to urge the pope to confirm Tournai's right to choose its own bishop rather than continuing to share a single prelate with the distant diocese of Noyon, and Innocent had sent back letters to the archbishop under whose administration the diocese of Tournai lay. The complex series of events by which Tournai's independence was secured is narrated in book 4 of the "Historiae Tornacenses,"

MGH SS 14: 340–6; and has been studied by M. Sdralek, "Zur Geschichte der Trennung der unierten Bistümer Noyon et Tournay," *Kirchengeschichtliche Studien* 1, fasc. 2 (1891): 66–72, 116–7.

5. Although Herman does not clarify the matter, "they" must refer to the canons of the cathedral of St. Mary of Tournai whose prerogative it would be to elect a new bishop. The canons seem to have anticipated that the pope's message to the archbishop was favorable to their case and they intended to press the matter by electing a new bishop and sending Herman back to Rome to seek his confirmation by the pope.

". . . lord abbot of St. Amand's . . ." St. Amand was widely revered as the apostle of Flanders. Born in Gascony, he became a monk and was sent from Rome in 626 to preach the gospel as bishop of the region. In 647, he founded two major monasteries: Blandin, near Ghent; and Elnon, near Tournai. At his death in either 679 or 684, he was buried at Elnon, which later took the name of St. Amand's. For some reason, Amand became the patron saint of brewers and vintners. Because of its patron's important role in the reestablishment of Christianity in the region, the presence of his relics there, and its rank as one of the oldest monastic houses in the region, the monastery of St. Amand enjoyed great prestige, and its abbots commanded particular respect.

6. Herman expected to wait from 26 April to 14 June of 1142, a period of some seven weeks. The papal administration moved very slowly, partly because it was still the popes' practice to oversee the business of the Church personally. The Church was just emerging from the conflict over lay investiture, and the popes were particularly careful to ensure that they controlled the Church in fact as well as in theory. Virtually every dispute and departure from traditional practice required the decision or confirmation of the papacy, and the popes personally presided over the curia in hearing the cases presented and in rendering judgment. Bernard of Clairvaux would later write to Pope Eugenius that his excessive involvement in administration weakened his ability to provide spiritual leadership.

7. Herman's concern was not an idle worry. Rome itself was not well-drained and was surrounded by marshes; diseases such as malaria, typhoid fever, and cholera were common. Summer was the season of local epidemics, and many visitors to Rome, both great and humble, never returned home. If Herman were to die in Rome, he would lose the chance of being buried with the other members of his community, within earshot of the church where the living brothers of St. Martin's offered up regular prayers for the souls of the dead. This was a serious matter for Herman, since the burial of the dead had been a major issue in St. Martin's early struggles. Moreover, the abbey's cemetery was becoming his kindred's necropolis. His mother and father were buried there, and his

three brothers would rest there along with several uncles, cousins, and their descent. If it happened that he could not be interred at St. Martin's, Herman was seeking to assure himself that he would at least be written down in St. Martin's register of those mentioned by name in the service for the dead. It is characteristic of Herman that he expressed a real fear in a humorous manner.

8. The distinction between inner and outer progress is that between the spiritual growth of the members of the community and the acquisition of the external resources to support them physically. Herman's account continually emphasizes the importance of material possessions to St. Martin's survival and growth, and yet he also recalls with pride and a certain nostalgia the days in which the little community of St. Martin's were paupers in a pauper church. Herman's mixed feelings reflect a contemporary ambivalence toward the wealth of the Church. Few monasteries were self-supporting, and most sought regular revenues to adorn their churches, to increase the number of brothers glorifying God through the holy offices, and to provide charity to the poor. But population growth, the expansion of manufacturing and the diversion of arable lands from agriculture to pasture, together with a deteriorating climate, were swelling the ranks of the poor to the point that famines in Flanders and its region were becoming more frequent, and the wealth of the Church was insufficient to deal with the problem. Demands that the Church give up its wealth and privilege were becoming increasingly vehement.

It should be noted at this point that Herman employs the word *religio,* or "religion," in many ways. It can denote discipline, zeal, faith, devoutness, the holy offices, spirituality, and a number of other things. We have translated the word in whatever manner seems best suited to the sense of the passage, but it should be remembered that, for Herman and his audience, *religio* referred to a range of qualities and actions, rather than to specific doctrines or institutions.

9. The patron of Herman's abbey was St. Martin of Tours (ca. 315–399), one of the most popular saints in western Europe. He was born in Pannonia, along the Danube frontier, and his father was an army officer. He became a Christian at the age of ten and an imperial cavalryman at the age of fifteen (ca.330). It was about this time that one of the most famous events of his legend supposedly occurred. Accosted by a freezing beggar, he gave him his military cloak and was subsequently rewarded with a heavenly vision. Martin left the army in 358, about the proper date for the retirement of a member of the cavalry, and joined the Church. In 371, he was called upon to become bishop of Tours. He died in 399, and his tomb became a famous shrine.

St. Martin's cavalry cloak (*capella*) was acquired by Charlemagne for his new palace church at Aachen, which was soon called the Capella after its most famous relic. Within a century, even village churches and other small establishments were referred to as *capella,* from which the modern word "chapel" is derived. Elaborating upon legends of Martin's attempts to spread the gospel in Pannonia and on his return to France, many districts throughout western Europe claimed that he had travelled through their territories, and various natural features throughout France were ascribed to his passage. Like all great symbols, St. Martin evolved with the needs of the times. By the eleventh century, he was portrayed with many of the trappings of the itinerant preachers of the day, and his concern for the poor had been elevated to one of his salient characteristics.

See Christopher Donaldson, *Martin of Tours, Parish Priest, Mystic and Exorcist* (London: Routledge & Kegan Paul, 1980), and Clare Stancliffe, *St. Martin and His Hagiographer: History and Miracle in Sulpicius Severus* (New York: Oxford University Press, 1983).

NOTES FOR CHAPTER I

1. Odo is one of the main figures of Herman's account, but Herman pays little attention to him after his consecration as bishop of Cambrai on 29 June 1105 ended his direct connection with the monastery of St. Martin's.

Odo was born at Orléans and pursued a scholarly career from childhood. He taught at the cathedral school of Toul until he was invited to be the master of the cathedral school of Tournai. He exercised this office from 1086 until 1092, when he became the first abbot of the newly-restored monastery of St. Martin's.

Odo's involvement with the bishopric of Cambrai took him into the middle of the struggle between the popes and rulers of Germany, and the antagonisms of the time are reflected in conflicting reports of Odo's actions. Although that preserved in the continuation to Herman's history was not favorable, it is worth summarizing.

Elected to wrest control of the diocese of Cambrai from the simoniac Bishop Walter, Odo eventually succeeded in this task by gaining the support of the emperor Henry V (1106–1125). There had been a civil war in Germany at the time, and the papacy had supported Henry V against his father, Henry IV (1056–1105). Henry V was victorious, and Odo accepted his regalia from the emperor while Henry was still in favor with the papacy. Henry and Pope Paschal II (1099–1118) soon fell out, however, over the issue of lay investiture. The pope condemned Odo for having accepted the crozier, the symbol of spiritual leadership, from the emperor, and for offering fidelity to the emperor for the property of the diocese. Odo withdrew to the monastery of Anchin, where he soon fell mortally ill.

Hearing of this, Abbot Siger of St. Martin's of Tournai and a group of his monks went to Anchin to ask the abbot for permission to take Odo back to the abbey he had restored. The abbot of Anchin, however, declared that he would not suffer one whom God had sent to him to be carried elsewhere.

Even aside from Odo's close connection with both establishments, his reputation was such that he would surely be venerated as a saint. Both Anchin and St. Martin's were eager to possess his tomb, although St. Martin's, which was poor in saintly relics, had perhaps the greater need since such relics were essential to the prestige of church or abbey. In this, as in many other regards, St. Martin's was still a pauper church. Meanwhile, the papal decision regarding Odo's status arrived; Pope Paschal declared that the papacy would never invest Odo as a bishop. Odo died shortly afterward, 19 June 1113, and was buried in front of the crucifix at Anchin. As expected, his sainthood was soon accepted throughout the region.

This may or may not be an accurate account, but it fits with many things that Herman appears to have suggested but left unsaid. If this is the case, Herman's view of the matter was that Odo had betrayed his own principles in the end, a harsh judgment upon his spiritual and intellectual father.

2. Herman is listing the early Capetian kings of France: Hugh Capet (987–996), Robert II the Great (996–1031), Henry I (1031–1060), and Philip I (1060–1108). As can be seen, one of the remarkable attributes of Hugh's successors was the length of their reigns.

3. The technical term for the post of head of a cathedral school was *scholasticus,* and *magister,* or "master," was the title of respect for a *scholasticus.* We have used the English term "master" throughout as best conveying both meanings.

Odo first taught at Toul, at the time both a center of learning and of ecclesiastical reform. This blend of scholarship and religious idealism was an important aspect of Odo's character throughout his life. In 1079, Pope Gregory VII had ordered all cathedrals to establish schools, and there was a considerable shortage of experienced and competent masters for some time. The bishop and cathedral chapter of Tournai called upon Odo of Orléans, an established and respected scholar and teacher to operate such a school there. Odo accepted and assumed the mastership of the cathedral school of Tournai in 1086. One might legitimately wonder why he had given up a position at a distinguished school such as Toul for a new establishment at Tournai. A number of factors may have been involved in his decision, but the fact that he was a member of the Avesnes family and therefore a kinsman of both Bishop Radbod and Castellan Everard doubtless played a role.

The bishop may have had still other things in mind. Not only was he introducing a kinsman into a chapter of canons dominated by a rival clan, but he was setting a man reared in the tradition of religious reform into the midst of a group that was failing to live up to the new standards of austerity of the age. Part of this failure may have been due to the fire that had destroyed many of the buildings of the cathedral complex in 1070. At any rate, the canons did not live communally as their Rule required but lived in their own homes with their own families. Not all canons were content with this laxity, and there had been sporadic previous efforts at reform. It is unlikely that Radbod was as concerned with the religiosity of the canons as with the limitations that stricter adherence to the Augustinian Rule would have placed on them. Communal living and celibacy would have separated them from their kinsmen and lessened the power that they could exert upon their ecclesiastical overlord.

4. It should be noted that Herman draws on the works of the historian Sigebert of Gembloux. Copies of Sigebert's *Chronica* were owned by many of the monasteries of the region, and several abbeys, including St. Martin's of Tournai, attempted to keep continuations of his account, which closed in the year 1011. This particular account is found in the continuation kept at the abbey of Anchin, "Auctarium Aquicinense," *MGH SS* 6: 394.

Students during the eleventh and twelfth centuries were wanderers, a custom that was made possible by their being in holy orders and because the language of higher education was standardized in Latin. In addition, the curriculum was more or less fixed by the "Seven Liberal Arts": the *trivium:* grammar, rhetoric, logic, and the *quadrivium:* arithmetic, geometry, astronomy, and music. Nevertheless, there were different textbooks used from place to place, different methods of teaching, different approaches to the subject matter, and some teachers who were simply better than others. So the medieval student went from place to place, taking the best that each school had to offer. The presence of a single outstanding scholar in a cathedral or monastery school could attract students from all over western Europe. Lanfranc had made the small Norman monastery of Bec an important center of learning almost single-handedly, and the presence of Anselm was later able to enhance Bec's position even more. The reputation of Peter Abelard drew students to Paris from all over Europe.

In addition, however, civil wars in Germany and the continued factionalism of the investiture controversy during the later eleventh century had arrested the promising development of the cathedral schools of Germany, and scholars from all over the Empire sought out the schools of France and the Lowlands where they could pursue their studies in greater security and relative tranquility. Odo's school at Tournai had benefited from this student emigration, and its growth was not necessarily due solely to the excellence of Odo's teaching.

5. Herman is introducing, by allusion, Odo's affinity for ancient Greek philosophy. The Peripatetics and Stoics were two famous schools of Greek philosophy. The Peripatetics ("those walking around") were the students of Aristotle of Stagira, who taught while walking about the Lyceum in Athens. The Stoic school, which eventually had a considerable influence upon early Christianity, was founded by Zeno the Athenian in about 300 B.C., and derived its name from the fact that Zeno used to teach in one of the *stoa,* or arcades, surrounding the city's marketplace.

Herman's statement that Odo discussed the zodiac and traced the Milky Way is a good indication that his education was primarily humanistic and relatively up to date, since the study of astronomy had traditionally been restricted to learning the method of determining the date of Easter, an essential skill for students training to become priests. In addition, staying up late at night was regarded by men and women of the Middle Ages as a special delight; such late-night star-gazing would have seemed particularly pleasurable to the reader or listener. This short description of Odo the teacher is thus more affectionate than would immediately appear to the modern reader.

Nevertheless, there is a certain jarring note to this pleasant passage if one knows, as Herman's audience certainly knew, that St. Eleutherius, founder of both Saint Martin's and the diocese of Tournai, had been beaten to death by Arian thugs and achieved martyrdom on that very spot in front of the church doors.

[Particular thanks are due Professor Stephen McCluskey of the University of West Virginia for his assistance in the translation of the astronomical references in this passage.]

6. "Anulus Odonem decet aureus Aureliensem." The continuator of Sigebert at Anchin mentions the presentation of this gift, suggesting that the incident indicates how much honor Odo could have enjoyed had he not abandoned the secular world for the monastic life. See *MGH SS* 6: 394. Herman may be reporting the incident with a literary purpose of foreshadowing later events.

First, the ring served as an example of the worldly praise that Odo found so attractive. In chapter five of this text, a reading of Saint Augustine led Odo to recognize that he was motivated primarily by a thirst for secular regard and that such a preoccupation led away from the path to heavenly glory. This realization triggered Odo's inner conversion. Once Odo had become a monk, Herman relates, he was repelled by gold and inspired by a line of poetry, "Tell me, bishops, what has gold to do with sacred things?" (chapter 68). Herman's audience was presumably aware that Odo had died under a cloud for having accepted the regalia of the bishopric of Cambrai, including the gold ring of his office, from the hands of a layman and enemy of the pope. In a structural sense, the gift of a gold ring by one of his students may have been intended as the first element in a series linking the three major stages of Odo's life: schoolmaster, abbot, and, by inference, ill-fated bishop-elect.

7. Entitled *On Connections in Discourse*; the term *complexione* is one often employed by Quintilian. Some of Odo's works may be found in *Patrologia Latina* (hereafter *PL)* 160: 140 ff., but they do not include those cited by Herman. The book of Substance and Essence dealt with the terms *res* and *ente,* important concepts in the Realist-Nominalist controversy. Herman is making the point that Odo was accomplished in the art of logical disputation even if he did not make it a dominant element in his method of teaching.

It is curious that Herman does not mention Odo's work, *De peccato originali,* in which he proves the existence of original sin with impeccable Realist logic. His argument is that all humans share a single substance, that descending from Adam and Eve. Since Adam and Eve corrupted that substance when they disobeyed the commandment of God, the substance of all humans is corrupt.

For a translation and annotation of this and another of Odo's theological works, as well as an excellent introduction and bibliography, Odo of Tournai, *On Original Sin and a Disputation with a Jew, Leo, Concerning the Advent of Christ, the Son of God. Two Theological Treatises,* trans. Irven Resnick (Philadelphia: University of Pennsylvania Press, 1994). Also see Irven Resnick, "Odo of Tournai's *De peccatio originali* and the Problem of Original Sin," *Medieval Philosophy and Theology* 1 (1991): 18–38.

8. Odo's colleagues in Tournai had apparently Germanized his name, but the inscription on the ring given to him indicates that his students continued to regard him as Odo of Orléans. *Odo* (which also took the forms of Eudes, Hugh, and Hugo) meant "mind" or "intellect," and *hard* or *hart* (cf. Barnhart, Bernard) "strong" or "powerful." So the combination "Odard" meant "powerful intellect."

NOTES FOR CHAPTER 2

1. The traditional teaching format and curriculum were intended primarily to train priests and, at their best, could provide a broad humanistic education based upon the study of ancient authors. There was an increasing demand for lawyers and administrators, however, and students wanted the training in the disputation and argumentation that could gain them advancement in these callings. This new pre-professionalism

coincided with the application of logic to problems of philosophy and theology and gave rise to new teaching methods. Rather than simply reading and explaining the text, teachers of the "new learning" would present arguments for and against a given proposition. Debate was an important part of such instruction, and students would be pitted against each other or even against the master in supporting or attacking various propositions. This must certainly have been more exciting for the students than the more passive learning favored by traditional masters. Herman suggests that Odo's students were already accustomed to the modern fashion of education when he pictures them circling the squares of Tournai engaged in disputation.

2. A reference to *Acts* 17:21. It is somewhat curious, after Herman's praise of the Hellenes, to note that he now compares Odo's students with the Athenians who invited Paul to speak. In any event, this shifting among masters was a normal occurrence within the educational system of the day. A number of Odo's students appear to have decided that Rainbert's method of instruction would be of greater benefit to them. It may well be that this rejection played a role in preparing Odo for an inner conversion. Odo was learning that public acclaim is a transitory thing.

3. Herman uses the word *phitonicus* to describe the deaf-mute in question. A phitonic suffers from a particular deformity in which the spine and neck are arched backwards, and the face is often thrown upward. Many sufferers from this condition are also deaf and mute. For some reason, phitonics during this period were believed to have the power of divination and were employed to find lost objects, to predict the outcome of events, and to provide guidance in the making of difficult choices. Herman repeats the story, while noting that the Church condemned consulting diviners as well as fortune tellers and other dealers in supernatural arts.

4. The significance of the diviner's second sign is easily understood, but the first sign seems more obscure. Herman suggests that Galbert interpreted as meaning that Odo's teaching, like the field of a good plowman, was fruitful, while that of Rainbert was as empty as the wind. There are other possibilities, however. The Latin word *exarare*, in addition to meaning "to plow," can also mean "to write" or, more specifically, "to write on a wax tablet," a common method of writing in Classical times. It may be that Galbert understood the diviner's gesture in this sense, as signifying that Odo was true to what the ancient authors had written. One of the factors in the success of a fortune-teller is often the ability to offer ambiguous answers. The questioner is left to interpret their meaning, and any failure is ascribed to the questioner's misinterpretation rather than the fortune-teller's lack of prescience.

5. Herman's defense of his introduction of the story of the diviner is

rather weak. If the diviner is not to be believed, then how does the story reprove the practitioners of the "New Learning"? Many of the passages in his account revolve about predictions and prophecies although Herman was well aware that belief in such things was against the teachings of the Church. If one believes that it is possible to predict the future or that omens foreshadow coming events, one denies that the future is changeable and contingent upon the will of God. If the future is not in God's power, then prayers for divine aid and protection are useless.

Herman's mention of Porphyry and Boëthius indicates another reason for his contempt for the "New Learning." Education in the trivium and quadrivium was generally conducted through lectures on one of a limited number of basic texts. Boëthius (d. 524) had long been the most popular of these, followed at some distance by Isidore of Seville (d. 636), Martianus Capella (d. ca. 424), Orosius (d. ca. 416), and Cassiodorus (d. 585). Porphyry's *Isagogue*, a third-century commentary on Aristotle, had been available but had enjoyed little popularity.

Although Boëthius had translated what works of Aristotle early medieval scholars had available in Latin, he was in fact a follower of the Platonic school of Idealism. The Platonists believed that humans recognized objects and qualities only because of their similarity to an innate although imperfect "recollection" of perfect forms of which physical objects are only rough approximations. Platonic Idealism was transformed into medieval Realism. Idealism was attacked by several teachers who used the Old Logic—the works translated by Boëthius—to question generally accepted truths. Although Herman was looking back to the beginnings of this movement, he was reacting to the degree to which this fashion had supplanted the Old Learning by the fifth decade of the twelfth century. It should be remembered that Herman began the history of his abbey, which is in many ways also the story of his youth, in 1142, the same year that Peter Abelard died. In his famous work *Yes and No,* Abelard had shown that the teachings of the Church Fathers, the basis of theological authority, conflicted on virtually every major point of Christian doctrine and had concluded that one had to determine religious truths by the use of reason.

The "New Learning" thus taught young men how to question, and every aspect of Herman's faith and education could be attacked as old-fashioned and erroneous by clever young men who knew little else than how to disprove the beliefs of others and who took delight in ridiculing traditional wisdom and learning. It is understandable that Herman viewed the new scholars with distaste. Many others no doubt shared his opinion.

There is a rich bibliography on the cathedral schools, their curricula, and accomplishments. Pierre Riché, *Écoles et enseignement dans le Haut*

Moyen Age: fin du Ve siècle–milieu du XIe siècle (Paris: Picard, 1989) studies the development of these institutions, and Ph. Delahaye, "L'organisation scolaire au XIIe siècle," *Traditio* (1947): 221–68, treats them at their height. Cora Elizabeth Lutz, *Schoolmasters of the Tenth Century* (Hamden, Conn.: Archon Books, 1977), deals with the schoolmasters of the period, and F. Beyls, "Le bienheureux Odon et l'école de Tournai au XIe siècle," *Semaine religieuse du diocèse de Tournai* 18, no. 12 (1875): 487–8, is a rather dated appreciation of Odo's role in this capacity. C. Stephen Jaeger, *The Envy of Angels: Cathedral Schools and Social Ideals in Medieval Europe, 950–1200* (Philadelphia: University of Pennsylvania Press, 1994), discusses the influences of the cathedral schools on the society of the time.

Many of the works used as texts in the cathedral schools are available in English translation. Boëthius, *The Consolation of Philosophy*, trans. V. E. Watts (Baltimore: Penguin Books, 1969), and Henry Chadwick, *Boëthius, The Consolations of Music, Logic, Theology, and Philosophy* (Oxford: Clarendon Press, 1981), present the texts from which Herman was taught. Edmund Reiss, *Boëthius* (Boston: Twayne Publishers, 1982), offers a full-scale study of the man and his works, and Noel Harold Kaylor, *The Medieval Consolation of Philosophy: An Annotated Bibliography* (New York: Garland Pub., 1992), provides a full bibliography. For some medieval commentaries on Boëthius, see Gilbert de La Porree, *The Commentaries on Boëthius*, ed. Nikolaus M. Haring (Toronto: Pontifical Institute of Mediaeval Studies, 1966), and Thierry of Chartres, *Commentaries on Boëthius, by Thierry of Chartres and His School*, ed. Nikolaus M. Haring (Toronto, Pontifical Institute of Mediaeval Studies, 1971).

Other medieval textbooks available in translation are Cassiodorus Senator, *An Introduction to Divine and Human Readings*, trans. Leslie Webber Jones (New York: Columbia University Press, 1946), Isidore of Seville, *Etymologies, Book II*, ed. and trans. Peter K. Marshall (Paris: Les Belles Lettres, 1983), Martianus Capella, *The Marriage of Philology and Mercury*, trans. William Harris Stahl, Richard Johnson, and E. L. Burge (New York: Columbia University Press, 1977), Paulus Orosius, *The Seven Books of History Against the Pagans*, trans. Roy J. Deferrari (Washington, D.C.: Catholic University of America Press, 1964), and Porphyry, *Isagoge*, trans. Edward W. Warren (Toronto: Pontifical Institute of Mediaeval Studies, 1975). A text of Peter Abelard's significant work is available in *Sic et non: A Critical Edition*, ed. Blanche B. Boyer and Richard McKeon (Chicago: University of Chicago Press, 1977).

6. Anselm was born in Italy in 1033 and studied in the Norman abbey of Bec under Lanfranc of Pavia. He entered the Benedictine order there and became the abbey's second abbot in 1078. He was called by

William II to the archbishopric of Canterbury after the death of Lanfranc and vigorously opposed William's seizure of church lands. Henry I
recalled Anselm from the exile into which William had sent him but he
soon broke with Henry over lay investiture and was again exiled,
1103–1107. A reconciliation was finally effected in which Henry gave
up his claim to the right of investiture. Anselm was appointed regent of
England in 1108, but died in the following year and was buried at Canterbury cathedral. He was one of the great intellects of the period, often
known as "the father of scholasticism," and was later recognized as a
"Doctor of the Church."

Herman notes later in his history that he was personally acquainted
with Anselm, probably through his uncle Baldwin, who had relinquished
the advocacy of Tournai to enter Anselm's abbey of Bec. Baldwin had
followed Anselm to England and had served as a canon of Canterbury
Cathedral.

The work to which Herman refers is the *Liber de fide trinitatis et de
incarnatione verbi, PL* 158: 259–84. Anselm directed this book against
the extreme Nominalist, Roscelin of Compiègne, who was Peter
Abelard's first teacher of philosophy. Roscelin had argued that if the persons of the Trinity were in fact a single God sharing a single substance,
then all had to be present in Christ and that there would have been no
deity left in heaven during the Incarnation. From this he concluded that
the Trinity was a group of three separate gods, each with its own nature
and substance. He was widely attacked for what was, in fact, heresy, and
later recanted, but not before bringing suspicion upon the entire Nominalist position.

Herman is thus not attacking merely teachers of the New Learning,
but Nominalist philosophy as well, as was only to be expected from one
trained in Boëthius' Idealism by a Realist such as Odo.

The passage also contains a rather savage pun. Anselm's words as
quoted by Herman were *Qui nonisi flatum universales putant esse sub-
stantias,* to which Herman added the paraphrase *"eos de sapientium nu-
mero merito esse exsufflandos."* Another way of translating the statement might be "Through nothing but wind do they consider universals
to be substances . . . and people with this sort of learning ought to be
blown away." The reader might recall the deaf-mute's alleged characterization of Master Rainbert's teaching.

For a general introduction to this philosophical controversy, see
Meyrick Heath Carre, *Realists and Nominalists,* (New York: Oxford
University Press, 1961), and *Five texts on the mediaeval problem of uni-
versals: Porphyry, Boethius, Abelard, Duns Scotus, Ockham,* trans. Paul
Vincent Spade (Indianapolis: Hackett, 1994). For the relationship be-
tween Platonic Idealism and the scholastic tradition, see Richard W.

Southern, *Platonism, Scholastic Method, and the School of Chartres* (Reading, U.K.: University of Reading, 1979).

NOTES FOR CHAPTER 3

1. As master of the cathedral school, Odo was responsible for his students' dress, grooming, and deportment while they were in the cathedral precincts. He was expected to concern himself with his charges' spiritual development as well as their intellectual growth and was thus already discharging some of the functions of an abbot. Later expectations that Odo would be a good abbot were no doubt based at least partly upon his reputation as a strict school master.

2. One of Everard's functions as castellan of Tournai was to hold a regular court for the citizenry, and this court had customarily been held in the cathedral cloister. This arrangement shows one small instance of the lay control over ecclesiastical property that had grown up over the years since the fall of the Carolingian Empire. Although the bishop was the titular lord of Tournai, the laity had gained the free use of the cathedral cloister for their courtroom. In many other cities and towns, such civil courts were held under the cover of the church porch.

3. One cannot help but feel that Herman intended this remark to be ironic. Many of his audience believed that Odo had allowed himself to be invested by Emperor Henry V in order that the emperor would oust his episcopal rival in Cambrai and that he had died in papal disfavor precisely because he had "strayed . . . from the path of rectitude for the favor . . . of a prince."

4. Odo found himself being deserted by some of his students in favor of more "modern" teachers, and at least one of the canons had already had doubts about the worth of his teaching. There were also detractors who questioned his spirituality. He had reached a point where his fame as a teacher was unlikely to grow greater and was, in fact, likely to diminish. Although Herman does not suggest that Odo realized this consciously, one must suspect that these were additional factors preparing him for inner conversion.

NOTES FOR CHAPTER 4

1. This is an extremely surprising statement. Odo was reputed to be a well-trained scholar, and one would expect that he would have read at least some of Augustine's work since Augustine was revered as one of the three original Latin Fathers. Besides, Herman has emphasized that Odo was partial to Plato, and Augustine was the greatest of the Christian Platonists. Even if this were not the case, as master of the cathedral school, Odo was a member of the canons living under the Augustinian Rule and should have had a greater interest in the founder of his rule.

2. Boëthius, *Libri V de consolatione philosophiae*, the text of which may be found in *PL* 53: 579–862. Herman notes that Odo preferred secular authors such as Plato, over ecclesiastical writers such as Augustine. Plato was, of course, more than just secular; he was pagan and could hardly be taught in a cathedral school. Odo instead lectured on Boëthius.

Severinus Boëthius was not only an eminent scholar but also a high official in the court of Theodoric, king of the Ostrogoths, ruler of Italy (493–525), and an Arian Christian. Theodoric suspected Boëthius of complicity in a plot to assassinate him and condemned him to death. Boëthius was imprisoned for a long time awaiting execution, and he used this time to write *The Consolation of Philosophy* as a preparation for his death. Interestingly enough, the work drew its inspiration almost entirely from the pagan, rationalist tradition rather than Christian belief. Nevertheless, since Boëthius was finally beheaded by order of the Arian monarch, he was considered a Christian martyr and enrolled on the calendar of saints. The favorite work of both Odo and Herman was an example of pagan philosophy that was, because of a combination of circumstances, quite acceptable to ecclesiastical authorities.

3. Herman portrays Odo as being captivated by Augustine's eloquence. This would seem to be rather frivolous for a scholar noted for his mastery of dialectic, but it is quite in keeping with Herman's portrayal. It also suggests yet another element in Odo's conversion. He had been captivated by Augustine's eloquence and had presented the work to his students as rhetoric, concerning himself with the form of the words rather than their meaning. His sudden insight must have come, then, as a great surprise and intellectual shock.

4. The passage that so moved Odo was the following:

Hinc fit ut peccans creatura superior creaturis inferioribus puniatur, quia illae tam sunt infimae ut ornari, etiam a turpibus animis possint atque ita decori uniuersitatis congruere. Quid enim tam magnum in domo est quam homo? et quid tam abiectum et infimum quam cloaca domus? Seruus tamen in tali peccato detectus ut mundandae cloacae dignus habeatur ornat eam etiam turpitudine sua. Et utrumque horum, id est turpitudo serui et mundatio cloacae iam conjunctum et redactum in quandam sui generis unitatem ita dispositae domui coaptatur atque subtexiturut eius uniuersitati ordinatissimo decore conueniat. Qui tamen seruus si peccare noluisset, non defuisset domesticae disciplinae alia prouisio qua necessaria mundarentur. Quid itaque tam infimum quam corpus omne terrenum? Hanc tamen corruptibilem carnem etiam peccatrix anima sic ornat ut ei speciem decentissimam praebeat motumque uitalem. Habitationi ergo caelesti talis anima non congruit per peccatum, terrestri autem congruit per supplicium, ut quodlibet elegerit sem-

per sit pulchra uniuersitas decentissimis partibus ornata, cuis est condi-tor et administrator deum. Namque optimae animae cum in infimis crea-turis habitant, non eas ornant miseria sua, quam non habent, sed usa earum bono. Si autem peccatrices animae permittantur habitare in subli-minis locis,/ inhonestum est, quia non conueniunt illis, quibus nec bene uti possunt nec ornamenti aliquid conferunt.

Il 'De Libero Arbitri" di S. Agostino. Studio introduttivo, testo, traduzione e commento. ed. Franco de Capitani (Milan: Catholic Uni-versity, 1987), book 3, chapter 27 [pp. 404–6].

5. Herman engages in a complex play upon words at this point. *Sen-tentia* ("sentence") may mean a passage in a book, a philosopher's opin-ion, or a judge's sentence, and all three of these meanings are applicable in Odo's statement. This is not the only instance in which Herman defus-es a moment of intense emotion with a quip.

6. Herman describes a dramatic scene. The cloister must have been crowded on the day of Odo's conversion. The entire student body of per-haps two hundred were present, and some the canons were perhaps viewing with some satisfaction Odo's new fascination with a clearly Christian philosopher. The schoolroom was doubtless in session, and Odo's lecture may have been punctuated by the occasional cries of a young student being beaten for inattention. After Odo reached that pas-sage where he felt that Augustine was writing directly for his personal instruction, he began to talk to himself in a fashion that many of the stu-dents probably considered a normal commentary and copied dutifully. Although still in the middle of his lecture, he turned and disappeared into the cathedral. It was probably a few moments before the scribbling students knew that he had gone and only then realized that what they had just copied was Odo's personal confession and renunciation of the world.

The intense experience of spiritual conversion is not easy to under-stand, but it was an important aspect of the life of the times. The influ-ence of conversions of which they knew or had witnessed and the possi-bility that they themselves might undergo a similar transformation, pro-foundly affected the actions and attitudes of medieval men and women. Karl F. Morrison, *Understanding Conversion* (Charlottesville: University Press of Virginia, 1992), provides a valuable introduction to this subject.

7. Odo clearly had personal funds since he had been able to purchase a book, a relatively expensive thing at the time, purely on speculation. One would suppose that the "money collected from everyone" may have been the tuition paid by his students. If that was in fact the case, Her-man fails to indicate whether the cathedral and canons had already been paid for the facilities used by the school, or whether the proper amount had been reserved for charity and hospitality. Herman's short reference

does suggest that Odo was behaving irresponsibly, but Odo was now animated by a new passion that left little room for minor considerations. Odo was giving all that he had to the poor, although this did not appear to have included his books.

It was perhaps more significant that he was now failing to provide the lectures for which his students had paid. Odo was burning his bridges behind him, but his students were bearing part of the price of his abandonment of the world. He was failing to meet his obligations, and this was not something that eleventh-century Flemish society viewed with indulgence. Herman's portrayal of Odo's new religiosity raises an interesting question. It is all well and good to scorn the things of things of this world, but should that scorn extend to other peoples' things? It may well be that many of the people of the time believed that it should.

8. Herman gives the anniversaries of the deaths of the founders of his community, the days on which a mass or prayers were said for the repose of their souls. Most monasteries had a necrology or obituary, a calendar in which the names of those to be remembered were listed day by day. For St. Martin's abbey, see U. Berlière, "Nécrologe del'abbaye de Saint-Martin de Tournai. Actes de confraternité, donations et fondations d'obits," *Documents inédits pour servir à l'histoire ecclésiatique de la Belgique,* I (1894): 133–246; Appendices: 247–61.

The closing phrase, *quintus eorum socius,* "their fifth comrade," is somewhat ambiguous, and the "Auctarium aquicinense," *MGH SS* 6: 394, states that Odo and his *four* associates were placed in St. Martin's. Nevertheless, several later passages refer to five followers. It may well be that Lamfred left the group, but was replaced by Godfrey and Roger, the brothers of Ralph and William, almost immediately. References to the number of the original congregation of St. Martin's have been allowed to stand with neither correction nor comment.

9. Odo and his companions would have made an excellent addition to any monastery or canonry. Odo was already well known, and his renunciation of secular life had gained him even greater fame. It cannot have escaped the notice of the citizens of Tournai that the monasteries of the region were in competition for Odo. The community upon which Odo's choice fell would gain a great deal of prestige, and prestige was essential to a monastery's prosperity. Moreover, Odo would come with his library, his teaching reputation, and a group of assistants. This was more than enough to establish an abbey school, and some abbots may have had visions of their community attracting students from distant places and growing in influence and reputation.

10. Canons recited the holy offices five times daily, instead of the monastic standard of seven. They ate meat occasionally and, despite the tenets of the Rule of St. Augustine, frequently held personal property,

travelled about at will, and married. Some canonries admitted rich and powerful laymen to their company and in some cities assumed functions reminiscent of the exclusive and influential private social clubs of Victorian London. For the standard to which canons were supposed to aspire, see Augustine of Hippo, *The Rule of Saint Augustine: Masculine and Feminine Versions*, trans. Raymond Canning (London: Darton, Longman & Todd, 1984), and George Lawless, *Augustine of Hippo and His Monastic Rule* (Oxford: Clarendon Press, 1987).

NOTES FOR CHAPTER 5

1. ... *modica ecclesia* ... *in monte modico constructa* is a slight pun. The name of the hill upon which the church stood appears to have been "Mons Modicus."

2. The Vandal devastation began in 407, but Herman is in fact referring to the Norsemen, whose raids devastated and almost depopulated southern Flanders near the end of the ninth century. Herman later suggests that the original St. Martin's was founded under the Merovingian monarchs and still fourished in the time of Charlemagne.

3. Herman frequently refers to St. Martin's as an *ecclesiola*, sometimes, it would seem, as an affectionate diminutive, and at other times to suggest its poverty and humility. The same word is used for its congregation of monks, and we have translated the word as seems appropriate within the context.

4. The earliest life of St. Piatus dates from the tenth century, and much of it is probably legendary. He is said to have been born in Benevento in Italy and to have preached Christianity in the district of Tournai. He became one of the victims of Diocletian's persecution and was beheaded in 287. He was venerated as a saint, and his body regarded as a holy relic, by the ninth century. During the Norse raids, his body was successively carried to Seclin, St. Omer, Chartres, and finally back to Tournai. He is venerated in all of these locations, as well as in Benevento. Piatus is regarded as an apostle to the region of Tournai and is the patron saint of its diocese. St. Piatus's church still stands south of the city, not far from the grounds that were once those of St. Martin's.

The churches and parishes of Tournai are discussed in Louis Cloquet, *Monographie de l'église paroissiale de St. Jacques à Tournay* (Lille: Desclee, De Brouwer, 1881); Paul Rolland, *L'église Saint-Quentin à Tournai* (Antwerp: De Sikkel, 1946) and *Les églises paroissiales de Tournai* (Brussels, Nouvelle sociètè d'edition, 1936).

5. That is, none of the offerings made at St. Martin's were expended on the upkeep or repair of that church but were taken to St. Piatus.

NOTES FOR CHAPTER 6

1. The "plague" was in fact an outbreak of ergotism in 1090. Ergot is a fungus that may infest old and damp rye kernels. It is self-limiting and soon dies away but leaves behind as a by-product an extremely potent toxin. This poison attacks the nervous and circulatory system leading to gangrene and extreme pain. For further information on such maladies, see Claude Moreau, *Moulds, Toxins and Food,* trans. Maurice Moss (New York: John Wiley & Sons, 1979).

2. This sickening odor is a characteristic of the gangrene that was turning the limbs of the sufferers black. The condition was a serious danger until relatively recently, and doctors and nurses customarily sniffed the bandages to discover if their patients' wounds had developed gangrene. The standard treatment until well into the twentieth century was immediate amputation of the affected portion of the body before the condition could spread.

3. The canons' action was a pivotal event in Herman's view, and much of what followed came about as a result of it. From the canons' point of view, they had to be able to go into the cathedral to say mass at the various chapels assigned to them and for many of which they and the cathedral had received endowments. Moreover, they avoided the expense and bother of burying dead who were neither residents of the parish nor able to compensate the cathedral for its services. But by so doing, they ignored their paramount obligations of feeding the hungry, giving drink to the thirsty, clothing the naked, and caring for the sick (Matt. 25). Moreover, given the increasing popular concern for the condition of the indigent and for an ideal of self-sacrificing spirituality, their action aroused the townspeople to what amounted to a popular revolt against the canons' authority. Herman emphasizes the importance of this episode by reiterating the theme of the ejection of the innocent at several points in his work.

It should not be forgotten, however, that the canons ruled the city of Tournai. A wave of communal rebellions by burgesses against their over-lords had arisen in France in the 1070s and was still underway. The public outcry for the reestablishment of St. Martin's was also part of a polit-ical struggle by the merchant laity of Tournai to gain greater control over their own affairs. There was yet another factor involved. The chap-ter of canons was controlled by members of a clan that we have called the Osmonds, and other members of the same family also coined the city's money, monopolized brewing in the area, managed the extensive church lands in the province, collected the taxes, and commanded the bishop's private army and police force. There was doubtless an element that would have wished to see such power and privilege more widely distributed.

4. The establishment of a liturgical procession as a response to plague followed the precedent set by Pope Gregory the Great (590–604), who inaugurated the procession that was believed to have ended a great plague in the city of Rome in 590. It should be noted that Bishop Radbod addressed his actions primarily to the laity, although the citizens had blamed the canons for their callousness. Although the involvement of the entire community in an effort to move God to mercy was an important aspect of such processions, Radbod may also have intended to quell the laity's rebellious mood. For a study of the institution of the Great Procession, see Jean Dumoulin, *La grande procession de Tournai (1090–1992): une réalité religieuse, urbaine, diocésaine, sociale, économique et artistique* (Tournai: Cathedrale Notre-Dame; Louvain-la Neuve: Université Catholique de Louvain, 1992).

5. The Great Procession is still held at Tournai on 14 September, but it has become primarily a folkloric festival, and, as was the case long ago, many participants are ignorant of the reasons for its establishment.

NOTES FOR CHAPTER 7

1. The paupers died and were buried largely without the benefit of clergy, but Herman suggests that the agonies they had suffered before they died had been adequate penance for whatever sins they may have committed in their lives. This revealing statement is the first indication that Herman was quite willing to accept the possibility of salvation outside the Church and without benefit of the sacraments. In chapter 61, Herman recounts that his father had renounced the world and become a monk primarily because he had lost faith in the power of the sacraments to secure salvation.

2. Herman uses the term *seniores urbis cives,* which might refer either to the nobles residing among the commoners in the town, or to a distinction within the population between the wealthy, or patriciate, and the generality of citizens. Given the aristocracy's involvement in trade, however, the distinction between the nobility and patriciate was probably not as great as it would have been elsewhere in western Europe.

3. Herman's statement that those buried in the cemetery of St. Martin's were praying for the restoration of the church may seem startling, but it is quite understandable. The wish that the dead "may rest in peace" presupposes that there are circumstances under which they might not rest in peace. The visions and apparitions that abound in Herman's account are evidence of the belief that the spirits of the dead could visit

the living and even continue to participate in secular affairs. The dead who were praying for the restoration of the abbey were the monks who had served there before its destruction, and Herman is thus emphasizing for his audience the continuity of the community serving God in St. Martin's abbey.

NOTES FOR CHAPTER 8

1. The later manuscript, MS BM Harley 4441, adds *pater illius Bernardi, de quo in prima constructione mentionem fecimus.* Bernard is first mentioned in chapter 52 of the earliest surviving version of *The Restoration*. This suggests that Herman had already tried arranging his materials in a different order.

2. The power of this story lies beyond the fact that Vidal, a poor man, had dared to answer back someone who, along with the bishop and castellan, was one of the most powerful men of Tournai. Claiming to predict the future was a dangerous act and could result in being hauled before the bishop's court on charges of heresy. Such a possibility lay behind Herman's "playful" inquiry. Vidal's prediction before a large group of witnesses of Herman's long life and his own impending death was something of an act of defiance in which Vidal implied that he did not fear the prior of the canons because he did not have long to live. The account gains an added significance later on, when the reader discovers that Herman was a leading member of the Osmond clan.

NOTES FOR CHAPTER 9

1. For Fastrad and his dates, see note 5 below.
There were many peasants who yearned for the chance to become free-holders. Once having been accepted as such, they could not be dispossessed if they paid their rents and renders and obeyed the customs of their village. It is surprising that Fastrad's wife should have undertaken to distribute this land without gaining his permission and to choose his tenants and assign them their holdings without his approval. He recognizes her right to do so and can only warn her that she is making a mistake. It would appear that the lands, and hence the post of advocate, were considered as private property descending in the Avesnes family as an hereditary tenure. If so, Fastrad had gained both by right of his wife.

2. Fastrad predicts that God will soon see to the restoration of St. Martin's and that its lands should rightfully be returned to the congregation when this comes to pass. This would have been more easily accomplished if the properties had been left without tenants.

3. St. Martin's abbey established two convents in Tournai soon after 1093.

4. This story suggests some of the difficulties involved in the restoration of St. Martin's lands. Despite Fastrad's piety, he seems to have regarded the lands he held in fief from the bishop of Tournai as his private property. The law and custom of the time required that the property of parents be distributed to their children. Fastrad's declaration that he would leave nothing to his sons should be taken as meaning that he would have given both their sons and their rights to the advocate's benefices to St. Martin's.

This was in fact how the dilemma was eventually resolved. The advocate Ralph commended his wife and children to God, and his wife commended the children to St. Martin's. Ralph was then technically without wife or children and free to dispose of his goods as he saw fit. He relinquished the advocate's benefices to the bishop of Tournai, and the bishop was then able to return the properties to St. Martin's. This arrangement also deprived the Avesnes family of much of the wealth and power of their traditional office of advocate and compensated the Osmonds in additional measure for the younger Fastrad's murder of their kinsman Tetbert.

5. The feast of St. Medard is 8 June. Born in about 500 in Picardy, Medard became a bishop and, in 531, established his seat at the fortified inland city of Noyon for protection from sea raiders. In 532, St. Eleutherius, bishop of Tournai, died; Medard was asked to take over the bishopric of Tournai and did so without relinquishing the see of Noyon. This peculiar arrangement of two diocesan sees, located over a hundred miles apart but united under a single bishop, lasted until 1146.

The Frankish King Clothar (558–561) conceived a special veneration for Medard and removed his body to the capital of Soissons, where the famous abbey of St. Medard was built. The body was later moved to Dijon and finally back to Noyon. Medard was a popular saint and the subject of numerous legends in the region.

The dates of the advocates of Tournai, and of Fastrad in particular, present many difficulties. *The Chronicle of Tournai* and local documents suggest that Fastrad became advocate in about 1065 and continued in this position until his death in 1093. See E. Warlop, *The Flemish Nobility Before 1300,* (3 vols.; Kortrijk: G. Desmet-Huysman, 1976) 2: 1169.

A possible reconstruction of the succession of advocates of Tournai might be as follows: Fastrad I was advocate in 1065 but died in June 1071 in the disorders accompanying the seizure of Flanders by Robert the Frisian. Bishop Radbod appointed Baldwin Osmond, one of Robert's supporters, to succeed him, and Baldwin relinquished his office sometime after 1082. Bishop Radbod then appointed Fastrad II d'Avesnes, son of Fastrad, as advocate, but the younger Fastrad was forced to flee after his murder of Prior Tetbert Osmond in about 1084. The office was given to Ralph Osmond, Tetbert's younger brother, who vacated it when he joined St. Martin's in September of 1094. Fastrad II returned about this time, paid Tetbert's kinsmen compensation, and was reappointed advocate.

NOTES FOR CHAPTER 10

1. The nobility of Flanders was an aristocracy of birth; landed estates were not necessary for the definition of noble status but did determine where in the scale of nobility a given individual belonged. The highest class held extensive lands and gave benefices to their vassals, the middle class of nobles had smaller estates and were vassals of the great lords, and the knights had smaller allodial holdings and were sometimes employed as warriors by higher lords. There seems to have been no feeling that members of the knightly class should not engage in trade and manufacturing, and some of them became quite wealthy through commerce. Despite the author's embellishments, there is no suggestion that Walter and Ralph were more than knights, although Ralph's appointment as advocate had elevated him to the middle rank of the aristocracy.

This particular premonition presents some difficulties. The outcry to restore St. Martin's was partly inspired by opposition to the power of the Osmonds who dominated the chapter of canons, and Ralph, and probably Walter, were members of the Osmond clan. It would seem unlikely that the account would have gained much currency at the time, but there may be more to the story than meets the eye.

2. These dreams, visions, and prophecies were coming from the laity and more particularly from the citizens of Tournai and its district. It may be that such reports were a form of public pressure upon the bishop and canons.

NOTES FOR CHAPTER 11

1. Charismatic preachers were characteristic of the times and commanded great respect. Four years after these events, another such figure, called Peter the Hermit, would lead a mass of peasants as an ill-fated vanguard of the First Crusade. In a more orthodox vein, Saint Norbert, founder of the Premonstratensian order and one of the primary forces in ending the investiture conflict, was sent by the pope to preach back to the faith the citizens of Antwerp who clung to an heretical belief in the divinity of Tachelm, is yet another spell-binder.

2. Acts 14:22, ". . . we must through much tribulation enter into the kingdom of God." It may have been an unconscious recollection of this argument that later led Odo to set "tests" of humiliation and endurance for those seeking admission to St. Martin's abbey.

3. Since Odo had already confessed publicly (chapter 4) that his great

weakness was the pursuit of praise, the bishop's line of argument would seem to have been adroitly chosen.

4. It would appear that the negotiations between the bishop and his chapter turned on the ecclesiastical revenues the abbey might enjoy. The two major sources of income were the endowments that accompanied the burial of rich laymen and the tithes from Church property. Radbod had already promised Odo that the abbey and its properties would be free of episcopal renders and was now attempting to convince the chapter to relinquish capitular obligations. The members of the chapter made the best deal they could under the circumstances, since they could not prevent the abbey from being reestablished and enjoying episcopal exemptions. Because part of the papal reform movement was to expand monastic immunities, and the canons might lose their right to revenues from properties acquired by St. Martin's in any event.

The canons probably remembered the public outcry of two years earlier when so many of the citizens announced their desire to be buried in the cemetery of St. Martin's, and agreed to be co-donors provided the bishop grant them the power to determine whether a layman or woman might be buried in St. Martin's. The value of this reservation would be reduced considerably when St. Martin's entered the Benedictine Order, since the canons could not prevent the burial of anyone who chose to be taken into the Order before death.

5. The freedom from episcopal exactions was expressed imprecisely and was an important factor in the later struggle between St. Martin's and the cathedral. The abbey contended that they were not required to pay tithes or other obligations to the cathedral incumbent on lands they acquired. This was one of the more controversial aspects of the monastic immunity that formed an important element in the papal-led reform movement at the close of the eleventh century.

6. It was not uncommon to include a list of contemporary rulers in the dating clause of a charter; the list appearing on the bishop's formed the basis for this passage. William the Conqueror, king of England, however, had died in 1087, and the ruler cited in the document was his successor, William II Rufus (1087–1100). The source of this error was doubtless Sigebert of Gembloux's *Chronica, MGH SS* 6: 366, which places the death of William I in 1092.

For the early documentation of St. Martin's, see C. Vleeschouwers, *Les cartulaires des évêques de Tournai: étude diplomatique et notes sur l'histoire et la composition de ces cartulaires ainsi que sur leurs scribes* (Brussels: Academie Royale de Belgique, 1977) and A. d'Herbomez, *Chartes de l'abbaye de Saint-Martin de Tournai* (2 vols., Brussels: Commission royale d'histoire, 1898–1901).

NOTES FOR CHAPTER 12

1. Count Robert I (1071–1093) bore the sobriquet "Frisio," "the Frisian." This chapter begins a long treatise on the political history of the dukes of Flanders from Count Baldwin V (1035–1067) to Count Thierry of Alsace (1128–1168), extending from chapter 12 to chapter 36. Although lengthened by several stories with various morals to be drawn, the account is tightly constructed, tracing the descent of Count Baldwin V and presenting the political history of northern France, England, and the Lowlands, 1067–1127. It would be easy to dismiss these chapters as a simple attempt to integrate disparate materials with the main account, but these passages should be taken together with the account of affairs in Germany, and some consideration paid to their common theme of intra-familial strife before discounting what Herman may have been attempting to portray.

For a full portrayal of Count Robert I, see Charles Verlinden, *Robert 1er, le Frison, comte de Flandre, étude d'histoire politique.* (Antwerp, "De Sikkel"; Paris, Campion, 1935).

2. The monastery of Hasnon was not located in Flanders, but at Valenciennes. Baldwin VI was also the count of Hainaut, 1057–1070.

3. The marriage took place in 1051. Although Herman refers regularly to the counts of Mons; we have consistently used the term Hainaut.

4. Leo IX (1049–1054) was a Lotharingian, a member of the family of the counts of Egisheim-Dagsburg and a cousin of Emperor Henry III. Leo effectively restored the position of the pope as leader of the western Church.

NOTES FOR CHAPTER 13

1. It should be remembered that Arnold had commended himself and his lands to the king of France and received Flanders in vassalage. Robert needed a strong ally should the French king decide to assert his claim to the county. One of the results of his alliance with the German emperor was the cession to Flanders of the lands between the Scheldt and Dender. This left the border lords whose castles defended that portion of the Flemish frontier with a greatly reduced function and led their sons to seek opportunity elsewhere. One such youth was Everard Ralph, who succeeded in gaining control of Tournai and the fortress of Mortain, commanding the confluence of the Scheldt and Scarpe.

Baldwin is first mentioned as advocate of Tournai in 1071 and apparently continued in the office until at least 1082. See Warlop, 2 (2): 1169. Herman mentions that he heard this story directly from Baldwin, his paternal uncle.

NOTES FOR CHAPTER 14

1. King Philip I of France (1060–1108) married Bertha, the daughter of Count Florence II of Holland (1091–1122).

2. William had in fact bequeathed a large sum of money to his youngest son.

3. . . . *contra se rebellantem.* Although Henry had seized the crown of England during Robert Curthose's absence on the First Crusade and ignored any claims his elder brother might have had under primogeniture, Herman characterizes Count Robert's attempt to assert what he considered to be his rights as "rebellion."

Herman will continue this picture of the descendants of Robert the Frisian warring against each other. Robert's sin of attacking his nephew is replayed with variations by his descendants.

4. Henry defeated Robert Curthose at the Battle of Tinchebrai in 1106 and imprisoned him for life in the castle of Gloucester.

NOTES FOR CHAPTER 15

1. The account is in error on this point. Edith was the daughter of King Malcolm III (1058–1093), and Edgar (1098–1107) was ruling Scotland at the time of the marriage in 1100. David I ruled from 1124 to 1153. According to legend, Henry found the name "Edith" difficult to pronounce, so she was re-christened Matilda. Henry's desire to marry Matilda was more than a matter of keeping his promise to the king of Scotland. Through her mother, Saint Margaret, Matilda was a great-grandniece of Edward the Confessor (1042–1066) and therefore a member of the royal house of Wessex. Until 1066, the English had traditionally chosen their monarchs from among the members of this family, and Henry was doubtless seeking a greater legitimacy for the Norman line.

2. The figure of Anselm of Canterbury looms large in Herman's account, perhaps because of the relationship of Baldwin, his uncle, to one of the most eminent figures of his days. See Richard W. Southern, *Saint Anselm: A Portrait in a Landscape* (Cambridge: Cambridge University Press, 1990), and *Saint Anselm and His Biographer; A Study of Monastic Life and Thought, 1059–c.1130* (Cambridge UK: Cambridge University Press, 1963) for studies by an eminent modern scholar who has devoted much of his life to the subject. See Eadmer, *Vita D. Anselmi archiepiscopi Cantuariensis. The life of St Anselm, Archbishop of Canterbury,* ed. R. W. Southern (Oxford: Clarendon Press, 1962) for a contemporary account. Several of Anselm's works are available in English translation, including *Why God became man = Cur Deus homo.* ed. and trans. Jasper Hopkins and Herbert Richardson (n.p.: Edwin Mellen

Press, n.d.), and *The Letters of Saint Anselm of Canterbury,* trans. Walter Frohlich (Kalamazoo, Mich.: Cistercian Publications, 1990–1993).

3. Roses were an important part of a monastery garden and were frequently classified as herbs because of their usefulness. Rose petals were used as flavoring in jellies and glazes, and for their scent in sachets and potpourris. Rose hips, the fruit of the rose, were particularly prized because of their tart flavor and were dried and added to boiling water or mulled wine to made a winter drink. Although medieval men and women were unaware of vitamins, they had chosen to supplement their winter diets with an extremely rich source of vitamin C. Until citrus fruits became widely available, rose hips were an important part of the common diet. The king's subterfuge was therefore quite believable. If the convent had possessed a particularly productive and aromatic variety of rose, William might well have asked for some seeds or slips to distribute to his own estates. Charlemagne had also been concerned with ensuring that the gardens of the imperial villas were well-stocked with the best varieties of herbs and vegetables.

4. It is a curious detail that the princess had continued to wear her nun's veil even after William Rufus had departed. It may be that the abbess herself had some doubts as to how to proceed once the girl had donned a veil.

5. The confrontation between King Henry and Archbishop Anselm took place in the year 1100, when Herman was about ten years old. It is unlikely that he was visiting England at such a tender age, so it is more probable that he means that he heard Anselm repeat the story. Anselm was in exile on the Continent from 1103 to 1107, and Herman might have met him at any time during this period.

NOTES FOR CHAPTER 16

1. Margaret bore only one son, William; Richard, the other prince, was illegitimate. Both drowned in the sinking of the White Ship while crossing the English Channel in 1120.

2. Emperor Henry V (1106–1125) married Matilda in 1114. They were married for over ten years, so there is no reason to believe that an untimely death prevented the Emperor from gaining an heir from Matilda. His death without a successor led directly to the great Guelf-Hohenstaufen rivalries that troubled the empire for the remainder of the twelfth century. The widow Mathilda married Geoffrey Plantagenet, count of Anjou; their son became Henry II, the first of the Plantagenet kings, who ruled England from 1154 to 1399.

3. Stephen was the son of Adele, daughter of William the Conqueror and sister of King Henry I. His father had been a leader in the First Crusade but had withdrawn just before the climactic battle of Antioch.

Urged by his wife to regain his honor, he returned to the Holy Land in
1101 and was killed at Ramalah, in battle against the Muslims.

4. The order of events in this passage is somewhat confused. Robert
of Gloucester had called Matilda to England in 1139, but it was only in
1141, after considerable fighting, that he succeeded in capturing
Stephen, and Stephen soon gained his liberty. The civil war continued
until 1153, when a compromise was reached by which Henry of Anjou,
Matilda's son and the first Plantagenet king of England, would succeed
Stephen. The entire issue was still unsettled, as Herman remarks, and
would not yet be settled when he departed on crusade in 1147.

NOTES FOR CHAPTER 17

1. The first marriage of Robert's daughter Gertrude was to Henry,
count of Brabant. This passage relates why she had no children by the
count.

2. Count Henry and his friends were apparently entertaining themselves by dividing up into two groups and staging a mock fight. Such
martial exercises were quickly developing into the tournaments that
would become so popular in the course of the next century, although the
Church officially condemned such events.

3. Gertrude's second husband was actually Thierry II, duke of Upper
Lorraine (1070–1115), but also a member of the house of Alsace. One of
their sons was Simon I, duke of Upper Lorraine (1115–1139), and another was Thierry of Alsace, count of Flanders (1128–1168).

NOTES FOR CHAPTER 18

1. Count Robert II (1093–1111) was one of the heroes of the First
Crusade and consequently bore the sobriquet "of Jerusalem."

2. Guy became Calixtus II, 1119–1124.

3. After the death of Count Robert, Clemence married Duke Godfrey
VII of Lower Lorraine (1106–1128). For this reason, she was later
known as "the duchess."

NOTES FOR CHAPTER 19

1. . . . *cum populo Dei proficiscitur.* It is uncertain whether Herman
is referring to the crusaders in general or to the poor who had led the
way under the leadership of Peter the Hermit, Walter the Penniless, and
other popular leaders. The belief that indigent pilgrims were peculiarly
"the people of God" was widespread and particularly strong in the Low
Countries. Herman's list of the crusaders is a bit curious; he includes
Raymond St. Gilles, from southern France, but ignores Godfrey of
Bouillon and his brother Baldwin, later king of Jerusalem and count of

Edessa respectively; the southern Norman leaders, Bohemond and Tancred; and—most surprising of all—Count Stephen of Blois.

NOTES FOR CHAPTER 20

1. King Louis VI the Fat (1108–1137) was the son of Philip I and of the step-daughter of Robert I of Flanders. The castle of Dam-martin was located in the present department of Seine-et-Marne.

2. The interment took place in Arras in 1111. St. Vaast, or Vedastus, was Clovis's religious instructor after the Frankish king's conversion in 496. He was made bishop of Arras and Cambrai in 510. Christianity had virtually disappeared in this area due to the Germanic invasions of the early fifth century and the expansion of the pagan Franks by the mid-century. St. Vaast worked to restore the faith and Church in the region. After his death in Arras in 540, his relics were much sought after. His body was moved from the cathedral to the monastery of St. Vaast, then to Beauvais in the 800s, and was finally returned to the cathedral of Arras.

NOTE FOR CHAPTER 21

1. The point of the passage is that the Flemish nobles promised to obey the laws but not to help to enforce them. Their reason for refusing seems to have been their belief that the peace could not be maintained. They were not inclined to become involved in a losing effort to keep order.

NOTE FOR CHAPTER 22

1. The thief was boiled alive with his sword still belted on as a demonstration that noble status would not save one from swift and savage justice.

NOTES FOR CHAPTER 24

1. This feast is that of the birth of St. John the Baptist, 24 June, very near the longest day of the year. A number of the larger fairs were held around Midsummer's Day, partly because of the good weather and relative ease of travel during that season, and partly because the long days allowed the maximum amount of time for business. Thourout is a village in West Flanders.

2. The kinsmen of the prisoners had sworn fealty to Count Baldwin and consequently could not harm him. They could, however, take vengeance on the count's men, and Baldwin's followers were afraid that they would do just that. The ability of aggrieved parties to seek satisfaction at the expense of the count's agents was an effective device for

maintaining the special status of the powerful and numerous noble kin-dreds, and in complicating the count's efforts to maintain peace.

3. *Sic ergo novem suspensis* . . . An understatement that requires the reader to imagine the desperate efforts of these brothers and cousins grappling in dark confines, struggling to hang each other. Contempo-raries must have been particularly impressed by the count's method of proceeding since, by setting kinsmen to kill each other, he had made it impossible for their other kinsmen to fulfill their obligation to seek vengeance for the deaths of their relatives.

4. This story, told with a certain relish, is an example of numerous medieval tales in which the hero punctiliously observes the letter of an agreement while offending grievously against its spirit. It is worth one's while to read the late medieval tales contained in *The Glorious Adven-tures of Tyl Ulenspieg l*, trans. Allan Ross Macdougall (New York: Pan-theon Books, 1944), and *Till Eulenspiegel: His Adventures,* trans. Paul Oppenheimer (New York: Garland, 1991), to gain an appreciation of this particular aspect of medieval life and thought. Till Eulenspiegel was a very popular comic figure whose appeal was that he took everything literally. When he paid for a cup of wine at a tavern, he took the cup away with him. When asked to wipe his feet before entering a house, he took off his muddy boots, wiped his feet with his hat, put the boots back on, and walked in.

The count had promised that he would not hang the prisoners and had accepted compensation from their families in lieu of punishing them. He kept his word precisely; his prisoners hanged themselves. Em-bedded in the grim humor of this episode was the message that wrong-doers could not expect to buy their way out of difficulty.

NOTE FOR CHAPTER 25

1. It will be recalled that Count Robert of Normandy and Count Robert of Flanders had been comrades-in-arms on the First Crusade.

NOTE FOR CHAPTER 26

1. Saint Canute, king of Denmark (1080–1086), was murdered at mass at the church of Odense in July 1086 while in the midst of prepar-ing a great fleet for the invasion of England. His saintly status was de-rived from the circumstances of his death rather than the nature of his life. Part of the drama of the murder of Charles derived from the fact that he died in the same fashion as his father.

Canute's claim to the English throne was strong, since he had de-scended in the male line from the Danish kings who had ruled England, 1017–1042, and could legitimately claim that William had usurped the throne from the usurper Harold Godwinson. His projected invasion was taken very seriously by William of England, and may have been the immediate cause of the Domesday Inquest and the Salisbury Oath.

Charles enjoyed the same claim as his father, and it was only strengthened after the sinking of the White Ship and the drowning of King Henry's only legitimate son in 1120.

NOTES FOR CHAPTER 27

1. The monastery of St. Bertin, originally called Sithiu, was located in St. Omer, Artois, France. It was an extremely influential establishment, particularly because of its close connections with several major English ecclesiastical centers. Its founder, St. Bertin, was born in Switzerland and became a monk of St. Columban. He was sent to preach the gospel in the region of Pas-de-Calais in 632, became abbot of Sithiu in 659, died and was buried there.

2. Germanic law and custom did not permit the alienation of land, even to the Church, to the damage of one's heirs. The knight was apparently claiming that his grandfather's donation to St. Bertin had been excessive and thus illegal. Count Charles ruled that any hereditary claim upon the property had been lost when the donor's son, the knight's father, had allowed the donation to stand.

NOTES FOR CHAPTER 28

1. The reasons for this conspiracy were complex. Bertulf was a member of a numerous clan descended from Erembald of Veurne. "New men," they had gained both position and power under Robert the Frisian and his successors. Bertulf was not only the prior of the royal church, but was also chancellor and collector of revenues of the county. His family had allied with noble families throughout the area despite the Flemish law that nobility required that both parents be of noble blood, and many Flemish nobles had sought their friendship and favor. The circumstances had allowed them to ignore their origins and encouraged them to claim property and position as hereditary rights.

Count Charles had attempted to rule Flanders during Baldwin's periodic forays into Normandy and was well aware of the Erembalds' power and ambitions. When he had consolidated his own position as count, he initiated a policy of reducing such men to their proper status and replacing them with his own appointees. It was Charles's intention to break the Erembalds at his Easter Court and to return them to their servile status. There were enough Flemish nobles irritated with court officials in general that the Erembalds had no hope of resisting the count's decree, so they decided upon assassination as the only course open to them.

2. Wednesday, 2 March 1127.

3. The events surrounding and succeeding the death of Count Charles

were meticulously recorded by Galbert of Bruges. His work is available in an excellent English translation accompanied by an invaluable introduction. See Galbert of Bruges, *The Murder of Charles the Good, Count of Flanders: A Contemporary Record of Revolutionary Change in 12th-Century Flanders*, trans. and ed. James Bruce Ross (New York: Harper Torchbooks, 1967).

Both contemporaries and later commentators drew numerous morals from the count's demise. It was observed that, by his death, Charles had atoned for the crime of Robert the Frisian in foreswearing himself by attacking his nephew and encompassing his death.

NOTES FOR CHAPTER 29

1. The sense of the passage is that Count Charles made it his habit to give the lame beggar alms whenever he was in Bruges. In short, the count recognized the beggar as an individual and made a special effort to provide for him. This was rather unusual for the times. The rich often took a number of small coins with them to hand out one by one to the beggars and paupers they encountered, but the identity of the recipient was irrelevant. The wealthy often discharged their Christian duty of providing charity impersonally, with an eye to their own salvation rather than the welfare of those whom they benefited. The count's action in this regard demonstrated the ideal of Christian charity, that one should cherish the poor because they are the brothers and sisters of Christ and Christ is present in them.

2. The church of St. Donatian, the castle church in which the count had been killed, was modelled after the palace church of Charlemagne at Aachen. Its floor plan was essentially round, with a balcony running the circuit of the interior. The count's throne was on this balcony, overlooking the altar and reached from the floor of the church by a flight of stone stairs. Charles was prostrate in prayer in front of his throne when he was killed, and the beggar crawled up the stairs to the spot where his body lay.

NOTE FOR CHAPTER 30

1. The troubles in Flanders were great indeed, but Herman seems unable to keep himself from palliating with a bit of wry humor the drama of the events he is recounting. The passage to which he refers is Rev. 20:7–10, which describes how Satan, in alliance with the barbarian kings, Gog and Magog, will persecute the people of God until he and his followers will be washed away by a rain of fire. This is two thirds of the letter. The final third, however, is contained in verses 11–15, narrating the day of resurrection, the last judgment, the sweeping away of the old world and the appearance of the New Jerusalem. In effect, Herman re-

minds his audience that events far more dramatic than a mere civil war are in the offing. Considering how easily the people of the age were moved to millennial fervor, Herman's sense of proportion is remarkable. See Norman Cohn, *The Pursuit of the Millennium* (New York: Harper Torchbooks, 1961).

NOTE FOR CHAPTER 31

1. Baldwin was addressing the "goodmen" (*boni viri*) or leaders of the middle class of Bruges, a term that we have translated as "citizens." The force that had gone out against Baldwin's army were not supporters of the murderers and their kin, but the municipal militia, prepared to beat back what they believed to be an attempt by the nobles to seize their city. Baldwin assured them that the army of nobles was not there to fight them or render them defenseless by destroying their fortifications. He expected them to understand the nobles' obligation to revenge the murder of their lord.

NOTES FOR CHAPTER 33

1. By "at the beginning," Herman means that Baldwin had joined the First Crusade. He died sometime about 1098 and was succeeded as count of Hainaut by his son, Baldwin III, who died in 1120.

2. Gerard was count of Geldern.

3. Her brother was Calixtus II (1119–1124). Clemence was particularly incensed because Baldwin was rejecting an alliance with the ducal family of Burgundy, a powerful family to which her brother's elevation had brought even greater prestige and influence.

4. The girl in question was Adelais of Burgundy, wife of Louis VI the Fat (1108–1137) and mother of Louis VII (1137–1180).

5. The following passage is an interpolation that interrupts Herman's account and obscures the point he was making. Baldwin and Yolanda's son was Count Baldwin IV of Hainaut, in 1127 the sole surviving descendant of Count Baldwin V of Flanders in the direct and legitimate male line. Moreover, he was a descendant in the lineage of Count Baldwin V's eldest son and therefore that of the rightful counts of Flanders. Herman discusses in chapter 35 how Baldwin argued his case before King Louis of France immediately following the murder of Charles the Good but was passed over. The matter might have been different if the young man had enjoyed the support of the duke of Burgundy. In any event, his case could scarcely have been furthered by his appeal to the husband of the woman he had once spurned. It would seem that romantic love, a concept only just beginning to be celebrated, was already regarded as a potential cause of the trouble.

NOTE FOR CHAPTER 34

1. Everard III Ralph lived well after Herman's departure on the Second Crusade. This chapter and the transition at the end of the previous chapter are clearly interpolations.

NOTES FOR CHAPTER 35

1. Prov. 21:1.

2. One might assume that Louis's wife had a role in the matter, but there were certainly other factors that the king had to consider, not least being the wisdom of allowing both Hainaut and Flanders to come under the control of a single ruler.

3. Baldwin's hereditary claim was undoubtedly superior, but there were other claimants. Four other great-grandsons of Count Baldwin V had survived Count Charles: William of Ypres (d.1165), Thierry of Alsace (d. 1168), William Clito (d. 1128), and Stephen of Blois (d. 1154). William Clito, Stephen, and Thierry, however, were descended through a female, and William of Ypres was illegitimate. There were also three great-great-grandsons: Baldwin IV of Hainaut, Arnold of Denmark, and Count Thierry VI of Holland (d. 1157). Arnold was descended through two females, and Thierry VI was the son of a step-daughter of a granddaughter of Baldwin V.

Baldwin IV of Hainaut was therefore the only representative of the male lineage of the ruling house of Flanders but had less support than others with weaker claims. William Clito was the sole survivor in the male lineage of William the Conqueror, hostile to King Henry of England, and was valued by the king of France for this reason. William of Ypres had acted first and had coerced oaths of loyalty from almost the entire county. His lack of powerful allies was the reason for Baldwin's willingness to defend his claim by the ordeal of combat.

4. Herman had recently become abbot of St. Martin's.

5. St. Christopher, "the travellers' saint," was one of the most popular saints of the Middle Ages. He was believed to protect those who venerated him against sudden death, a possibility which medieval men and women particularly feared since it prevented the dying person from enjoying the benefits of last rites. The legend of Christopher ("Christ Carrier" in Greek) carrying the child Jesus across a stream is well-known, but that of his martyrdom has been largely forgotten.

6. The church had been polluted by the murder and had to be cleansed and reconsecrated before it would be fit to hold Count Charles's body. The occasion provided the king of France with an oppor-

tunity to gain prestige through association with his martyred vassal, already widely accepted as a saint.

7. Galbert of Bruges, chapter 77, relates how those who were removing the body lit a fire near the count's tomb and burned frankincense and thyme in it to overcome the stench they anticipated. The body was removed on 22 April 1127.

8. This is a rather startling statement for a former abbot to make to his community, but Herman appears throughout his work to have found displays of public emotion distasteful.

9. The re-interment took place on 25 April 1127, only three days (or four, after the Roman system of counting) after the removal of the count's body on 22 April.

10. Although execution by precipitation was not unknown in France and Normandy, it had not been practiced in Flanders. There was an underlying symbolism to this form of execution. Count Charles had ordered this castle to be built, and its fortifications were a visible expression of his power. By forcing the Erembalds' followers to jump from the tower, King Louis had arranged that the manner of their deaths would serve to re-affirm the authority of the counts of Flanders. As was the case with Baldwin's execution of the ten thieving knights, the rebels' kin was also punished by being unable to seek vengeance for their deaths since they were jumping to their deaths, not being pushed. In addition, of course, the method had the advantages of being novel and of being conducted in full public view.

11. Galbert of Bruges, chapter 57, recounts the manner of the execution of Prior Bertulf on 11 April. He was stripped except for his trousers and bound with two long ropes, by means of which he was pulled from place to place toward the market-place of Ypres, being pelted with rocks and filth and struck with sticks as he passed. When he reached the gallows, his arms were outstretched and his hands secured on the gallows, and his neck placed in a fixed noose so that he could just reach the ground on his tiptoes. His trousers were then pulled down around his feet, and a great crowd mocked and threw rocks at him. When his executioner, William of Ypres, gave the command, the people who had come to the market to buy fish rushed upon Bertulf, striking him with clubs and baling hooks, and kicking his feet from under him so that he swung by his neck. As he was dying, the guts of a dog were tied around his neck and its muzzle stuffed in his mouth. His body was then tied to a cart wheel and hung from a tall tree for everyone to ponder on. Given these particulars, one can appreciate Herman's tendency to understatement.

NOTES FOR CHAPTER 36

1. The citizens of Lille rebelled against Count William on 1 August
1127. The offense that sparked open hostilities was seemingly slight but
struck directly at the rights that the Flemish middle class had laboriously
obtained and which the count had sworn to respect. 1 August was the
day of the great fair in Lille. Merchants had come from many distant
places to buy, sell, and trade in the market square of the town. They
were under the protection of the citizens of Lille, and the conduct of
those at the fair was overseen by the town's market officials. This conduct was defined by municipal regulations and a collection of merchant
customs known as "dusty-foot" law that would eventually evolve into
complex codes of corporate and contract law.

The fairs were essential functions in distributing commodities and
providing outlets for long-distance traders carrying luxury goods that
had been passed from hand to hand from Africa, China, the East Indies,
Siberia, Greenland, and other exotic places. They were also a celebration of the rising power of the middle class and provided the leaders of a
city or town with an opportunity to display their power, wealth, and defenses.

In many ways, prestige was as important to the merchant classes as it
was to the nobility.

Count William Clito appears not have understood this. Being told
that an escaped serf of his had been seen in the market place at Lille, he
ordered some of his Norman soldiery to enter the market and seize the
man. The citizens could not tolerate such an affront to their rights and
dignity, particularly in front of so many visitors, so the city militia drove
off the count and his men. The count quickly laid siege to the city and
forced the municipality to pay a fine of fourteen hundred silver marks.
This hardly endeared Count William to the burgesses of Flanders, and
other towns soon rose up in arms. See Galbert of Bruges, chapter 93 ff.

2. Dacia was a Roman province in the territory of modern Romania,
but it was also a name for what is now known as Denmark.

3. Henry was heir to the county of Champagne and the cousin of
Count Stephen of Blois. The dissolution of this betrothal was almost a
political necessity for King Louis. He must have known ever since the
sinking of the White Ship in 1120 that Stephen of Blois might claim the
English throne and would have been anxious to avoid a marriage alliance between the count of Flanders and a potential king of England.

His support for William Clito may well have been to establish his
protege, a direct male descendant in the elder line of William the Conqueror, as count of Flanders in order to provide the young man with a

base of power from which to threaten England, as well as to frustrate any possibility of an alliance between the two. The latter possibility was very real since the economies of the two regions were steadily integrating. The Flemish needed shipments of food from England since their own land no longer produced sufficient foodstuffs for its inhabitants, and they needed the particularly fine English fleeces to supply their burgeoning textile industries. The English, for their part, needed foreign exchange, especially since the English upper classes were in the process of converting their drinking preference from locally-brewed malt beverages to imported wines.

NOTE FOR CHAPTER 37

1. There is some bitter fun in this passage. Representatives of the citizens of Tournai had promised Bishop Radbod that the whole town would support Odo and his companions if they would reside in St. Martin's. The townsfolk kept the letter of their promise but hardly honored its spirit. The city provided the residents of St. Martin's the same sort of precarious charity offered to those indigents whose infirmities precluded their begging through the streets in person.

NOTES FOR CHAPTER 38

1. The precentor was the leader of the cathedral choir, an important post since the holy offices that formed one of the clerics' major functions were sung. It seems fairly certain that Siger was an Osmond, which explains his violent opposition to his son's joining the community of St. Martin's. Not only did St. Martin pose a threat to the wealth and prestige of the cathedral chapter and the Osmond clan that dominated the chapter, but it had been established against the canons' will by Bishop Radbod and was ruled by Odo, members of the Avesnes family that had not yet made restitution for Fastrad Avesnes' murder of Tetbert Osmond about nine years earlier. Young Alulf's attempts to join Odo's congregation clearly indicated that there was a division within the Osmonds and may indicate one of the sources of that conflict.

Herman calls Alulf a *clericus,* but he was clearly a mere boy and so his status must have been that of a student in Odo's school. In his account of Odo's career as master of the cathedral school, Herman discussed his teaching of advanced and mostly foreign students, but it should be remembered that he also directed the grammar school in which the sons of the townspeople were enrolled. He had had five years to win over these boys, and Alulf's eagerness to join him at St. Martin's, together with the story of Thierry Osmond recounted below, suggests that he had been successful in doing so.

2. The "paupers" whom Emory had come to comfort were to Odo

and his colleagues. Abbot Emory seems to have been advising Odo for some time and to have been eager to see St. Martin's converted into a monastic congregation.

3. The clerical reforms initiated by Pope Leo IX had been directed primarily at introducing monastic discipline into the ranks of the secular clergy through a strict observance of the Rule of St. Augustine. Several previous reformers in the district of Tournai had retired from the city to found Augustinian congregations, and Odo had simply followed these precedents with the exception that his community was established just outside one of the city's main gates. The community at St. Martin's still lived under the same Augustinian Rule as the canons of the cathedral of St. Mary's. They wore the same white habit as the canons and had no greater claim to religiosity. Moreover, they were under no obligation to persevere in the community and were still under obligation to their kindred.

The tenor of the passage suggests that Abbot Emory had been building up to this moment for some time and had seized upon Alulf's plight as an opportunity to persuade Odo to join himself and his followers to the Benedictine Order. Some of the reasons he offers seem a bit far-fetched, but the matter was a complex one. Perhaps Emory's most telling argument was set forth in his first words, when he called Odo "Master." Despite Odo's conversion, fasting, and present poverty, he was still—Emory pointed out—only a school teacher who had quit teaching.

4. Once having taken the monastic vows of poverty, chastity, and obedience, the residents of St. Martin's would be divorced from their families and kindred, and would represent an even greater challenge to the relative laxity of the chapter of canons. They had good reason to fear that some attempt might be made to prevent this from happening.

5. The "Auctarium aquicinense" dates St. Martin's adoption of the Benedictine Rule to 1093; *MHG SS* 6: 394. The fact that the destitute abbey of St. Martin's happened to have twelve sets of monastic garments on hand suggests that the decision to join the Benedictine Order may not have been as spontaneous as Herman states.

6. Local churches passed part of their income to the person or institution that "owned" them. These rents and renders were paid on each altar in the church. Men and women would leave property to a church or a chapel in a church so that masses and prayers might be offered there in perpetuity for the repose of their souls, and the income from these endowments, as well as the obligations that they entailed, were often transferred in one way or another. Archdeacon Herman had acquired the income from the endowments of five altars in local churches to give to his son. Adam would have enjoyed the income, but would also have offered the masses and prayers at St. Mary's that these endowments had been intended to secure.

This custom points up the dilemma in which the canons found themselves when the church was crowded with paupers suffering from ergot
poisoning. The canons had good incomes, but were supposed to earn
them and could not do so unless they could reach their altars. The obligations to render up prayers for the dead and to comfort the dying were
both incumbent upon them, and, at times, they could not do both.

7. Odo is generally credited with having played a significant role in
the monastic reforms of the late eleventh and early twelfth centuries. See
Ch. Dreine, "Odon de Tournai et le crise de cénobitisme au XII⁰ siècle,"
Revue du Moyen Ége latine 4 (1948): 137–54.

8. ". . . books of St. Gregory portraying the Fathers . . ." probably
refers to the *Magna Moralia*.

9. Since Herman notes in chapter 31 that Alulf's anniversary was the
fifth of the nones of March, then he died on 25 February, 1142, shortly
after Herman had left for Rome.

10. During the summer months, when the time between the evening
and morning offices was quite short, monks might be allowed to catch
up on their sleep with an afternoon nap.

NOTES FOR CHAPTER 39

1. The *Institutes* and *Collations* cited by Herman were doubtless the
works of John Cassian dealing with monasticism and the religious life,
and *The Lives of the Fathers* may have been *The Lives of the Desert Fathers,* a series of anecdotes concerning the practices of the early an-
chorites of Egypt. See John Cassian, *Conferences,* trans. Colm Luibheid
(New York: Paulist Press, 1985); Graham Gould, *The Desert Fathers on
Monastic Community* (New York: Oxford University Press, 1993); *The
Lives of the Desert Fathers: The Historia monachorum in aegypto,*
trans. Norman Russell (London: Mowbray; Kalamazoo, Mich.: Cistercian Publications, 1981); and *The Desert Christian: Sayings of the
Desert Fathers: The Alphabetical Collection,* trans. Benedicta Ward
(New York: Macmillan, 1980).

Odo and his congregation were studying religious life conducted at a
very high level of asceticism and were becoming increasingly dissatisfied
with their actual circumstances. Herman views their attitude with some
distaste, as he does enthusiasm and passion generally. The reader might
also wonder about the matter, since the sounds of children playing and
girls singing distracted them from their meditation and led them to long
to go to a place in which the contemplative life might be easier to follow.
A popular story of the time tells of a pious monk walking along a road
and finding himself drawing near some nuns walking in the other direction. He averted his eyes as he passed them so that he would not even
look at a woman. He was rebuked by one of them, who told him not to

be so pleased with himself; if he had been truly contemplative, he would never have noticed that they were women. Asceticism is supposed to overcome obstacles, not be overcome by them.

2. When Odo's monks spoke of a "desert," they meant any isolated and deserted place. By stating that Odo's followers were motivated by an overly enthusiastic reading of *The Lives of the Fathers*, Herman makes them appear somewhat silly by neglecting to explain the context in which they were acting. This was an era of monastic reform and experimentation in which varied interpretations of the Benedictine rule were giving rise to new orders, and it was not unreasonable for Odo and his followers to consider the meaning of the religious life and to study ways in which they might achieve such a pattern of living.

Only eleven years earlier, Bruno, a former master of the cathedral school at Reims, had led a few followers into the "desert," in this case an isolated valley in the diocese of Grenoble. Here they built a monastery that became known as La Grande Chartreuse and established the Carthusian order. The reputation of the order grew swiftly, but only the most zealous embraced it. The Carthusians lived in individual cells and assembled for a common meal only on holy days, much like the early communities of the desert fathers. They fasted on bread and water three days a week and abstained from meat entirely. They would not accept property outside of their "desert," and so remained paupers in a very real sense.

Odo and his congregation had set themselves to the task of reading and studying their situation in order to devise a rule of religious discipline that would meet their particular needs and suit their special circumstances. Their lack of property and endowments was one of their major problems. The congregation of St. Martin's did not own even their church and the lands on which it stood. They were distracted in their prayers and meditation because the church of St. Martin's had become a popular place of public worship and the grounds around it were still used as a public park and playground. The clothes and books they packed in their wagon were in fact the congregation's only possessions. Given the background of the congregation and their situation, their enthusiasm to migrate to the wilderness was neither foolish nor lacking in precedent.

3. This affair was a complex matter, and the critical event in the restoration of St. Martin's, but Herman does not provide the information necessary for the reader to understand what was happening. It is clear, however, that the monks' actions were more deliberate and carefully planned than appears at first sight. The reader will find in chapter 64, for instance, that the abbot of St. Amand's had sent monks to maintain the church of St. Martin's and expected Odo and his followers to re-

turn. Given the importance of the event in the history of St. Martin's, one might expect that Herman had some reason to make it appear poorly-planned and foolishly executed.

4. The reaction of the townspeople would appear to be rather exaggerated; Herman does not make it clear why the disappearance of the monks should have created such consternation.

5. The reader should note that Everard and the lay leaders of the city immediately treated the matter as if it were an act of war by the bishop. One of the greatest weapons in the hands of townspeople in their struggles against ecclesiastical control lay in their complete authority over the city's defenses. They could refuse to allow anyone passage through the city gates and could thus cut the bishop off from his cathedral. This would have been a drastic thing to do and would probably have resulted in the interdict of the city and widespread excommunications. The message from Tournai threatened Bishop Radbod with just such exclusion, however, and demonstrated how seriously the citizens regarded the matter.

Herman has presented his audience with a puzzle at this point. Why did he picture Odo's migration as impulsive and unplanned, when it is clear that arrangements had in fact been made, or secretive, when the townspeople were able to find out rather easily what Odo was doing? And why had the townspeople panicked when then first discovered that Odo and his followers were gone, and then chanced excommunication and interdict to ensure that they would be returned?

6. Horses were a symbol of nobility. By refusing to take to the saddle, Odo and his followers were affirming their humility.

7. The main commercial square of a town of the period usually lay just outside the gate, where land was less expensive than in the constricted confines of the walled precinct. To appreciate the scene that Herman is describing, one must imagine a busy square, enclosed by shops, warehouses, hostelries, and taverns except where the road from the north entered the compound. The plaza sloped up toward the south, where the great gate of the city stood open.

Everyone must have been aware that something was afoot, and the square was probably crowded when Odo's dusty monks entered under the escort of the mounted militia of Tournai. The emotional scene that Herman describes thus took place in what was almost a stage setting, in the full view of hundreds of witnesses.

Some modern readers grow suspicious of the posturing, declamations, and displays of immoderate emotion recorded by medieval chroniclers, but should recognize that private dealings and personal agenda had ultimately to be expressed in public acts. The excessive emotion and exaggerated actions were those of men and women playing out their roles in the public dramas that constituted an important element in medieval society.

8. It seems hardly likely that Odo and his monks had returned at the exact day and time of the beginning of the Great Procession purely by accident.

9. One need not take the number of people in the procession seriously; six was one of Herman's favorite numbers.

NOTES FOR CHAPTER 40

1. For the monastery of Bec, see Sally N. Vaughn, *The Abbey of Bec and the Anglo-Norman State, 1034–1136* (Woodbridge, Suffolk: Boydell Press, 1981).

2. This account ignores the appointment of Fastrad II as advocate of Tournai, his murder of Tetbert, and flight from Tournai. It was this circumstance that led to the appointment of Ralph, Tetbert's younger brother, as advocate.

3. This passage is based upon Bishop Radbod's charter restoring its ancient possessions to the abbey of St. Martin. Herman later explains that Ralph had renounced the world and begged Odo for admission to the congregation of St. Martin's. Ralph accompanied Odo to Noyon, and it was there that Bishop Radbod issued the charter. The matter had been completely settled when Odo and his congregation returned to Tournai. See A. d'Herbomez, *Chartes de l'abbaye de Saint-Martin de Tournai* (2 vols.; Commission royale d'histoire, 1898–1901), 1: doc. no. 1, dated 1094.

4. Bishop Radbod's charter acknowledged the antiquity of the abbey and granted it the right to recover other property to which it might have a valid claim. At this point, however, Herman begins a long digression recounting his search for evidence of St. Martin's original foundation, followed by a reconstruction of the events surrounding its abandonment, and closing with an account of the church of St. Piatus of Seclin, from which St. Martin's had acquired a tooth of its founder as a relic.

NOTE FOR CHAPTER 41

1. Herman's discussion of the search for proof of the antiquity of St. Martin's begins in the year 1117.

NOTES FOR CHAPTER 42

1. Souppes-sur-Loing, between Nemours and Chateau-Landon.

2. *Tornio* in the Latin text.

3. The interest of the peasant in having the monks reclaim their property reflects the generally better treatment enjoyed by tenants of ecclesi-

astical lords. "Life is better under the Cross" was a popular saying at the time.

NOTES FOR CHAPTER 43

1. *MGH SS* 14: 293, n. 3, referring to *Vita Sancti Eligii,* 1: 32, notes that it was King Dagobert who provided the means to construct the tomb.

2. The inhabitants of the region were still half-pagan, and St. Eligius was very active in discovering saints' relics and promoting their veneration. The French practice to which Herman refers was that of dividing the body of a saint up into many separate relics. Peter Brown, *The Cult of the Saints-Its Rise and Function in Latin Christianity* (Chicago: University of Chicago Press, 1981), presents a study of the origins of the veneration of saints and offers several insights into the attraction exerted by their relics.

3. From its abrupt interjection into the main account, the story of the miraculous imprint of the hoof of St. Martin's horse would appear to have been an interpolation by Herman's continuator. Martin was one of the most venerated saints of the period, and many places were eager to claim some connection with him.

4. Lothar II ruled 613–629; his son, Dagobert I, ruled Neustria, Burgundy, and Soissons 629–639; and his grandson, Clovis II, was king of Neustria and Burgundy 639–657. Herman's dating of the beginning of Eligius' episcopacy to the third year of Clovis's reign appears to be in error; he was elevated in the eleventh year of the reign of Clovis II.

NOTES FOR CHAPTER 44

1. The owner of land enjoyed dominion over the property, while the resident held only the rights of tenancy. Herman is suggesting that the descendants of some tenants of St. Martin's may have usurped dominion during the period in which there had been no community at St. Martin's to exercise lordship. Such people would naturally say that they owned the land in question and, without documentary proof that the land had belonged to St. Martin's and that their ancestors had been tenants of the monastery, this land could not be reclaimed. Possession is, as they say, nine points of the law.

Herman suspected that the canons of St. Mary's of Tournai were hiding the precious documentation as part of their feud with St. Martin's. Whether or not this was the case, it would have been to the canons' advantage for such a story to be spread around. Many people who were uncertain of their own descent might well support the canons for fear that the discovery of St. Martin's documentation would show them to be

descended from serfs. It that were to happen, they could be returned to
the status of slaves

NOTES FOR CHAPTER 45

1. With the disappearance of the corporate body of the monastery
community, there was no lord to whom those possessing the abbey's
lands owed service. The properties were thus allods by definition: lands
not received from a superior lord and unencumbered by rents, renders,
or service.

NOTE FOR CHAPTER 48

1. Nicasius became the first archbishop of Reims and established the
church of St. Mary's there in about 400. He is said to have been killed in
his cathedral, along with a number of his congregation, during the invasion of the Alans and Vandals in 407. The traditional regnal dates of
Merowech, however, are 448–457. Herman is confusing the attacks of
the Vandals, 407–409, with those of the Huns, 451–453.

NOTES FOR CHAPTER 49

1. Sigebert of Gembloux, *Chronicon, MGH SS* 6. Sigebert's Chronicle
was continued at several monsteries, including St. Martin's.

2. This passage is found in the *Chronicle* of Sigebert of Gembloux,
MGH SS 6: 343.

3. See Sigebert of Gembloux, *Chronicon, MGH SS* 6: 374. The
Viking invasions of the Lowlands and their effect upon the historiography of the region has been studied by Albert d'Haenens, *Les invasions
normandes en Belgique au ixe siècle. Le phénomenè et sa répercussions
dans l'historiographie medievale* (Louvain: Bibliotheque de l'Université
& Publications Universitaires de Louvain, 1967).

NOTE FOR CHAPTER 50

1. *MGH SS* 14: 296, n. 2. Waitz suggests that the work in question
was *The Chronicle of St. Vaast,* based on *The Annals of St. Vaast* and
preserved in a codex of Marchiennes. He notes that the section of *The
Chronicle of St. Vaast* dealing with the period after 860 is missing.

NOTES FOR CHAPTER 51

1. Herman's tone throughout this passage is generally condemnatory
of the monks who fled. This particular statement recalls the biblical story
of Esau giving up the rights of the first-born son in exchange for a bowl
of stew. But where did these refugee monks acquire "hereditary properties"? Is he speculating that the monks' personal endowments to the

abbey had reverted to them with the dispersal of the community? This would seem to conflict with his general contention that the properties owned by the original abbey of St. Martin should by all rights be returned to its reconstituted corporation.

2. A monk normally pledged himself to serve God by living in accordance with the rules of the community into which he had been admitted. In the case of St. Martin's, however, that community had been dissolved. Herman suggests that those monks of St. Martin's who had fled to Souppes reformed themselves into a monastic community and re-instituted its rule of communal life. This was not unparalleled. There was a community of monks at Cluny who had fled there to escape the unsettled conditions in Spain.

NOTES FOR CHAPTER 52

1. The story is a strange one. Herman appears to be implying that some spirit—perhaps that of the Virgin Mary—allowed Bernard to see those possessions of St. Martin that had been taken by the canons and intermingled with their own in the cathedral treasury. The silence imposed upon Bernard would then suggest that Mary did not wish these treasures to be taken from her church. If this is an accurate interpretation, the tale foreshadows the compromise finally imposed upon the canons and the monks of St. Martin's.

2. The monks may have refrained from digging in the second spot because the main road leading from Tournai to Courtrai lay at the western edge of the monastery's precincts. If they had been seen digging there, it would have been difficult to prevent passers-by from suspecting that they were digging for treasure and starting to search for themselves. There was also a problem that Herman does not consider. The right to treasure trove generally belonged to the ruler of the land in which it was found, and Prince-Bishop Radbod of Tournai could have claimed anything the monks of St. Martin's uncovered.

NOTE FOR CHAPTER 53

1. This terse passage summarizes one of the many complex disputes over the ownership of relics that marked the times. St. Martin's apparently supported the clerics of Seclin in their attempt to recover the body of St. Piatus because Seclin had been a part of the parish of St. Martin's abbey until St. Eleutherius had made it independent. The agreement between St. Martin's and Seclin on the one hand and the cathedral of Chartres on the other was that the church of Chartres should be allowed to keep a part of the body and the rest was to be returned to Seclin. St. Martin's received a tooth from the body once it had been returned, per-

haps partly because of the aid they gave Seclin's cause and partly as a settlement of whatever claims they might have had to a share of the body. It may be that Herman had played some role in this settlement since he had been at the Vatican early in the same year that the body of St. Piatus was returned.

...*magna cum custodia servatur*... It is quite possible that the clerics of Seclin watched over the body of St. Piatus so well in order to prevent its theft. The theft of relics was not uncommon during the period. The great reliquaries in which holy objects were kept were designed not only to glorify their contents, but also to make them more difficult to steal. See Patrick J. Geary, *Furta Sacra: Thefts of Relics in the Central Middle Ages* (Princeton, N.J.: Princeton University Press, 1978), for a full discussion of this less than edifying aspect of the veneration of relics in the Middle Ages.

NOTE FOR CHAPTER 54

1. Herman is not referring to murders, but to mercy killings. Unable to bear the pain, sufferers would beg others either to amputate their limbs or to kill them. Such homicides were difficult for the clergy to evaluate since they knew that the sufferers often killed themselves. The killing of a victim of ergot poisoning not only relieved him of unimaginable suffering but also might save him from the sin of suicide. Such thinking, however, led into uncomfortably deep theological waters.

NOTE FOR CHAPTER 55

1. Bishop Radbod had managed to extricate himself from the position that Odo's threatened migration had placed him and had no doubt discovered that Ralph's commitment to St Martin's—the event that made the resolution of the matter possible—had occurred after Odo had already set his plan into operation. If Bishop Radbod had been relieved at Odo's arrival with the solution of the problem already in hand, he now knew that Odo had not been assured of this when he had undertaken his venture. Radbod determined to end Odo's relative freedom by ordering him to submit his community to some established order of discipline, one that would curb his propensity for extremes and would fix the community permanently in place.

When Odo fell ill in 1113, he sought refuge in Anchin rather than St. Martin's. The passage suggests a possible reason for this choice, that he considered himself to be a monk of Abbot Emory of Anchin.

NOTE FOR CHAPTER 56

1. Maubeuge is located about twelve miles south of Mons.

NOTES FOR CHAPTER 57

1. The scriptural text of this prayer may be found in Luke 1:28, 42.

2. That is, they had a grandparent in common. Canon law required that married couples not be within seven grades of consanguinity; in other words, not have a common great-grandparent.

3. The village of Berlaimont lies about eight miles northwest of Avesnes. There had been bad blood between the count and Isaac, and Isaac took advantage of an invitation issued to Theodoric by his overlords to join a hunt. He gathered men and combed the woods, finally finding Theodoric separated from the rest of the hunting party and without fighting weapons. The count was cut down, and there was considerable suspicion that the matter had been arranged by his overlords. See the *Chronicon Laetiense,* ed. Johann Heller, *MGH SS* 14: 496 for a more complete account of the event.

4. Goswin of Avesnes died in 1127, and the lordship of Avesnes passed to Walter Pulkans, son of Fastrad, the advocate of Tournai and murderer of Tetbert Osmond. Walter married Ida, the daughter of Everard Ralph, the castellan of Tournai, and combined the lordship of Avesnes with the posts of castellan and advocate of Tournai.

5. The phrase "as long as he lived" indicates this passage is the work of Herman's continuator. Walter did not die until sometime after 1149, after Herman had already left the scene.

6. Everard's wife was a sister of Bishop Radbod and hence their daughter was descended from the Avesnes family. It would seem that the name "Ida" was traditional in the line.

7. Theodoric died some time before 1149.

8. Walter's third son was Goswin, who was advocate of Tournai from 1149 until his death sometime before 1166. The male descent of Fastrad as advocates ended with Goswin, and he was succeeded by his son-in-law, Anselm II of Aigremont.

9. Everard was bishop of Tournai 1173–1191.

10. The year was probably 1149 or shortly thereafter.

11. The continuator ends his interpolation at this point and provides a transition back the Herman's account. Although the account of Walter's entrance into St. Martin's is widely separated from that of Ralph's conversion, the two events would appear to have taken place at almost the same time. Ralph joined Odo's congregation immediately after their return from Noyon and their acceptance of the rule of Anchin, and the account of Walter's admission is also placed after the congregation had accepted a rule. Both Walter and Ralph participated in the year's silence that probably began in late September of 1094.

NOTES FOR CHAPTER 58

1. This passage is somewhat more complex than appears at first sight. By German custom, property held in dominion could not be alienated in perpetuity by gift or donation. Except for transfer by inheritance, a price had to be paid for it. The practice developed of transferring property in exchange for a symbolic gift, often a war horse or hunting hawk. The proprietor would publicly announce that he had accepted something of worth, state the value that he placed upon it, declare this to be the price of the property to be transferred, and then state that he relinquished the property completely and in perpetuity to the giver of the price. For a fuller consideration of this practice, see Lynn H. Nelson, "Horses and Hawks: The Accommodation of Roman and Customary Law in Early Aragon and Navarre," *Res Publica Litterarum* 11 (1988), 215–9.

This custom played an important role in Germanic legend; Erwig, the first king of the Goths, was said to have liberated his people from servitude in Scandinavia for the price of a horse and a hawk, while Count Fernán González gained the independence of Castile for the same payment. Herman's narration of the incident places his father within an heroic tradition.

2. Herman will repeat this image. This sort of work was regarded as highly demeaning for a noble, and his kinsmen and followers are portrayed as bewailing his degradation. Herman generally portrays humility as the virtue most difficult for the nobles to acquire and the most admirable quality for them to display.

NOTES FOR CHAPTER 59

1. Herman's narrative jumps back in time in order to provide the full background of his father's conversion and entry into the congregation of St. Martin's abbey. Although the exact year is uncertain, the assassination of Tetbert may have occurred sometime around 1084.

2. As a prince-bishopric, Tournai coined its own money, and Theodoric held the lucrative post of minter, one that made him in effect the most important banker in the city. See Marcel Hoc, *Histoire monétaire de Tournai* (Brussels: Sociètè royale de numismatique de Belgique, 1970), and R. Serrure, "L'atelier monétaire des évêques de Tournai," *Bulletin mensuel numismatique et d'arquéologie* 2 (1882–1883): 5–17.

3. The three brothers were members of the Osmond family, and related to Herman and Siger, leaders of the cathedral canons. Although Herman does not elaborate, his father held the bishop's brewing monopoly;

his uncle, Theodoric was the bishop's minter; another uncle, Tetbert, was the bishop's prior, or business agent; and still another, Gunther, was prior of the cathedral's chapter of canons. Baldwin, the fifth brother, had been the bishop's advocate.

There were many possible causes for Fastrad's dislike of Tetbert. In the absence of the bishop, and Bishop Radbod was probably at Noyon a good part of the time, there was an inevitable conflict between the advocate and prior since both were supposed to defend the bishop's interests. Herman's statement that Fastrad resented Tetbert's protection of the bishop's poor tenants suggests that Fastrad wished to collect full tolls, rents, and renders, and that Tetbert was inclined to excuse those who were unable to pay. If Fastrad could seize the lands of the bishop's delinquent tenants, he could redistribute them—as his mother had done—to new tenants of his choice, but Tetbert was obstructing his ability to do so.

4. That is, Fastrad became godfather to Tetbert's son. Such a relationship was normally close and bound the parents and godparents in intimate ties. Herman suggests that Fastrad had accepted a holy trust with the sole purpose of betraying this trust by making his godson an orphan.

5. The Feast of St. Bartholomew, 24 August, was one of the more popular feast days in the region of Tournai where it was associated with the harvest of spring-planted grain. The detail of Fastrad kissing Tetbert to identify him to his killers is an obvious allusion to Judas and Jesus in the Garden of Gethsemane. The fact that Tetbert was murdered while performing an act of charity made Fastrad's treachery even more reprehensible.

6. Herman fails to explain why Tetbert should appear to a poor priest rather than a member of his family. The point that Tetbert had kept a concubine after the death of his wife adds a poignant note to the account. Since Fastrad had acted as godfather at the christening of the infant, and only a short time passed between that event and Tetbert's murder, the mother seems likely to have died in childbirth. Fastrad thus not only killed the infant's father, but orphaned it. The child must have been Gunther, who later became prior of the cathedral chapter and the major adversary of St. Martin's abbey.

7. The final reconciliation of Fastrad and the kinsmen of Tetbert took place sometime in the future. Since there is no documentary evidence of an advocate of Tournai between Ralph and Fastrad II, the reconciliation may have taken place in 1094 or early 1095, when Ralph had relinquished the advocacy and renounced the world to enter St. Martin's. Herman's next chapter returns to the period immediately after the initial peace initiated by the priest Ranier.

NOTES FOR CHAPTER 60

1. The class of *milites* was the lowest of the three orders of Flemish nobility. There were variations within this class, however, and the upper level of knights merged into the middle level of vassals who held benefices and supported knights of their own. The post of prior was the ecclesiastical equivalent of the secular vassal, and the families of both Ralph and Mainsendis were thus situated in the upper ranks of the knights and the lower ranks of the vassals.

2. Herman may portray his young brother as speaking with incongruous maturity, but he is making a serious point. The sale of prebends was a common form of simony that Gregorian reformers did their best to end. Bishop Radbod's apparent lack of concern for the ecclesiastical regulations serves the literary purpose of foreshadowing his eventual fall on the charge of having purchased his bishopric.

This is a significant passage even apart from this consideration. The prebend brought the donor or his designate maintenance for life in the canonry. By urging Ralph to acquire one for his son, the canons were in effect promising to take Theodoric as one of their number when he came of age. Gunther, Siger, and Herman, all kinsmen of Ralph, must have arranged the matter since admission required a favorable vote of the chapter. Ralph's rejection of the plan was another indication of growing tensions among the Osmonds.

Young Theodoric's speech provides yet another clue to the means by which the citizens of Tournai were finally brought to support St. Martin's. Where would a five-year old have learned of the rules governing the sale of prebends; with the canons entering his classroom to congratulate him in the presence of his surely envious schoolmates, how did he acquire the assurance to repudiate the opinion of his uncles; and what caused him to decide that he would be fattening on his father's soul if he accepted this gift? Finally, in what fashion did he acquire the bitter rhetoric with which he explained his position to his father. The answer, of course, is in his schoolroom and from his school masters. Herman has concentrated upon Odo's activities in the cathedral, but Odo was also in charge of the grammar school, and his followers taught there. Herman may be suggesting that Odo was capturing the loyalties of the children of the grammar school.

NOTE FOR CHAPTER 61

1. Ralph had lost faith not only in the efficacy of the sacraments, but also in the spiritual leadership of his kinsmen, canons of the cathedral of

St. Mary's. He sought the advice of Prior Walter secretly because he was
aware that he was repudiating the wisdom of his kinsmen and of the
sacramental system upon which their power and prestige were based.
The eternal torments of Hell were very real for Ralph, as they were for
most medieval men and women, and he now believed that his kinsmen
had almost condemned him to eternal agony.

NOTES FOR CHAPTER 62

1. Mainsendis apparently followed the custom of carrying a supply of
alms with her to distribute throughout the day, but often gave the entire
sum to the monks of St. Martin's.

2. Herman several times remarks in passing that the abbey grounds
were a favorite place for children to play. It is pleasant to note that what
was once the abbey precinct is now a municipal park, the site of the city
hall, zoo, museums—and a playground. Such continuity is rather remarkable.

3. Herman rarely gives precise dates, and so the chronology of events
is somewhat uncertain. It would seem, however, that Ralph and Mainsendis decided to renounce the world sometime in 1092 before 4 March,
the date of Odo's conversion, and their fourth son must have been born
in about September of that year. Since Theodoric was five years old at the
beginning of 1092 and almost seven when he joined St. Martin's, the
events of chapter 62 most probably took place in early 1094.

It would appear that Theodoric's entering St. Martin's disrupted their
plans considerably, since Ralph did not implement his decision to abandon the world until Odo's flight in August 1095 forced his decision. Herman states that his parents remained continent for a year and a half after
their decision to seek the contemplative life, but three and a half years
passed before they actually did so. Their plan had been to enter a
monastic community as a family, and they appear to have hesitated for
some time before Ralph entered St. Martin's.

4. The care and upbringing of their young charges had been a matter
of monks' special concern and attention from the time of Benedict of
Nursia. The boys of a monastery may have received the best training,
diet, and general care in Europe, a point well made by Patricia A. Quinn
is the title of her book, *Better Than the Sons of Kings: Boys and Monks
in the Early Middle Ages* (New York: P. Lang, 1989).

NOTES FOR CHAPTER 63

1. Although Herman begins this chapter with the words *eodem anno*,
it can scarcely have been the same year of 1094. Instead of being barely
seven, Thierry was now eight years old. A year had passed, and Herman
is dealing once again with the events of 1095.

2. A variant text of this passage suggests that the treasury may have been bridge tolls. There is no indication of why Ralph was holding back these funds, or what violence he had visited upon the canons.

3. Herman uses the words *comitem peregrinationis* for Odo's group, suggesting that Ralph may have thought that they were in fact bound for some distant site or even on crusade.

4. The story of Zacheus, the publican, may be found in Luke 19. Although Herman fails to explain the situation clearly, this passage constitutes a discovery scene in which much that has gone before is explained. As is customary with Herman, he inserts a pun into a critical scene. "Publicanus," in its scriptural usage, meant "tax-gatherer" but, by Odo's time, had already begun to assume its later meaning of "tavern-owner." Ralph Osmond was a tax-gather by virtue of his position as advocate, but he was also the chief tavern-owner of Tournai through the bishop's grant to him of a brewing monopoly. These events were discussed in chapter 39, but Herman now reveals what lay behind those events.

5. Bishop Radbod's wonder was occasioned by Odo appearing with a member of the Osmond clan and a leading citizen. He suggested that there was now no reason for Odo to consider leaving Tournai, since he had won the day. He further advised Odo that he should not delay in gathering Ralph into his fold, since there was still a chance that Ralph might change his mind and enter another abbey.

6. The previous discussion of Odo's three-day stay with Bishop Radbod in Tournai states only that the monks were allowed to recuperate before returning to Tournai. In fact, the foundation charter of the abbey of Saint Martin's consists of a grant from Bishop Radbod, recognizing that the monastery was an ancient establishment now restored, giving the monks the right to recover its old possessions, and relating how Advocate Ralph had turned over the fiefs of his office to the bishop, who was now returning them to St. Martin's. This transaction took place in Noyon; the entire matter had been settled before Odo and his followers had returned to Tournai.

7. That is, she was not affected by the fear that she might have to prove herself in similar fashion.

8. In fact, Mainsendis sent for Theodoric precisely so that he would be present to take charge of his nephews. Although Herman says that the children remained with their uncle "a long time," he has nothing else to say about this period of his life. Since he was now five years old, he probably spent much of his time being schooled at St. Martin's.

9. One loaf was a day's ration, and two loaves was the normal day's pay for an itinerant farm worker.

10. This scene illustrates something of the "testing" that Odo was conducting. Mainsendis could not travel the streets alone and had atten-

dants with her. The point was not that those being tested were emulating the truly poor, but that they were accepting humiliation. Given the intense appreciation at the time of the dignity of station, such scenes of voluntarily endured degradation must have a powerful effect upon observers. It might be noted that Ralph, a brewer and tavern owner, was ordered to work as a tavern handyman. It may well be that Odo's other "tests" also had special significance for observers.

11. *curs, curtem:* "court," an independent farmstead. Such farms could be sizeable and complex agricultural units. Many developed into towns and villages and left their names behind them in such place-names as Harcourt.

12. "Horses of great price" is the term used by Herman for war horses. It is a common conception, found in many textbooks, that feudalism developed as the result of the introduction of a large breed known as the Great Horse from the East, perhaps Persia. Such horses supposedly required a great deal of grain as feed, and thus necessitated the reorganization of western Europe into manors producing a surplus of grain and the growth of a class of military landowners who alone could afford to maintain this unique breed of horse.

The original "Great Horse" appears in fact to have been the stock known as the Black Horse of the Lowlands, an indigenous or at least very old, breed of western Europe. It is interesting to see that, in the late eleventh and early twelfth centuries, plow horses and war horses were selected from the same herd. The major difference may have been that the latter group were the larger members of the herd and were fattened up, thereby giving them more mass, before sale.

See R. H. C. Davis, *The Medieval Warhorse: Origin, Development and Redevelopment* (London: Thames and Hudson Inc., 1989), for a recent work upon the subject.

13. It is true that Bishop Radbod had returned to St. Martin's the lands that had been held by the advocates. It may be remembered from chapter 9 that Ida, wife of Fastrad I, had distributed the advocate's empty lands to various tenants. The abbey had a claim upon rents, but no land upon which to raise their own food.

NOTES FOR CHAPTER 64

1. The fire took place in 1066; see *Annales Elnonensis, MGH SS* 5:13.

2. Abbot Hugh was aware of Odo's plan and expected Odo and his monks to return. The fact that there were five monks of St. Amand's in the abbey of St. Martin's, and that the holy offices continued to be observed there, presents quite a different picture from that offered by Herman in chapter 37.

NOTES FOR CHAPTER 65

1. Easter fell on 14 April in 1118, suggesting that Henry entered St. Martin's in 1096.

2. That is, Ralph and John advanced together through the various steps leading to ordination.

NOTES FOR CHAPTER 66

1. See chapters 33, 34, 39, 57. Count Robert was successful in defeating Everard, but could not dislodge him from his positions in Tournai and Mortain. The matter was settled when Count Robert recognized Everard as lord of Mortain and one of the twelve peers of Flanders, high lords who defended the frontiers of the county.

2. A cynic might note that these acts of charity also provided Everard with the money to pay his troops and so keep up his struggle. One should remember, however, that prisoners rank with the poor, hungry, thirsty, naked, and ill as the brethren of Christ.

NOTES FOR CHAPTER 67

1. . . . *de horis pulsandis . . . sollicitudinem gerebat.* The job of keeping the time in a monastery must have been worrisome indeed. According to Latin custom, the night and day were each divided into twelve hours, and religious observances, the offices and masses, were scheduled for certain hours.

The community began its day with the office of Prime (later called Lauds), the first hour of the day. The third hour of the day was struck for Terce, which was followed by a mass; Sext was said at the sixth hour and was followed by a high mass, presumably about noon; Nones was called at the ninth hour, and Compline at dusk, the twelfth hour of the day. At some time between the sixth and ninth hour of the night, the community was called from their beds to celebrate the Nocturnes (also called Matins or Vigils), a service that could last as long as two hours and was something of a burden to sleepy monks. After Matins, there was time to wash and shave before being called to Prime.

There were also other scheduled activities. The community gathered in a chapter meeting daily, following the mass after Terce, for a sermon, discussion of monastery business, and confession of faults. If the monastery ran a school, its opening and closing had to be signalled. Meals also had to be called, one in the winter shortly before Nones, and two in the summer, before Sext and before Compline.

All of this created a complex schedule even without an abbot who was fond of calling special chapter meetings. And to add to the complexity, the winter daybreak at St. Martin's could be as late as 9:00, and the sun could set well before 4:00. A winter's day could be as little as six hours duration, and a summer's day as long as eighteen hours. And yet, each day and each night had to be divided into twelve equal hours, and the various calls sounded at the proper time.

Thus, maintaining the schedule was a difficult task normally handled by two monks at a time and rotated through the community. The fact that Ralph handled the task by himself on a permanent basis is rather extraordinary. Such men developed something of the highest importance to the Western civilization. In order to distribute the tasks and offices throughout the day in more a reasonable manner, the monks at about this time developed the concept of a day and night composed of twenty-four equal and invariable hours. Even this did not lift the entire weight of his responsibilities from the shoulders of the monastery's time-keeper. It is not surprising to note that the first mechanical clocks were constructed in monastic communities.

2. Herman has referred more than once to the belief that the dead pray to God. Ralph's account demonstrates that it was also believed that the souls of the dead could leave their resting places, since this manifestation was not part of a dream. Herman does not specify whether these souls were thought to be those of the many paupers buried in St. Martin's cemetery whose souls had been purged of sin by the agony of their deaths, or of the monks of the first foundation of St. Martin's. It seems most likely that all of those buried at St. Martin's were considered to be a single fellowship. In any event, it would appear it was believed that those souls whose rest was less than perfect might continue to visit the world of the living.

NOTES FOR CHAPTER 68

1. *Dicite, pontifices, in sancto quid facit aurum?* The words were aimed at simony and ecclesiastical cupidity, but Odo chose to interpret them as questioning the validity of the long tradition of fashioning sacred objects from gold. This would appear rather self-righteous in view of the fact that St. Eligius, the putative founder of St. Martin's, had been a goldsmith fashioning precisely those golden crosses that Odo now affected to disdain.

Herman probably had Sigebert of Gembloux's *Gesta abbatum Gemblacensium* in mind when he wrote this passage. Sigebert quotes the same poem in discussing the deeds of Abbot Olbert (d. 1048). Olbert also felt that gold had no place in holy things, but he also considered that laymen could not see spiritual beauty as well as monks could and were happiest when they saw the things that they loved richly adorned.

Besides, Olbert noted that these riches formed an emergency reserve and could be sold to buy food for the starving in times of need.

Olbert was more farsighted than Odo had been. The abbot of Gembloux stored the surplus in years of bountiful harvests, knowing that hard times would surely come. When a great famine struck in 1044, he was able to assist a large number of needy. Odo, by contrast, took little thought of the future and made no attempt to build up a reserve of food or riches. Instead, he gave away what was given to St. Martin's and allowed the congregation to grow in an uncontrolled fashion. See Sigebert of Gembloux, *Gesta abbatum Gemblacensium,* cap. 41, *PL* 160: 624, C–D. Nevertheless, it should be noted that Odo was striving after poverty, one of the pressing spiritual ideals of the time. See Irven Resnick, "Odo of Tournai and Peter Damian. Poverty and Crisis in the Eleventh Century," *Revue Bénédictine* 98, 1/2 (1988): 114–40. Finally, one must remember that planning for the future was not one of the virtues emphasized by Scripture; the lilies of the field toil not, nor do they spin.

2. *Et eum qui venit ad me non eiciam foras.* John 6:27. The abbot of Anchin later used the same phrase in refusing a group of monks from St. Martin's, probably including Herman, who had asked to be allowed to take Odo back to St. Martin's to die. At the same time, the quotation is a reminder of the canons' driving the ergot-poisoned and dying paupers from the precincts of the cathedral of St. Mary's. Finally, the same quotation prepares the audience for a tale to follow shortly, that of Herman's mother, Mainsendis, being unjustly ejected from her convent.

3. This "test of ancient times" was an obvious recollection of the labor of Sisyphus. King of Corinth, Sisyphus was condemned in Hades to roll a great rock to the top of a hill. As soon as he reached the peak, however, the weight of the rock would become too much for him, it would roll back down the hill, and he would have to begin again. The labor of Sisyphus was the epitome of fruitless toil. Herman may be suggesting that Odo derived his inspiration from pagan myth.

4. In fact, one third of the chapter of canons of St. Mary's of Tournai joined the congregation of St. Martin's. The division among the canons regarding reform was settled in this fashion, and members of the Osmond family came to dominate the abbey.

5. The text gives Chalons.

6. There is no clue as to why the sight of rich and dignified men milking and making cheese should have seemed so funny. There is probably a good deal of fun and joking in medieval works that modern readers no longer even recognize as being comical. It is also possible, however, that Herman was being sarcastic.

7. Since they apparently did not eat meat, Herman is probably referring to milk, butter, and cheese.

NOTES FOR CHAPTER 69

1. It is unclear whether Eremburg was his sibling or his sister in Christ. Given the fact Herman did not take kinship and lineage lightly, and that kin stuck together in Herman's place and time, it seems much more likely that she was in fact the daughter of Odo's parents. No trace of this convent has survived; see *MGH SS* 14: 307, n.1.

2. Herman appears to be saying that Odo had chosen to subject Mainsendis to the pain of living under the orders of another woman in what was once her house, rather than giving her a position of responsibility consonant with her background, wealth, nobility, and dedication. This is but one of many examples of Herman's ambivalent portrayal of Odo. He must, for instance, have been aware that many people would not find his examples of the humiliation of wealthy and noble converts at Odo's hands at all uplifting or comical. The words by which he described the man struggling to move the massive stone suggest that Herman himself did not find them all that amusing.

3. This was irregular in that confession was supposed to be a matter between the individual and his or her confessor. By dealing with Mainsendis in this fashion, Eremburg was treating her like a loose and lascivious woman who could not be trusted to be alone with a man, even a priest, and even when deathly ill. Eremburg showed herself to be more interested in the exercise of her power than the limits that common decency should have placed upon that power.

4. Eremburg did not mean that Mainsendis was excommunicated in the technical sense of the word, since only the bishop could cut a person off from the community of the faithful. Eremburg could, however, cut Mainsendis off from the community of nuns she governed. By so doing, however, she sinned against Mainsendis in the same fashion that the canons had offended against the dying paupers they had ejected from the cathedral.

5. In other words, Mainsendis claimed that her final words to the priest had, in fact, been about her sins, just as Eremburg had ordered.

6. It would appear that the sisters working in the kitchen would simply throw their waste water out the door, where it would run down the stairs. Mainsendis's situation was somewhat reminiscent of those aspirants whom Odo required to stand under the icy water flowing of the eaves of houses.

There are some difficulties with this account. Although the mother superior had ordered that she be ejected, Mainsendis was placed in the courtyard, which was still within the precincts of the house. If she had been placed outside of the convent, Theodoric the Minter would soon have learned of her plight and rescued her. Moreover, it seems hardly likely that Eremburg would have taken such a grave step against someone as important and well-connected as Mainsendis without informing Abbot Odo. In any event, there was clearly more to the matter than Herman states.

7. Henry's invocation of Saint Alexis was particularly apt. The legend of Saint Alexis, a Roman noble of the fourth century, was extremely popular during the Middle Ages. The legend recounts how Alexis left his wife on their marriage night and went to Edessa as a pilgrim, giving up all of his wealth, living as a pauper, and begging his food through the city's streets. After seventeen years, he returned home but was not recognized. He was allowed some shelter and lived for another seventeen years under a staircase in his father's house, often with rainwater dripping on him. He was recognized only after his death when his autobiography was discovered on his person. His voluntary poverty, and particularly his suffering contempt and discomfort in his own home were regarded as particularly admirable.

Mainsendis, too, had given up her spouse and all her wealth, begged her food in the city, become a pauper, and suffered contempt and discomfort in her own home by being lodged under a staircase where water ran down upon her.

8. There is no suggestion that Odo did anything more than countermand his sister's orders.

NOTES FOR CHAPTER 70

1. The famine of 1094–1095 was particularly severe in the Lowlands. See Fritz Curschmann, *Hungersnöte im mittelalter* (Leipzig: Teubner, 1900), pp. 123–5. The life of the poor in medieval Europe was precarious under any circumstances and grew much worse with even the slightest scarcity of food. For the poor in general, see Michel Mollat, *The Poor in the Middle Ages. An Essay in Social History,* trans. Arthur Goldhammer (New Haven: Yale University Press, 1986), and for analysis of the phenomenon of famines in general, see Ronald E. Seavoy, *Famine in Peasant Societies* (New York: Greenwood Press, 1986). It should be noted that Western Europe was entering a period of altered climate, the study of which was initiated by Emmanuel Le Roy Ladurie, *Times of Feast, Times of Famine: A History of Climate Since the Year 1000,* trans. Barbara Bray (Garden City, NY: Doubleday & Company, Inc., 1971).

2. One might assume that the monks' year of silence began with the arrival of their mentors from Anchin, perhaps one or two weeks after their return to Tournai. Their year would have been completed about 29 September 1096, St. Michael's day, and the exhaustion of St. Martin's supply of food occurred more than likely sometime in the early months of 1095.

The famine had been growing for some time; the wave of ergotism in 1090 had been an early indication of what was happening. The ergot toxin is spread when old and mouldy rye is consumed, and such grain would have been eaten, even by beggars, only if there had been a shortage of more suitable supplies. Famine grows cumulatively by degrees, and the population tries to stretch its store of food to the next harvest. The general cycle of grain production saw the first plowing and planting of winter wheat in the late autumn, another plowing during the winter, and the planting of summer wheat, the harvest of winter wheat in June, and that of summer wheat in August or September.

The famine of 1094–1096 began with a very poor fall harvest in 1094. This was followed by a wet winter that made plowing and sowing difficult and almost ensured that the 1095 crop of summer wheat would be short. The cold and wet weather lasted unusually long, and the harvest of winter wheat was poor. With the shortfall of the summer wheat harvest in the September 1095, there had been three consecutive crop failures, and there was not enough food to sustain the population until the next harvest in June 1096.

The price of grain rose sharply, and what reserves existed were concentrated in the hands of the wealthy and the landowners. Churches and monasteries were obligated to devote a tenth of their income to feeding the poor, but, with a diminution of private charity, the entire burden now fell upon institutions that were short of food themselves.

3. This episode was a critical event in the history of the abbey of St. Martin, and is worth extended consideration.

The immediate complaint of the community was that Abbot Odo had not sought their advice, which a Benedictine abbot was supposed to do in matters touching on the welfare of the monastery (See *The Rule of St. Benedict,* chapter 3). The community obviously had other grievances against Odo, part of them due to the fact that they were now themselves better acquainted with the manner in which a well-ordered monastery ought to be managed. In the larger monasteries, the abbot often had two priors. One was in charge of the internal affairs of the community: monastic discipline, the singing of offices, teaching, and overseeing the spiritual progress of the individual monks. The other prior, or sometimes a lay agent, managed the monastery's properties, collected rents and renders, oversaw labor, ensured the supplies of food, clothing, and fuel needed by the community, maintained the monastic buildings, and supervised the construction of new ones. These exacting duties were sometimes shared between a prior and a cellarer. The abbot was expected to represent the abbey in acquiring property, privileges, and relics.

The community was therefore requesting two things. The first was that Odo take charge of the internal life of the monastery and presumably end the strict rule of the priors from Anchin, but that he restrict himself to Cluniac standards of discipline and follow the example set by Abbot Hugh of Cluny. The second was that Odo relinquish the external management of the monastery. One of the fundamental policies of a well-ordered monastery was to acquire wealth in order to accommodate more members, and Odo's decision not to accept traditional donations such as gold, tithes, or the rents of churches had already cost the abbey important resources.

In the community's eyes, Odo had shown himself to be incapable of ruling the monastery without guidance. The authors of the time generally describe good abbots as being able to balance charity with foresight. Odo had shown himself to be charitable enough but lacking in providence. Had they inquired further into the situation, however, they might have been less quick to humble their abbot.

The famine that was afflicting northern France and Flanders was more than a local shortfall; it was the result of a wide-spread and severe crop failures. After collecting its harvests and tithes, the cellarer of the monastery of Gembloux found that he had less than two months' supply of food at his disposal and quickly began buying grain from whoever would sell it to him. (See Sigebert of Gembloux, *Chronicon, MGH SS* 6: 367.) The lack of food soon sparked class conflict in the countryside. Landowners, fearing that their own households would suffer want, loaded demands upon their tenants. When the harvest was been brought in and the day to pay their renders had arrived (probably Michaelmas, 29 September 1095), many peasants could not meet their obligations. The landowners were ready and, on the very same day, forced their tenants to agree to doubled renders in the future. (See Gottschalk, *Gesta abbati Gemblacensis continuatio, MGH SS* 8: 547.) The paupers, driven to desperation by hunger, retaliated against the rich with theft and arson (Sigebert, *MGH SS* 6: 367). None of this created more food, and increasing numbers of corpses were found along the roadsides and in dark places in the woods. Not only the poor, but workers and artisans also, perished (Gottschalk, *loc. cit.*). The cemeteries were not large enough to accommodate the dead, and they dug deep ditches in many places and piled the corpses in them.

Perhaps the last straw was another outbreak of ergotism. The first sufferers appeared at the church of St. Gertrude near Nivelles in France, but their numbers swiftly increased. (See Ekkehard, *Chronica universale, MGH SS* 6: 213.) Having endured famine, pestilence, civil war, the devastation of war, and now a return of this terrifying affliction, many of the peasants and paupers of northern France and Flanders were desperate and ready to follow anyone who would point the way out their misery.

These were the conditions that gave rise to the Peasants' Crusade. In addition to the numbers of paupers who began the trek to the Holy Land without much direction, five large groups assembled, each from a different area and each under a different leader. The Flemish were led by a rather mysterious "King" Tafur, and they became the most terrifying of the crusaders, not least for their practice of roasting and eating their enemies when lacking other food. Tafur is variously described as a native of the Ardennes, as a Norman knight, a hermit, or a wandering preacher. Tafur and his followers are studied by L. A. M. Sumberg, "The 'Tafurs' and the First Crusade," *Mediaeval Studies* 21 (1959). The story is briefly recounted in Norman Cohn, *The Pursuit of the Millennium* (New York: Harper Torchbooks, 1961), pp. 45–9. David Nicholas, "Of Poverty and Primacy: Demand, Liquidity, and the Flemish Economic Miracle, 1050–1200," *American Historical Review* 96 (1991): 20, n. 19 emphasizes that the Tafurs were drawn from the entire southern Low Countries, and not Flanders alone.

The paupers who flocked to St. Martin's were not only desperate; some of them were dangerous. This may have had something to do with Odo's decision not to try to turn any gifts of gold into ornaments but to distribute it to the "poor." The presence of gold in the abbey would have been a constant temptation to the desperate and sometimes lawless men and women passing by. The cathedral of St. Mary and the townsfolk of Tournai were relatively safe behind the walls of the city; the monastery of St. Martin's was defenseless. Although Odo may have been inspired purely by charity, his openness may well have protected the monastery from the dangers that surrounded it.

4. The cellarer had the responsibility of maintaining provisions for the monastery. This could extend to managing the working of monastic land and supervising the collection of rents and renders, as well as dispensing the funds necessary to purchase supplies. It was the cellarer who determined the amount of food and money that was to be devoted to charity and hospitality.

The choice of Walter, Ralph, and Henry to manage the abbey's affairs of the monastery was significant. All three had entered the community from lay life and were neither priestly nor academic in their backgrounds. They represented the middle class of the city of Tournai and belonged to extensive and wealthy kindreds. If the citizens of Tournai had hoped for a "people's church" to balance the cathedral canons and the prince-bishop, they had gotten their wish.

5. Herman is making a wry comment in describing the aid the citizens gave William, Ralph, and Walter Hubert. They gave the monks food, *eos exhortantes et confortantes, hilares et letos ad fratres remittunt.* This is, of course, how the monks were supposed to treat the paupers who came begging at their gate.

NOTES FOR CHAPTER 71

1. It is difficult to convey the sense of suffering that Herman was attempting to describe. Bread was of central importance to the people of the time; the most common prayer of the era, the Lord's Prayer, included the request to "give us this day our daily bread...," the presence of Christ incarnate was manifested in a piece of bread, and one's status was reflected in the kind of bread that one ate. Only the wealthy could afford to eat wheaten bread exclusively, and most of the congregation of St. Martin's came from this social level. The famine had dropped them from that class, so that they had reached the point of eating oats and straw, food scarcely fit for animals. Their emotional distress may have been as painful as their physical want.

See Piero Camporesi, *Bread of Dreams: Food and Fantasy in Early Modern Europe,* trans. David Gentilcore (Chicago: The University of Chicago Press, 1989), for speculation upon the effects of having flax, hemp, and poppy grains added to the medieval "staff of life."

2. Prov. 27:7. "Someone who is full may refuse honey from the comb, but to the hungry even bitter food tastes sweet."

3. This passage is an addition to the original text, and places Odo in a particularly poor light. Members of the community had to be abandoned because his lack of foresight. Moreover, since the property that had been donated by the women entering St. Martin's should have ensured that they would be protected and attended, Odo had reneged on his obligations to them. His failure in this regard recalls his disregard of his obligations to his students. This is yet another instance in of the recurring theme of ejection. The women had come to Odo for refuge from the world, and he had forced them back out into it.

NOTES FOR CHAPTER 72

1. This passage interrupts the narrative and is doubtless a later interpolation. It is worth inclusion, however, since it suggests where Ralph obtained at least some of the money that he used to establish the farmsteads that are subsequently discussed.

2. Adjacent to the village of St. Maur.

3. One of the reasons that Ralph was able to embark on this ambitious program of land acquisition was no doubt the partial depopulation of the land due to the famine and the numbers who had left on the crusade. Where he obtained the people to live on these farmsteads and speed the plows is difficult to determine.

NOTES FOR CHAPTER 73

1. . . . *nonulla ornamenta Tornacensis ecclesie pro sui redemptione vendita suis adiutoribus dedit . . .*

2. That is, he would have to find two other bishops who would swear with him that he was innocent of having bought his bishopric.

3. Instead of having to obtain two compurgators, Radbod was allowed to place his hand upon the Bible and swear on his own behalf. The inference is clear that he had tried to buy the support of two bishops and, when they withdrew at Anselm's advice, he used other means to gain supporters to argue for a lighter oath.

4. This is a rather loose translation. The Latin reads . . . *ecce tibi predico, quod de hoc anno cum honore non exibis.*

5. Radbod was unable to confess his sins and gain absolution because the paralysis had robbed him of the use of his tongue. There is more than a touch of irony in the detail that Bishop Radbod, so glib and persuasive, was unable in the end to plead for his own salvation. For additional analyses of this account, see E. de Moreau, "La légende de la mort tragique de Radbod II, èvêque de Noyon-Tournai," *Annales de la Fédération archéologique et historique de Belgique. Congrès de Namur de 1938* (Namur: La Fédération archéologique et historique de Belgique, 1939), pp. 3–7.

NOTES FOR CHAPTER 74

1. The names of Baldwin and Tetbert suggest that the individuals were members of the Osmond clan, just as Guerric or Weric was a name traditional among the Avesnes family.

2. Additional and alternative text is provided by *MGH SS* 14:301: ". . . and the lands and vineyards of Pinon. When we held them for many years, we sold them for sixty pounds to the canons of the church of Premonstré, because they weren't very profitable for us. With the money, we bought a tract of land on the sea, which returned us three marks every year as long as we held it. The monks of Ter Duyn, however, hoping that it would be of more use to them, asked that it be given to them and obtained it. In exchange, two altars, Beverna and Lebdenghin, were given to us by Lord Bishop Simon of Tournai. They easily pay four marks every year."

3. Walter of Tournai was bishop 1166–1171.

NOTE FOR CHAPTER 75

1. *MGH SS* 14:310, n. 13, notes that this grant was made in the year 1103. Bishop Baldwin of Noyon (1098–1113) was, of course, also bishop of Tournai.

NOTES FOR CHAPTER 76

1. This account is somewhat confused by its sudden switch of chronology and the references to two Priors Ralph, one of St. Martin's and the other of St. Amand's. After he had become a monk, Peter used to remind Prior Ralph, the Norman, to remember the poor. During the famine of 1094–6, when he was still a canon and apparently the almoner of the cathedral of Noyon, Peter had distributed the same amount of food that had been given out in more prosperous times. He appeared to have had divine aid in his efforts to feed the poor, so Prior Ralph, the Norman of St. Amand, was inclined to follow his advice in this regard.

2. For the history of this priory, see L. A. Gordière, *Le prieuré de Sant-Amand de l'ordre Bénédictins, dépendant de l'abbaye de Saint-Martin de Tournay, situé dans l'ancien diocèse de Noyon sur le terroir de Marchemont* (Compiègne: Lefebvre, 1886).

3. Peter's place of burial held a special significance. The porch of the church was the place where alms and food were distributed to the poor and needy. Peter was buried near a place that would recall his concern for the poor.

4. In chapter 4, Herman names Gerbert, Ralph, William, and Lamfred as Odo's original four followers. It would appear that Ralph and William's two brothers soon joined the group. The congregation must have had a sizable proportion of Normans in its first years.

NOTES FOR CHAPTER 77

1. Herman was no doubt genuinely concerned for his monastic brother, but it would appear that he was also interested in comparing Godfrey's condition with that of the ailing abbot. Siger died on 30 January 1127 after a year's illness, so Godfrey's death probably occurred sometime in 1126.

2. The opening words of the Athanasian Creed.

3. The monks apparently struck a wooden block rather than ringing a bell to call the congregation. A well-cured block of hardwood emits a bell-like sound when struck.

4. The usefulness of the works probably lay in the fact that they could be placed in front of the monks, who could then follow the read-

ings. Hymnals of similar size and clarity of script were produced throughout medieval Europe and even by the Indian converts of Paraguay. Over the years, many such books have been divided into single pages and sold as souvenirs.

NOTES FOR CHAPTER 78

1. Ingelran was bishop of Laon 1098–1104. Since the grant of St. Amand had been made in 1103, Ralph's expedition to Laon must have occurred in 1104.

2. Note that Herman avoids speaking of these acquisitions as purchases.

NOTES FOR CHAPTER 80

1. Herman again portrays Odo ambiguously. Odo did not thank God for securing the welfare of his congregation but for securing his own. An abbot had many responsibilities, not the least of which was to attend courts and councils and secure donations and endowments for his abbey. Odo appears to have abandoned all of these functions to Ralph. Far from providing religious leadership, Odo seems to have indulged his own penchant for scholarship. Much as he had abandoned his teaching responsibilities when he underwent conversion, he now abandoned his monastic responsibilities for study. His achievements endured, however, and his contribution to the establishment of one of the finest libraries of its time and region is discussed in A. Boutemy, "Odon d'Orléans et les origines de la bibliothèque de l'abbaye de Saint-Martin de Tournai," *Mèlanges Félix Grat*, 2 (Paris, 1949): 179–222.

2. The increased availability of books and a greater concern for their textual accuracy were two aspects of the twelfth-century renaissance. In his description of the scriptorium of St. Martin's, Herman provides an excellent picture of how that movement occurred. It is interesting to note that the first four authors he mentions are Jerome, Gregory, Augustine, and Ambrose, the four "Fathers of the Latin Church" and that none except Isidore of Seville were the standard texts that had formed the basis for monastic and cathedral school education for the past three centuries.

3. Herman is clearly aware that the reform congregations of the Cistercians and Premonstratensians had ended the preeminence of the Order of Cluny and seems to be suggesting that that preeminence had been partly the result of a lack of competition.

NOTE FOR CHAPTER 81

1. Lam. 5:15–16.

NOTE FOR CHAPTER 82

1. Odo became bishop of Cambrai on 29 June 1105, thirteen years after having accepted the abbacy of St. Martin's.

NOTES FOR CHAPTER 83

1. The complexities of the Investiture Controversy are clearly explained by Uta-Renate Blumenthal, *The Investiture Controversy. Church and Monarchy from the Ninth to the Twelfth Century* (Philadelphia: University of Pennsylvania Press, 1991).

2. Guibert was the anti-pope Clement III, 1080 and 1084–1100.

3. This and other important aspects of the Council of Clermont in 1095 are overshadowed by the preaching of the First Crusade shortly after the meetings of the council had ended.

4. The text reads . . . *pluribus annis episcopatui superbe presidet.* . . . *Superbia,* "pride," is not an admirable quality but one of the seven deadly sins; it is the sort of pride that "goeth before a fall." *Superbe* might have been translated as "arrogantly" but for the fact that this passage is generally supportive of the validity of lay investiture.

5. See Uta-Renate Blumenthal, *The Early Councils of Pope Paschal II, 1100–1110* (Toronto: Pontifical Institute of Mediaeval Studies, 1978), for a study of Paschal's policies.

6. Odo's career as bishop of Cambrai is a part of the history of the Investiture Controversy, a history filled with invective, half-truths, and whole lies. It is consequently difficult to determine what happened during his episcopacy. Herman may have been biased against Odo's actions as a reform bishop and his continuator was clearly so. Another treatment, also negative, may be found in the Latin text edited by Charles de Smedt, *Gesta pontificum cameracensium. Gestes des évêques de Cambrai de 1092 a 1138, d'apres un ms. du XIIe siècle donné a la Bibliothèque nationale par le duc de La Tremoille* (Paris: Librarie Renouard, H. Loones successeur, 1880), as well as the *Gesta Odonis episcopi Cameracensis,* ed. Georg Waitz, MGH SS 14: 210–1.

NOTES FOR CHAPTER 84

1. Liège was a princely bishopric. Although a part of the Holy Roman Empire, its wealth and power were controlled by its prince-bishop. The existence of such states was one of the reasons that the emperors were so determined to keep some degree of control over the selection of the bishops of the land.

2. The text gives *Moselle.*

3. Herman may have read the letter in Sigebert's *Chronica, MGH SS* 6: 369–71.

Herman had great difficulty accepting the papal reform movement of the late eleventh century. He found the papacy's opposition to lay investiture contradicted by a long history of precedent and felt little sympathy for papal policies that pitted sons against their fathers. The reader should remember Herman's appreciation of his father's loss of faith in the efficacy of the sacraments (chapter 61), his joking reference to pious reading (chapter 35), and his willingness to suggest the human failings of the Blessed Odo. Herman appears to have been an independent thinker, but he must also have been influenced by the work of Sigebert of Gembloux, an eloquent spokesman on behalf of lay involvement in ecclesiastical appointments.

There is, however, another and less obvious point to Herman's discussion of these matters. In his ardor to advance the independence of the Church from lay influence, Paschal had set son against father, a sin that Herman found particularly difficult to overlook.

NOTES FOR CHAPTER 85

1. Henry IV, originally duke of Bavaria, ruled as Holy Roman Emperor from 5 October 1056 to 31 December 1105. His son, Henry V, ruled from 6 January 1106 to 23 May 1125.

2. Emperor Henry married Mathilda, the sole legitimate child of Henry I of England, in 1114. Had Henry survived, he could have claimed England through her.

3. Events did not occur as rapidly as Herman pictures them. Emperor Henry died in 1125, some eleven years after his marriage to Mathilda. Herman compresses the time period in the same fashion in chapter 16.

4. According to the terms of the privilege of Ponte Mammolo, the pope assured Henry an imperial coronation, which took place 12 February 1111, the right to investiture with ring and staff, and that he would never excommunicate Henry.

NOTES FOR CHAPTER 86

1. That is, Saint Norbert sacrificed more and demanded more of himnself than the relatively mild Rule of St. Augustine required.

2. Norbert was born in 1080 in the Rhenish town of Xanten and lived a worldly life as a court functionary until 1115. It was not the perfidy of his master that caused him to abandon the world, but being thrown from his horse during a sudden thunderstorm. The event seems to have affected him as deeply as another storm would bring about a drastic change in young Martin Luther. Norbert immediately entered the

Benedictine abbey of Siegburg where he soon was made a priest. Dissatisfied with the laxity of Siegburg, however, he left the monastery.

In 1118, he gave all of his property to the poor and walked barefoot
and dressed in rags to the South of France where he was granted an audience with the pope and given license to preach anywhere in Christen-
dom. In 1121, he and thirteen comrades founded a monastic community
at Prémontré, from which he travelled through France, German, Bel-
gium, and the Netherlands, arousing popular enthusiasm by his powerful and bitter condemnations of the excesses of the age. The saint in rags
soon became known as a worker of miracles.

It was at this time that a former notary named Tachelm proclaimed
himself a prophet and appealed to the lower classes of Flanders and Brabant by his fiery and mystical speeches against the wealth of the Church.
He soon dominated the region, acting like a king and proclaiming himself to be God. Although Tachelm was murdered in 1115, his influence
had been so great that the artisans of the city of Antwerp continued to
revere his memory and reject the orthodox Church. In 1124, the papacy
sent Norbert to Antwerp to win back the loyalty of the city. See Norman
Cohn, *Pursuit of the Millennium* for a discussion of Tachelm's heretical
movement as well as other of the sudden enthusiasms of the day.

After becoming archbishop of Magdeburg, Norbert personally convinced Emperor Lothar to abandon imperial claims to the right of investing bishops with the ring and crozier. By doing so, he brought the
long investiture conflict to an end. It is worth noting that, despite these
accomplishments, he was not canonized until 1582.

See the late medieval biography provided by John Capgrave, *The Life
of St. Norbert,* ed. Cyril Lawrence Smetana (Toronto: Pontifical Institute
of Mediaeval Studies, 1977).

3. The long and complex history of this conflict is clearly summarized
by Uta-Renate Blumenthal in *The Investiture Controversy,* a work that
also provides an excellent bibliography of the subject. Odo's role is a
matter of dispute, and the reader would do well to consult Irven
Resnick's introduction to *On Original Sin and A Disputation.*

NOTES FOR CHAPTER 87

1. St. Martin's abbey also served as a parish church for the southern
suburb of Tournai, and the canons denied the abbey's right to bury anyone except members of their community and residents of their own
parish. This meant that the community could not receive the burial donations of laymen who wished to be buried at St. Martin's rather than in
their own parishes. Bishop Radbod had agreed not to allow the abbey to
bury people who properly belonged to the parishes or cathedral of Tournai, and the canons were now enforcing this provision in the most

sweeping manner possible. Their insistence upon this point recalls the statements by townsfolk in the aftermath of the canon's ejection of the dying paupers in 1090 that they wished to be buried with those sufferers.

2. Herman does not provide the bases of the canons' claims, but they might have argued with some justification that Bishop Radbod had granted the church of St. Martin's to Odo, who was a member of the chapter, as a place to live under the canonical rule of St. Augustine, and that Odo had continued to be a member of the chapter of canons even though detached from the community. When Odo left for the bishopric of Cambrai, he also left the fellowship of canons, and properties in his possession automatically reverted to the chapter. They might have answered the argument that St. Martin's had become a Benedictine house by pointing out that the privilege that had reestablished St. Martin's, and of which they had been co-donor, made no provision for the abbey's adopting an order other than the Augustinian.

3. Tetbald had been previously been prior of the cathedral of Rouen; see chapter 74.

4. Although Herman portrays this privilege as the result of Odo's intercession, it was in fact part of a papal policy of favoring regular clergy.

5. The "something worse" was the strife within the Osmond kindred. Such violence was a possibility that struck at the heart of a basic institution of Flemish social life. The rule of law was made effective by the threat of the revenge that might be exacted by the relatives of the injured party. No such force restrained conflict between kinsmen, and so the armed conflict between Ralph and Gunther was, for the people of Tournai, a glimpse into a world without law or loyalty.

NOTE FOR CHAPTER 88

1. *MGH SS* 14: 317, n. 1 states that the date of the document is uncertain. The controversy was part of a general policy of Paschal to gain monasteries greater independence of local bishops. The Cluniac monastery of Afflighem, situated between Ghent and Brussels, received an initial confirmation from Paschal in 1105. See "Auctarium affligemense," *MGH SS* 6: 400. The cartulary of Saint Martin's contained several letters from the pope dated 1108, directing that the conflict be settled.

NOTES FOR CHAPTER 89

1. Abbot Siger could hardly have expected the reputation of Garulf's previous prowess to stop the canons' troops, and he may have been relying upon the prestige of his kinsmen to protect him from physical harm. Whether the canons' men were simply ignorant of Garulf's connections, or whether the canons had decided to meet Abbot Siger's challenge, the

beating administered to Garulf escalated the conflict considerably. The contest between the canons and the monks was now drawing in their kinsmen, and their secular relatives were unlikely to be as sparing of human life as the ecclesiastics had been up to this point. There was considerable danger that the laity of the town was being drawn into opposing camps and that a true civil war might ensue.

2. There was a symbolism underlying this savage act. The rotting feet of those suffering from ergot poisoning were often amputated in an attempt to end the pain and save their lives. Even when this was not done, the sufferers' feet sometimes simply fell off. By chopping off the feet of the canons' lay adherents, Garulf's relatives reminded the canons that this entire affair had begun with the canons' ejection of dying men, women, and children from the cathedral. It is also likely that they were appealing to public opinion by reminding those citizens not as yet involved of the original reason for the call to restore the monastery of St. Martin's.

3. At the time this brawl took place, the stories of the assistance given by St. George on his white horse to the crusaders during the battle of Antioch were still fresh in the people's memory. For quite some time, the victors in virtually every battle claimed to have seen a mounted and armed saint riding in the sky in their support. The vision at Tournai was more appropriate than many since St. Martin had been a commander in the Roman imperial cavalry.

4. The reader might note how easily Herman slips into talking of this battle as having been between "them" and "us." He would have been about sixteen years old at the time of the clash and, although a monk virtually all of his life, he still betrays excitement about worldly conflict some forty years after the event. Even monastic discipline seems to have provided a imperfect constraint upon the violent tenor of the times.

NOTES FOR CHAPTER 90

1. The statement that the abbey had not yet completed its twentieth year would place the struggle sometime before May 1112, but there is considerable evidence to suggest 1108 is a more resonable date. Herman is unlikely to have been mistaken in this matter, since he and St. Martin's were of about the same age. It may be that Everard's words were metaphoric; upon completion of its twentieth year, the abbey would pass from youth to adulthood, and the death of the young is particularly regrettable.

2. Everard, a layman, at this point condemns a grant to St. Martin's made by Pope Paschal II, and he does so on the grounds of justice and piety. Herman was old enough to have been present and to have understood Everard's points, and their repetition in his history is a both criti-

cism of the pope and a reminder that laymen could indeed play a constructive part in ecclesiastical affairs.

3. See *MGH SS* 14: 317, n. 3; the document recording this reconciliation has been dated 17 July 1108.

4. The reconciliation of Gunther, leader of the faction of the Osmonds supporting the canons, with the Osmonds of St. Martin's, forms an appropriate conclusion to this account. From this point on, both the abbey and cathedral, and the Osmonds of each, would join forces to gain the diocese of Tournai independence from that of Noyon. Despite the wealth and extent of Tournai, the canons of Noyon had been electing its bishops. It was not just the intervention of Everard, but their common commitment to a new cause that reunited the Osmonds and the Church in Tournai.

NOTE FOR EPILOGUE

1. An anonymous monk of St. Martin's attempted to continue Herman's account up to his disappearance on the Second Crusade, taking much of his material from other sources and concentrating on the ongoing attempts of the canons of Tournai to divorce themselves from the diocese of Noyon and gain the right to elect their own bishops. Although this account contains some useful and interesting material, it is largely derivative, and I have chosen to summarize it as an epilogue rather than present the text. See "Herimanni liber de restauratione monasterii S. Martini Tornacensis, Continuatio," ed. Georg Waitz, *MGH SS* 14: 318–27.

NOTE FOR APPENDIX 1

1. Arnold was cruelly executed, his followers hunted down, and his memory generally vilified. Under such circumstances, it is difficult to determine what his actual policies and goals may have been, but George W. Greenaway, *Arnold of Brescia* (New York: AMS Press, 1978), makes a good attempt at doing so.

NOTE FOR APPENDIX 4

1. Scholarship on medieval childhood has grown considerably in recent years. Shulamith Shahar, *Childhood in the Middle Ages* (London: Routledge, 1990), provides an introduction to the subject, and Klaus Arnold, *Kind und Gesellschaft in Mittelalter und Renaissance: Beiträge und Texte zur Geschichte der Kindheit* (Paderborn: Schoningh: Martin Lurz, 1980), adds interesting source material. Although focused on a considerably later period than Herman's Tournai, David Nicholas, *The Domestic Life of a Medieval City: Women, Children, and the Family in*

Fourteenth-Century Ghent (Lincoln: University of Nebraska Press, 1985) presents an interesting portrayal of family life in a medieval Flemish town.

NOTES FOR APPENDIX 5

1. Any statements concerning the cathedral chapter of Tournai must be based upon the works of Jacques Pycke, *Le Chapitre cathedral Notre-Dame de Tournai de la fin du XIe a la fin du XIIIe siècle: son organisation, sa vie, ses membres* (Brussels: Nauwelaerts, 1986), and *Repertoire biographique des chanoines de Notre-Dame de Tournai, 1080–1300* (Bruxelles: Nauwelaerts, 1988).

2. Everard married one daughter of Advocate Fastrad, and Goswin Osmond, son of Theodoric the Minter, married another, so the three most powerful local families were finally united. Their positions were eventually concentrated in the person of Fastrad's son, Walter, who became at one and the same time castellan and advocate of Tournai, lord of Avesnes, and count of Brabant.

3. "Auctarium affligemense," *MGH SS* 6: 400.

4. General monastic responses to conflict are studied in a multi-part comparative article by Barbara Rosenwein, Thomas Head, and Sharon Farmer, "Monks and Their Enemies: A Comparative Approach," *Speculum* 66 (1991): 764–96, while the situation in Tournai particularly is the subject of Albert d'Haenens, "Moines et clercs à Tournai au début du XIIe siècle," *La vita comune del clero nei secoli x e xi*, 2 (Milan, 1959): 90–203.

5. In the letter inserted by Herman, Paschal warns Balderic against doing or saying anything to stir up the matter.

SELECTED BIBLIOGRAPHY

Abelard, Peter. *Sic et non: A Critical Edition.* Edited by Blanche B. Boyer and Richard McKeon. Chicago: University of Chicago Press, 1977.

Annales Elnonensis. MGH SS 5:13.

Anselm of Canterbury. *Opera omnia. PL* 158–59.

———. *The letters of Saint Anselm of Canterbury.* Translated by Walter Frohlich. Kalamazoo, Mich: Cistercian Publications, 1990–1993.

———. *Liber de fide trinitatis et de incarnatione verbi. PL* 158: 259–84.

———. *Why God became man = Cur Deus homo.* Edited and translated by Jasper Hopkins and Herbert Richardson. N.p.: Edwin Mellen Press, n.d.

———. *Epistola de incarnatione verbi.* Edited by Francis Schmitt, O.S.B. Bonn: P. Hanstein, 1931.

Arnold, Klaus. *Kind und Gesellschaft in Mittelalter und Renaissance: Beiträge und Texte zur Geschichte der Kindheit.* Paderborn, Schoningh: Martin Lurz, 1980.

Auctarium affligemense. MGH SS 6: 398–405.

Augustine of Hippo. *The Rule of Saint Augustine: Masculine and Feminine Versions.* Translated by Raymond Canning. London: Darton, Longman & Todd, 1984.

———. *Il 'De Libero Arbitri' di S. Agostino. Studio introduttivo, testo, traduzione e commento.* Edited by Franco de Capitani. Milan: Catholic University, 1987).

Benedict of Nursia. *The Rule of St. Benedict.* (Many editions and translations.)

Berlière, U. "Abbaye de St. Martin de Tournai" *Monasticon belge.* I (fascicle 1): Province de Hainaut. Liège: Maresdous, 1897. Anastatic reprint, Liège, 1961: 271–93.

———. "Nécrologe de l'abbaye de Saint-Martin de Tournai. Actes de confraternité, donations et fondations d'obits," *Documents inédits pour servir à l'histoire ecclèsiatique de la Belgique.* Vol. 1, 133–246. Appendices, 247–61. N.p., 1894.

Berthod, D. "Hériman de Tournai," *Histoire littéraire de la France* 12 (Paris, 1869): 279–88.

Bethune-Sully, Etienne, baron de. *Testaments tournaisiens et comptes d'exécutions testamentaires. XIIe siècle–XVIIe siècle.* Aalst: Chez l'auteur, Brusselsesteenweg 75, 1970.

Beyls, F. "Le bienheureux Odon et l'école de Tournai au XIᵉ siècle." *Semaine religieuse du diocèse de Tournai* 18, no. 12 (1875): 487–8.

Blumenthal, Uta-Renate. *The Early Councils of Pope Paschal II, 1100–1110.* Toronto: Pontifical Institute of Mediaeval Studies, 1978.

————. *The Investiture Controversy. Church and Monarchy from the Ninth to the Twelfth Century.* Philadelphia: University of Pennsylvania Press, 1991.

Böethius. *Libri V de consolatione philophiae. PL* 53: 579–862.

————. *Opera.* Edited by Ludwig Bieler. Turnholt: Brepols, 1984.

————. *The Consolation of Philosophy.* Translated by V. E. Watts. Baltimore, Penguin Books, 1969.

Boutemy, A. "Les miniatures de la Vita Anselmi de Saint-Martin de Tournai et leurs origines." *Revue Belge d'Archéologie et d'Histoire de l'Art* 13 (1943): 117–22.

————. "Odon d'Orléans et les origines de la bibliothèque de l'abbaye de Saint-Martin de Tournai." *Mèlanges Félix Grat.* 2 (Paris, 1949): 179–222.

Boziere, Aime Francois Joseph. *Tournai ancien et moderne: ou, Description historique et pittoresque de cette ville, de ses monuments, de ses institutions, depuis son origine jusqu'a nos jours.* Brussels: Culture et civilisation, 1974.

Brown, Peter. *The Cult of the Saints-Its Rise and Function in Latin Christianity.* Chicago: University of Chicago Press, 1981.

Camporesi, Piero. *Bread of Dreams: Food and Fantasy in Early Modern Europe.* Translated by David Gentilcore. Chicago: University of Chicago Press, 1989.

Capgrave, John. *The Life of St. Norbert.* Edited by Cyril Lawrence Smetana. Toronto: Pontifical Institute of Mediaeval Studies, 1977.

Carre, Meyrick Heath. *Realists and Nominalists.* New York: Oxford University Press, 1961.

Cassian, John. *Conferences.* Translated by Colm Luibheid. New York: Paulist Press, 1985.

————. *Conferences.* Edited by E. Pichery. Paris: Editions du Cerf, 1955–1959.

————. *Iohannis Cassiani De institvtis coenobiorvm et de octo principalivm vitiorvm remediis libri XII. De incarnatione Domini contra*

Nestorivm libri VII. Edited by Michael Petschenig. Vienna: F. Tempsky, 1888.

———. *Opera omnia. PL* 49.

Cassiodorus, Senator. *An Introduction to Divine and Human Readings.* Translated by Leslie Webber Jones. New York: Columbia University Press, 1946.

———. *Opera.* Turnholt: Brepols, 1958–1973.

Chadwick, Henry. *Böethius, The Consolations of Music, Logic, Theology, and Philosophy.* Oxford: Clarendon Press, 1981.

Chronicon Laetiense. Edited by Johann Heller, *MGH SS* 14: 496.

Cloquet, Louis. *Monographie de l'église paroissiale de St. Jacques a Tournay.* Lille: Desclee, De Brouwer, 1881.

Cohn, Norman. *The Pursuit of the Millennium.* New York: Harper Torchbooks, 1961.

Curschmann, Fritz. *Hungersnöte im mittelalter.* Leipzig: Teubner, 1900.

Davis, Ralph H. C. *The Medieval Warhorse: Origin, Development and Redevelopment.* London: Thames and Hudson Inc., 1989.

Delahaye, Ph. "L'organisation scolaire au XIIᵉ siècle." *Traditio* (1947): 221–68.

Didier, J. C. "Herman de Tournai (1095–1147)." *Catholicisme* 5 (1958): col. 661.

Dierkens, Alain. *Abbayes et chapitres entre Sambre et Meuse: VIIe–XIe siècles: contribution a l'histoire religieuse des campagnes du haut Moyen Age.* Sigmaringen: J. Thorbecke, 1985.

Donaldson, Christopher. *Martin of Tours, Parish Priest, Mystic and Exorcist.* London: Routledge & Kegan Paul, 1980.

Dreine, Ch. "Odon de Tournai et le crise de cénobitisme au XIIᵉ siècle." *Revue du Moyen âge latine* 4 (1948): 137–54.

Dubois, Jacques, O.S.B. *Histoire monastique en France au XIIe siècle: les institutions monastiques et leur évolution.* London: Variorum Reprints, 1982.

Dumoulin, Jean. *La grande procession de Tournai (1090–1992): une réalité religieuse, urbaine, diocésaine, sociale, économique et artistique.* Tournai: Cathedrale Notre-Dame; Louvain-la Neuve: Université Catholique de Louvain, 1992.

Eadmer. *Vita D. Anselmi archiepiscopi Cantuariensis. The Life of St Anselm, Archbishop of Canterbury.* Edited by R. W. Southern. Oxford: Clarendon Press, 1962.

Ekkehard. *Chronica universale. MGH SS* 6.

Galbert of Bruges. *The Murder of Charles the Good, Count of Flanders: A Contemporary Record of Revolutionary Change in 12th-Century Flanders.* Translated and edited by James Bruce Ross. New York: Harper Torchbooks, 1967.

Geary, Patrick J. *Furta Sacra: Thefts of Relics in the Central Middle Ages.* Princeton, N.J.: Princeton University Press, 1978.

Génicot, L. G. *La maison d'Avesnes. Histoire généologique et sociale, des origines à Gautier II.* Louvain: Université Catholique de Louvain, Mémoire de license en histoire moderne, 1967.

Gesta Odonis episcopi Cameracensis. Edited by Georg Waitz. *MGH SS* 14: 210–11.

Gilbert de La Porree. *The Commentaries on Böethius.* Edited by Nikolaus M. Haring. Toronto: Pontifical Institute of Mediaeval Studies, 1966.

Gordière, L. A. *Le prieuré de Sant-Amand de l'ordre Bénédictins, dépendant de l'abbaye de Saint-Martin de Tournay, situé dans l'ancien diocèse de Noyon sur le terroir de Machemont.* Compiègne: Lefebvre, 1886.

Gottschalk. *Gesta abbati Gemblacensis continuatio. MGH SS* 8.

Gould, Graham. *The Desert Fathers on Monastic Community.* New York: Oxford University Press, 1993.

Greenaway, George W. *Arnold of Brescia.* New York: AMS Press, 1978.

d'Haenens, Albert. *L'Abbaye Saint-Martin de Tournai de 1290 à 1350, origines, évolution et dénouement d'une crise.* Louvain: Bibliothèque de l'Université, Bureau du Recueil, 1961.

———. *Les invasions normandes en Belgique au ixe siècle. Le phénomenè et sa répercussions dans l'historiographie medievale.* Louvain: Bureaux du Recueil, Bibliothèque de l'Université & Publications Universitaires de Louvain, 1967.

———. "Moines et clercs à Tournai au début du XIIᵉ siècle." *La vita comune del clero nei secoli x e xi.* 2 (Milan, 1959): 90–203.

———. *Comptes et documents de l'abbaye de Saint-Martin de Tournai: sous l'administration des gardiens royaux (1312–1355).* Paris: Palais des Academies, 1962.

d'Herbomez, A. *Chartes de l'abbaye de Saint-Martin de Tournai.* 2 vols. Brussels: Commission royale d'histoire, 1898–1901.

Herman of Tournai. *Herimanni liber de restauratione monasterii Sancti Martini Tornacensis.* Edited by Georg Waitz. *MGH SS* 14: 274–317.

———. *Herimanni liber de restauratione monasterii S. Martini Tornacensis. Continuatio.* Edited by Georg Wairz. *MGH SS* 14: 318–27.

———. *Historiae Tornacensis partim ex Hermimanni libris excerptae.* Edited by Georg Waitz. *MGH SS* 14: 327–52.

———. *Vita Sancti Ildefonsi Toletani. Acta Sanctorum SS Benedict* 2: 520–22; 3d ed.: 498–500.

Hoc, Marcel. *Histoire monétaire de Tournai.* Brussels: Société royale de numismatique de Belgique, 1970.

Isidore of Seville. *Etymologies, Book II.* Edited and translated by Peter
   K. Marshall. Paris: Les Belles Lettres, 1983.
————. *Opera omnia.* PL 81–84.
Jaeger, C. Stephen. *The Envy of Angels: Cathedral Schools and Social
   Ideals in Medieval Europe, 950–1200.* Philadelphia: University of
   Pennsylvania Press, 1994.
Kaylor, Noel Harold. *The Medieval Consolation of Philosophy: An An-
   notated Bibliography.* New York: Garland Pub., 1992.
Ladurie, Emmanuel Le Roy. *Times of Feast, Times of Famine: A History
   of Climate Since the Year 1000.* Translated by Barbara Bray. Garden
   City, N.Y.: Doubleday & Company, Inc., 1971.
Lawless, George. *Augustine of Hippo and His Monastic Rule.* Oxford:
   Clarendon Press, 1987.
Lutz, Cora Elizabeth. *Schoolmasters of the Tenth Century.* Hamden,
   Conn.: Archon Books, 1977.
Martianus Capella. Edited by James Willis. Leipzig: B. G. Teubner Ver-
   lagsgesellschaft, 1983.
Macdougall, Allan Ross, trans. *The Glorious Adventures of Tyl Ulen-
   spiegel.* New York: Pantheon Books, 1944.
Martianus Capella. *The Marriage of Philology and Mercury.* Translated
   by William Harris Stahl, Richard Johnson, and E. L. Burge. New
   York: Columbia University Press, 1977.
Memoires de la Société historique et litteraire de Tournai. Vols. 1–25.
   Tournai: 1853–[95].
Mollat, Michel. *The Poor in the Middle Ages: An Essay in Social Histo-
   ry.* Translated by Arthur Goldhammer. New Haven: Yale University
   Press, 1986.
Moreau, Claude. *Moulds, Toxins and Food.* Translated by Maurice
   Moss. New York: John Wiley & Sons, 1979.
Moreau, E. de. "La légende de la mort tragique de Radbod II, èvêque de
   Noyon-Tournai." *Annales de la Fédération archéologique et his-
   torique de Belgique. Congrès de Namur de 1938,* 3–7. Namur: La
   Fédération archéologique et historique de Belgique, 1939.
Morrison, Karl F. *Understanding Conversion.* Charlottesville: University
   Press of Virginia, 1992.
Nelson, Lynn H. "Horses and Hawks: The Accommodation of Roman
   and Customary Law in Early Aragon and Navarre." *Res Publica Lit-
   terarum* 11 (1988): 215–19.
Nicholas, David. "Of Poverty and Primacy: Demand, Liquidity, and the
   Flemish Economic Miracle, 1050–1200." *American Historical Re-
   view* 96 (1991): 17–41.
————. *Medieval Flanders.* London: Longman, 1992.

———. *The Domestic Life of a Medieval City: Women, Children, and the Family in Fourteenth-Century Ghent.* Lincoln: University of Nebraska Press, 1985.

Odo of Tournai. *On Original Sin and a Disputation with a Jew, Leo, Concerning the Advent of Christ, the Son of God.* Translated and annotated by Irven Resnick. Philadelphia: University Pennsylvania Press, 1994.

———. *Opera omnia. PL* 160 (1854): 1053–160.

Oppenheimer, Paul, trans. *Till Eulenspiegel: His Adventures.* New York: Garland, 1991.

Orosius, Paulus. *The Seven Books of History Against the Pagans.* Translated by Roy J. Deferrari. Washington, D.C.: Catholic University of America Press 1964.

Porphyry. *Isagoge.* Translated by Edward W. Warren. Toronto: Pontifical Institute of Mediaeval Studies, 1975.

Pycke, Jacques. "Bibliographie relative à l'histoire de Tournai." *Annales de la Société historique et littéraire de Tournai* 24 (1974): 129–436.

———. *Bibliographie d'histoire de Tournai des années 1977 à 1985: une bibliographie informatisee au CETEDOC.* Tournai: Archives du Chapitre cathedral, 1987.

———. *Le Chapitre cathedral Notre-Dame de Tournai de la fin du XIe à la fin du XIIIe siècle: son organisation, sa vie, ses membres.* Brussels: Nauwelaerts, 1986.

———. *Repertoire biographique des chanoines de Notre-Dame de Tournai, 1080–1300.* Bruxelles: Nauwelaerts, 1988.

Quinn, Patricia A. *Better Than the Sons of Kings: Boys and Monks in the Early Middle Ages.* New York: P. Lang, 1989.

Reiss, Edmund. *Böethius.* Boston: Twayne Publishers, 1982.

Resnick, Irven. "Odo of Tournai and Peter Damian. Poverty and Crisis in the Eleventh Century." *Revue Bénédictine* 98,1/2(1988): 114–40.

———. "Odo of Tournai's *De peccatio originali* and the Problem of Original Sin." *Medieval Philosophy and Theology* 1 (1991): 18–38.

Riché, Pierre. *Écoles et enseignement dans le Haut Moyen Age: fin du Ve siècle–milieu du XIe siècle.* Paris: Picard, 1989.

Rolland, Paul. *Les origines de la commune de Tournai. Histoire interne de la seigneurie épiscopale tournasienne.* Brussels: Lamertin, 1931.

———. *Cathedrale de Tournai.* Vol. 1. *Peintures murales romanes. La chapelle paroissiale et le cloître.* Antwerp: De Sikkel, 1944.

———. *L'église Saint-Quentin a Tournai.* Antwerp: De Sikkel, 1946.

———. *Les églises paroissiales de Tournai.* Brussels: Nouvelle société d'edition, 1936.

Rosenwein, Barbara; Thomas Head; and Sharon Farmer. "Monks and Their Enemies: A Comparative Approach." *Speculum* 66 (1991): 764–96.

Russell, Norman, trans. *The Lives of the Desert Fathers: The Historia monachorum in aegypto*. London: Mowbray, 1981.

Scaff, Villy. *La sculpture romane de cathedrale Notre-Dame de Tournai*. Tournai: Casterman, 1971.

Schwartzenbaum, Elizabeth B. *The Romanesque Sculpture of the Cathedral of Tournai*. Ph.D. diss. New York University: 1977.

Sdralek, M. "Zur Geschichte der Trennung der unierten Bistümer Noyon et Tournay." *Kirchengeschichtliche Studien* 1, fasc. 2 (1891): 66–72, 116–17.

Seavoy, Ronald E. *Famine in Peasant Societies*. New York: Greenwood Press, 1986.

Serrure, R. "L'atelier monétaire des évêques de Tournai." *Bulletin mensuel numismatique et d'arquéologie* 2 (1882–1883): 5–17.

Seymour, Charles. *Notre-Dame of Noyon in the Twelfth Century; A Study in the Early Development of Gothic Architecture*. New York: Norton, 1968.

Shahar, Shulamith. *Childhood in the Middle Ages*. London: Routledge, 1990.

Sigebert of Gembloux. *Chronicon. MGH SS 6*

———. *Gesta abbatum Gemblacensium*. Cap. 41, PL 160: 624, C–D.

Smedt, Charles de. *Gesta pontificum cameracensium. Gestes des évêques de Cambrai de 1092 a 1138, d'apres un ms. du XIIe siècle donné a la Bibliothèque nationale par le duc de La Tremoille*. Paris: Librarie Renouard, H. Loones successeur, 1880.

Southern, Richard W. *Platonism, Scholastic Method, and the School of Chartres*. Reading, U.K.: University of Reading, 1979.

———. *Saint Anselm and His Biographer; A Study of Monastic Life and Thought, 1059–c.1130*. Cambridge, U.K.: Cambridge University Press, 1963.

———. *Saint Anselm: A Portrait in a Landscape*. Cambridge, U.K.: Cambridge University Press, 1990.

Spade, Paul Vincent, trans. *Five texts on the mediaeval problem of universals: Porphyry, Böethius, Abelard, Duns Scotus, Ockham*. Indianapolis: Hackett, 1994.

Stancliffe, Clare. *St. Martin and His Hagiographer: History and Miracle in Sulpicius Severus*. New York: Oxford University Press; 1983.

Sumberg, L .A. M. "The 'Tafurs' and the First Crusade." *Mediaeval Studies* 21 (1959): 224–46.

Thierry of Chartres. *Commentaries on Böethius, by Thierry of Chartres and His School.* Edited by Nikolaus M. Haring. Toronto, Pontifical Institute of Mediaeval Studies, 1971.

Vaughn, Sally N. *The Abbey of Bec and the Anglo-Norman State, 1034–1136.* Woodbridge, Suffolk: Boydell Press; [ca. 1981].

Verlinden, Charles. *Robert 1er, le Frison, comte de Flandre, étude d'histoire politique.* Antwerpen, "De Sikkel"; Paris: Campion, 1935.

Vleeschouwers, C. *Les cartulaires des évêques de Tournai: étude diplomatique et notes sur l'histoire et la composition de ces cartulaires ainsi que sur leurs scribes.* Brussels: Academie Royale de Belgique, 1977

Waitz, Georg. "Hermann von Tournai und die Geschichtschreibung der Stadt." *Forschungen zur deutsche Geschichte* 21 (1881): 429–48.

Ward, Benedicta, trans. *The Desert Christian: Sayings of the Desert Fathers: The Alphabetical Collection.* New York: Macmillan, 1980.

Warlop, E. *The Flemish Nobility Before 1300.* 3 vols. Kortrijk: G. Desmet-Huysman, 1976.

The Restoration of the Monastery of Saint Martin of Tournai was designed and composed in Sabon by Kachergis Book Design of Pittsboro, North Carolina. It was printed on 60 lb. Booktext Natural and bound by BookCrafters, Chelsea, Michigan.